Getting Through Security's systematic examination of a particular security regime (airports) and ramified exploration of a particular realm of expertise (counterterrorism) prepares the way for a strikingly insightful examination of issues at the heart of the contemporary security state. Highly distinctive in style, structure, sources, and originality of thought, this book reads and should be read across disciplines—anthropology, cultural studies, law, political science, and sociology. Perhaps as significantly, *Getting Through Security* is the product of a highly successful collaboration, arising from conversation, thinking and writing together, in ways that frankly I, or any anthropologist, would envy. In a sense, achieved collaborations are as important for anthropology today as the topics that they might address.

George Marcus, author of *Ethnography Through Thick and Thin and coauthor of Collaborations Now*

In *Getting Through Security* Mark Maguire and David Westbrook have crafted a masterful account of the people and ideas that animate security culture. The book is a *tour de force*, but of an unusual sort: written not merely as a review of the relevant scholarship, but as a generous invitation to the reader to reflect on the modern state, the media, bureaucracy, and expertise in relation to fundamental ideas about the resilience and vulnerabilities of the contemporary social order.Drawing on scores of examples of successful and failed attacks, the authors challenge basic assumptions underwriting the politics and practices of security. They also provide glimpses of the multinational group of actors, of current and former police, military, terrorism and counter terrorism experts as well as consultants, managers, and bureaucrats who populate what Maguire and Westbrook term the "secret college:" the formal and informal networks in which the strategic and tactical of issues of security are relentlessly scrutinized and appraised. *Getting Through Security* thus opens familiar and unfamiliar terrains to expansive forms of anthropological inquiry and ethnographic reflection.

Douglas Holmes, author of *Economy of Words: Communicative Imperatives in Central Banks and Integral Europe: Fast-Capitalism, Multiculturalism, Neofascism*

This intriguing book takes the reader into the dispersed worlds of security, exploring by way of ethnographic glimpses and reflexive exercise, what 'security' in the broader sense, as a 'horizon for certain kinds of thought and institutional action', is. Ultimately, the book is about the uncanniness of not knowing, of being out of control, in a state of fear, yet attempting to come to grips with uncertainty and risk. In the end, it is not just about security and the officials who deal with security as a profession, but about modes of navigating with only fragments of maps at hand. A gripping and extra-ordinary read!

Christina Garsten, Principal, Swedish Collegium for
Advanced Study, and Principal Investigator,
Global Foresight, Stockholm University

This short book does much more than pull back the curtains that shroud airport security. *Getting Through Security* humanizes the security officials who, through long hours of boredom punctuated by sudden minutes of terror, become practicing ethnographers to keep the skies safe. It's a fascinating read for any air traveler interested in pondering the dilemmas faced by the security bureaucracy.

Michael Glennon, author of *National Security and
Double Government*, and former Legal Adviser,
Senate Foreign Relations Committee

Getting Through Security provides unique insights into the vexing issue of security in the 21st century, an issue we confront not only in airports, but also in finance and other digital spaces. Almost everyone with experience in facets of "security" recognizes that cross disciplinary approaches are required for meaningful solution development, but that is easier said than done. Maguire and Westbrook raise uncomfortable questions about the nature of security, fittingly illustrated with a variety of global examples.

Jimmie Lenz, Director, Master of Engineering in
FinTech and Master of Engineering in Cybersecurity,
Irene and Frank Salerno Visiting Professor of Financial
Economics, Pratt School of Engineering,
Duke University

Getting Through Security is an essential guide for understanding the critical vulnerabilities in modern bureaucratic institutions.

John Symons, Department of Philosophy, University of Kansas

Getting Through Security

Getting Through Security offers an unprecedented look behind the scenes of global security structures. The authors unveil the "secret colleges" of counterterrorism, a world haunted by the knowledge that intelligence will fail, and Leviathan will not arrive quickly enough to save everyone. Based on extensive interviews with both special forces and other security operators who seek to protect the public, and survivors of terrorist attacks, *Getting Through Security* ranges from targeted European airports to African malls and hotels to explore counterterrorism today. Maguire and Westbrook reflect on what these practices mean for the bureaucratic state and its violence, and offer suggestions for the perennial challenge to secure not just modern life, but humane politics.

Mark Maguire has long had extraordinary access to a series of counterterrorism programs. He trained with covert behavior detection units and attended secret meetings of international special forces. He found that security professionals, for all the force at their command, are haunted by ultimately intractable problems. Intelligence is inadequate, killers unexpectedly announce themselves, combat teams don't arrive quickly enough, and for a time an amorphous public is on its own. Such problems both challenge and occasion the institutions of contemporary order. David Westbrook accompanied Maguire, pushing for reflection on what the dangerous enterprise of securing modern life means for key concepts such as bureaucracy, violence, and the state. Introducing us to the "secret colleges" of soldiers and police, where security is produced as an infinite horizon of possibility, and where tactics shape politics covertly, the authors relate moments of experimentation by police trying to secure critical infrastructure and conversations with special forces operators in Nairobi bars, a world of shifting architecture, technical responses, and the ever-present threat of violence. Secrecy is poison. Government agencies compete in the dark. The uninformed public is infantilized. *Getting Through Security* exposes deep flaws in the foundations of bureaucratic modernity, and suggests possibilities that may yet ameliorate our situation.

Mark Maguire is Dean of Maynooth University Faculty of Social Sciences, and former Head of the Department of Anthropology. He has edited a number of recent collections on the anthropology of security, most recently *Spaces of Security* (NYU Press, 2019) with Setha M. Low.

David A. Westbrook is Louis A. Del Cotto Professor, University at Buffalo School of Law, State University of New York. His books include *Navigators of the Contemporary: Why Ethnography Matters* and *Deploying Ourselves: Islamist Violence and the Responsible Projection of US Force*.

Getting Through Security

Counterterrorism, Bureaucracy, and
a Sense of the Modern

Mark Maguire and
David A. Westbrook

Routledge
Taylor & Francis Group

NEW YORK AND LONDON

First published 2021
by Routledge
52 Vanderbilt Avenue, New York, NY 10017

and by Routledge
2 Park Square, Milton Park, Abingdon, Oxon OX14 4RN

Routledge is an imprint of the Taylor & Francis Group, an informa business

© 2021 Taylor & Francis

The right of Mark Maguire and David A. Westbrook to be identified as authors of this work has been asserted by them in accordance with sections 77 and 78 of the Copyright, Designs and Patents Act 1988.

Library of Congress Cataloging-in-Publication Data
A catalog record for this title has been requested

ISBN: 978-0-367-61303-7 (hbk)
ISBN: 978-0-367-61302-0 (pbk)
ISBN: 978-1-003-10510-7 (ebk)

Typeset in Bembo
by Taylor & Francis Books

Mark dedicates this book to Eileen. She knows the unusual "field" of security, and understands the excitement of finding out new things, even if that means going on some unusual trips.

David dedicates this book to Amy, who deeply understands that "security" is at best an oft-broken promise, and who bravely carries on nonetheless.

Contents

Preface

We (the authors) met in the context of "Global Foresight," a multiyear, multinational and multidisciplinary project directed by Christina Garsten, professor of social anthropology at Stockholm University and Principal, Swedish Collegium for Advanced Studies. The Program is funded by the Riksbankens Jubileumsfond, The Swedish Foundation for Humanities and Social Sciences, perhaps best known for establishing the "Nobel" in Economics. The Jubileumsfond was itself established by the Riksbank, Sweden's central bank, which happens to be the oldest such bank in the world.

Over the past decade, Mark's ethnographic research has explored several dimensions of contemporary security, and elements of his work are discussed herein. In 2011 he was granted access to a UK airport counterterrorism training program that focused on behavioral assessment, covert surveillance, and the close protection of VIP passengers. Later, he carried out six months of ethnographic field work with an airport police force, and thereafter contributed to their professional training. Starting in 2015, with the Demo, i.e., the NATO demonstration described in the Prologue, he has been exploring public behavior during the first minutes of terrorist attacks in Ireland, the UK, France and Kenya, all mentioned here. Public behavior is a recognized gap in security knowledge, but it is also a problem for counterterrorism security at a much deeper level: where security meets the public, the limits of the contemporary are visible. Mark's work is especially interested in airports, but also other public spaces and sites where a host of security bureaucracies, from local police to NATO appear. In such institutions, "security" is both a preoccupation and a mystery. While a violent event, a failure of security, may at least initially seem clear enough (upon examination, events are usually unclear, even after the fact), how should institutions begin thinking about security as such? Mark discovered an approach, if not an answer: ethnographic activity is written into the work of police and other security professionals attempting to know the "culture" in which they work, and to think about it. Security is by nature regulatory, and so the purpose of officials doing native ethnography, as it were, often is to create standards, to think about improvements, and most explicitly, to articulate what will be said in the training of new professionals.

This "paraethnographic" sense that contemporary practices were already ethnographic had been theoretically articulated through years of discussion among George Marcus, Douglas Holmes and David, who wrote it up in *Navigators of the Contemporary: Why Ethnography Matters*. Mark had read *Navigators*, and so he and David began talking about what ethnography might do, indeed already was doing, in the security context. Across several publications, David speculated that a paraethnographic approach might be useful for the prudential regulation of financial institutions (where "security," albeit in a different sense, is also a problem), but Mark's work was actually happening.

Conversely, Mark wondered, what might "paraethnographic" security conversations mean for ethnography? Especially if such conversations led to changes in security practices? In particular, ethnographic participation in security policy formation seemed to move ethnography from the relative distance and moral calm of academic observation and analysis to a far more political, and therefore vexed, practice, neatly bracketed by Weber's two late lectures, *Science as Vocation* and *Politics as Vocation*. What might all this mean, not only for how academic anthropology conceived of its own enterprise, but for how social sciences more generally conceived of the state, and perhaps even how ostensibly democratically legitimated officials conceived of their own work in situations where democracy was attenuated at best? We have had a lot to discuss.

Methodologically, the idea has been to use Mark's work as both basis and context for discussions of what security means, and more broadly, what modern means, and how ethnography might contribute. David has observed Mark conducting fieldwork, and met many of his interlocutors. Both of us have written on security and military matters before. Nonetheless, many of these interlocutors, especially soldiers and other professionally dangerous men, have forced our text to include troubling questions about violence, meaning and morality. In a Nairobi hangout we laughed with the security professional who described the life of "serving lattes" he narrowly avoided, but we did squirm when stories that told of prowess and virtue gave way to tales of violent acts and horrors witnessed. And the stories are fascinating, not just for the sorts of drama that our time understands cinematically (although there is that), but for the sense of forces at play under the surface, the sometimes violent spookiness of the contemporary. And here, to forestall an objection that will be explored in detail below, lies the possibility of serious internal critique.

Mark recast his field notes, added a fair bit of memory and analysis, into a collection of essayistic fragments, which we have used for raw material. As all this material was discussed and rehashed, themes emerged, and are reflected in individual chapters.

This book is thus a second order ethnography, which relies on fragments of Mark's fieldwork, but in David's case, mostly at one remove, "looking over his shoulder." Although he did the actual fieldwork, reviewing his efforts, Mark has had to explain what he thinks it all means to David, which raises problems of its own. One should not make too much of this point. Any multi-sited ethnography will be impelled to abstraction in order to maintain its integrity (how does this site relate to that?). And Mark personally did most of the fieldwork in question. Still, the questions addressed here are explicitly societally abstracted rather than locally situated. The direction is from the ethnographic to the sociological or even philosophical. In consequence, we have written about the modern vis-à-vis Weber, understood both as a set of highly conventional conceptions and as we have attempted to rethink the questions for ourselves. What does it mean to live in airports, literally terribly safe?

Acknowledgments

Ethnography and book publishing are collaborative enterprises, and this book could not have been written without the help of many people. We are grateful. Security tends to be a secretive business, however, and many people to whom we are obliged have no wish to be thanked here. We have tried to thank you privately, and we hope that you recognize your contributions to the text. Lorcan has been a deep ethnographic subject, the key liaison to others, and an important discussant. Sadhbh, "Woz", Alan, Peter, Serge and many others gave their time, support and insights; they took a risk when they opened the door to ethnographic research. They allowed us into their worlds in order to give them (and us) a chance to think about things differently.

Turning to those we should thank publicly: our mutual friend Christina Garsten brought us together ("you'll like him"), and hosted quite a few interminable conversations, which formed the basis for our collaboration. Her project, "Global Foresight: Anticipatory governance and the making of geo-cultural scenarios," also funded substantial portions of the research that went into this book.

Doug Holmes made a decisive intervention in the late stages of writing this manuscript, which, we believe, has made the text both more accessible and more effective.

Dean Birkenkamp's enthusiasm make the publication process (once again for David) as pleasant as possible.

Prologue

At 07:55 a CCTV recorded Ibrahim el-Bakraoui, a well-known street thug with terrorist links, and two other men arriving at the airport by taxi. The men placed their luggage on trollies and entered the terminal building. Three abreast, they pushed their trollies through the departure hall. A senior security officer passed between them, would later recall half-registering something "odd," but continued towards his office nonetheless. Perhaps it was nothing. Momentary experience quickly becomes memory, and memory is a trickster. At 07:58, el-Bakraoui stopped at the Delta Airlines check-in area, shouted something, and detonated his nail bomb. People fled in all directions. Some were lucky and escaped. Others were not so lucky. Najim Laachraoui, a failed electrical engineering student, a "foreign fighter," and, for several years, a Brussels airport worker, was a few dozen yards away. When the first explosion ripped through the airport, he took aim at the fleeing civilians and ran at them with his explosives-packed trolley. The bag with the explosives fell off the trolley before detonating, lessening the impact and resulting in fewer deaths.

At that point, a third attacker was far more alive than he should have been. CCTV footage shows el-Bakraoui and Laachraoui walking towards their victims. Each man apparently wears a single black glove on his left hand. In the same footage, we also see Mohamed Abrini, a former baker and petty criminal, dressed in a light jacket and wearing a floppy hat. When the bombs went off, however, Abrini hid behind a pillar, abandoned his own suitcase bomb, and joined the crowd fleeing the airport. Hours later, the bomb squad discovered his suitcase, filled with triacetone triperoxide (TATP), near the Air France desk. The suitcase exploded as the bomb squad began their inspection. Abrini became a suspect at large in the capital of Europe. For days, Europe lived in fear of the mysterious "l'homme au chapeau," the man with the hat.

As the attack unfolded at Zaventem Airport, confusion prevailed throughout the region. The mobile phone network went down. The emergency system was unusable. Security officials scrambled to establish command-and-control. An email ordering the closure of the metro system was sent but never read. Meanwhile, Ibrahim el-Bakraoui's younger brother Khalid (who had an extensive criminal record) walked through central Brussels wearing a backpack. He made his way down into the Maalbeek Metro station, just a ten-minute-stroll from the headquarters of the European Commission and the European Parliament building. At 09:11 he detonated his own nail bomb. In all, 33 civilians and three suicide bombers died, and over 300 people were injured, many dozens seriously.

There was supposed to be yet another suicide attack, but Swedish national Ossama Krayem changed his mind at the last minute. In 2005, when he was just eleven years old, Krayem participated in a documentary film celebrating successful integration activities. Ten years later he sent a relative a photograph in which he posed in front of an ISIS flag in Syria brandishing an AK47. He had, clearly, taken a different path. But in many ways, Krayem did not matter. The terrorist attack on 22 March brought a halt to the center of Europe. Bureaucrats were locked into their offices and hotels, unable to use the telephone network, and even if they did venture out, all public transport, trains and flights had stopped. The still CCTV image of el-Bakraoui, Laachraoui and Abrini (with his floppy hat) circulated. Where was l'homme au chapeau? And why were the other two wearing only one left-hand glove? Later, it was discovered that the CCTV image was misleading – poor pixilation and shadowing gave the illusion of gloves. But the battle over truth was fought on many levels. Hashtags appeared like mushrooms after the rain. Questions were asked about prison sentences, home-grown radicalism, and racism. Brussels was clearly more vulnerable than people had presumed. Technical and political matters collided in the airport. Analysts demanded that security be "pushed out" into landside, far from the terminal. There was also a desire to reopen the airport as soon as possible, to show strength and resolve, but the airport police went on strike, insisting that security could not be guaranteed.

Those concerned with security often sound a rather abstract warning, to be specified by context: "It [a coordinated terrorist attack] could happen here [in Brussels]." In fact, it did happen here, dozens of people killed with nails in the sometimes ostentatiously peaceful capital of Europe, not just the continent but the European Project, which so many people believe to be a crowning achievement of modern politics. Nail bombs, in contrast, must be premodern, somehow. Even in Brussels, however, such attacks were hardly unimagined. On the contrary, by the end of 2015, European security services were on high alert, anticipating what might be next, and in that simple-minded sense, too, modern.

★★★

Summer of 2015, the VIP day of a NATO-funded counterterrorism training program on combatting Marauding Terrorist Attacks (MTAs)

After invitations to the VIP day had been sent, but before the event itself, terrorists in Paris killed cartoonists in what came to be called the Charlie Hebdo massacre. Evidently the organizers of the counterterrorism training program, two internationally respected experts, possessed unusual foresight. During the week long program, footage of the events in Paris was often replayed. The general tone of the program was one of seriousness. More attacks were felt to be imminent (as proved to be the case), and discussion often turned to "worst case scenarios."

By noon the core group of about thirty attendees left the classroom to meet the VIPs: a handful of senior police officers, military chiefs, political figures, and various policy influencers. The national army's chief of staff arrived, received salutes, and greeted the civilians in order of importance. Then he turned to one of the organizers and nodded a command.

"Right," the organizer of the demonstration of counterterrorism (the "Demo") bellowed, "Outside, up the steps, and no talking!" Attendees hurried outside and up some makeshift steps onto the back of a flatbed truck that had been set up as a viewing platform. Before them lay an urban scene – several brick buildings along a pedestrian street, with a confectionary shop and a gasoline filling station. A number of people seemed to be going about their daily business. A man and woman refueled their car; a mother pushed her child in a stroller; a mixed group of teenagers chatted next to a bench on a small grass square. The knowledge that the scene was an exercise – and a demonstration of prowess, and a political performance – rather than an actual attack gave it the horrifyingly distant yet real feel of a public broadcast about the threat of nuclear war.

It is unclear exactly what happened next, but a car with several young men came to a stop along the fake road, slightly outside of sight. Moments later, a police car came into view, slowed, stopped near the gas station, and turned back towards the young men in the parked car. Instantly, the men emerged from the vehicle with weapons and began firing at the police car. The noise was shattering. One of the police officers stumbled out of his vehicle, fell to the ground and unsuccessfully attempted to drag himself to cover. The police car, one door still open, reversed at speed. For a moment, the attackers seemed to pause as if they no longer knew what to do. Then they began to fire indiscriminately; one man threw a grenade. The man and woman at the gas station both fell to the ground where they remained motionless. The teenagers scattered in all directions screaming, one almost colliding with the mother who was now cradling her child in her arms. By now, the noise was genuinely distressing, a cacophony of crying, screaming, pleading, and gunfire, made even more disturbing by the nonchalant movements of the men who hunted other humans.

Before long, another police car arrived. This was one of the larger, more powerful looking estate cars that one sees in capital cities or near airports. It blocked the road, and two armed police officers went to the back of the vehicle to retrieve heavy weapons, but they did not engage the attackers. An ambulance arrived but it too remained at a distance, behind the police barricade. The whole enactment was transfixing. But suddenly an event organizer materialized from nowhere and bellowed, "Ten minutes. Feels like an hour, eh? But only ten minutes so far." "They can't go in," a French security officer explained, "You see, they have to contain; they can't become the victims too."

Soon a deep mechanical sound split the skies somewhere beyond the horizon. In less than one minute, two bottle-nosed Dauphin helicopters appeared overhead. One helicopter instantly vomited out a dozen men on climbing ropes, while the other seemed to keep watch, before landing at some prechosen point and disgorged medics and more armed men. They formed up into two groups behind ballistic shields – called "bullet catchers" – and seemingly without command they dropped their weight slightly and, weapons pointed forward and to the side, advanced like a single entity. The two teams were hard to follow, obscured as they moved. The disorganized crackle of the attackers' gunfire gave way to what sounded like short bursts of more organized fire. By the time the dead, dying and wounded actors were being triaged, the audience on the back of the truck found its voice. The spell was broken. "Ten minutes!" people exclaimed over and over before formulating a reaction that foregrounded their own areas of expertise. The organizer asked the attendees to return to the building where the training program was scheduled to continue, but shrewdly left time for VIPs to absorb what they had seen, while special forces members mingled and answered technical questions.

In the hours that followed, the Demo was pronounced a success. For some, the demonstration was shocking, partly because of the noise of the gunfire, but mostly because watching the performance felt like stepping through a portal into a world that was hitherto only suspected, or rumored, where the horrific was the workaday reality. Participants in the training program from elite special forces or medical teams discussed all manner of technical details, from the precise movements of "the unit" to the emergency response equipment. This was a realm of tactics in response to plots and machinations, sudden violence, and arcane disciplines practiced in secret.

The VIPs, especially the senior police and political figures, were soon looking at their smart phones in anticipation of their next appointment. From their perspective, the Demo was a theatrical performance intended to deliver a range of messages. Not only was terrorism possible, even likely, there were things to be done about it – counterterrorism was also possible, effective, and impressive. There were entire disciplines, secret colleges, devoted to preventing the kind of terrorist violence that had become so familiar from global news. And surely it was the responsibility of politicians to employ such disciplines to safeguard against such threats? Surely, in the event of an attack, politicians who had not taken precautions would be held derelict, and punished accordingly?

Underneath, however, an even more chilling message lurked: "We've been lucky ... so far!" Anders Breivik murdered 69 people, mostly children, on Utøya Island, but he was little more than a "nutter with a hunting rifle." The Kouachi brothers were certainly better armed when they murdered Parisian cartoonists, but they were still "rank amateurs." Utøya Island, the Charlie Hebdo offices, these were horrific attacks for sure, but, from an expert perspective in the cold light of day, things could have been far worse. The Demo portrayed what could happen if "low level" attackers marauded for ten minutes before Leviathan intervened. Those in attendance were invited to imagine the scene of an attack carried out by peers of the counterterrorism forces who had just demonstrated their prowess. What would an attack by the "real deal," men professionally trained in what is euphemistically called the delivery of kinetic force, that is, killing, look like?

***

Nairobi Airport, February 2019

Nairobi is not the beating heart of global integration, but it is an international city, a nodal point in the contemporary. At the Jomo-Kenyata International Airport, a few weeks after the al-Shabab attacks on the DusitD2 hotel and office complex, lessons drawn from the Brussels bombings and other incidents are routinely enacted. Quite some distance from the terminal, the cab is first (at least first physically) searched. Passengers get out of their cars to walk past heavily armed guards; divest themselves of phones, wallets, passports and the like, which are placed on conveyer belts and screened; walk through a metal detector; pass more guards; reinsert phones, wallets, passports, and the like; and get back in their cabs. A few hundred meters on, passengers and their luggage are deposited, still about a hundred meters away from the terminal. Upon entering the airport proper, people are searched again, and luggage and other belongings also are screened again. Would-be passengers may then look for the right queue to check baggage. Having done so, passengers proceed to a passport check, with a brief interview. If successful, passengers continue on toward the gates, but not before going through another checkpoint, where their bodies and hand luggage are screened yet again.

Such procedures are normal, familiar, and even rather boring. Nairobi airport, like every other major airport in the world, assumes the existence of terrorism, and takes extensive countermeasures. More than airports are at issue, of course. Public spaces, critical infrastructure, much of global culture generally are variously shadowed by the threat of terrorism, and governed by the imperatives of security, sometimes more, sometimes less. Not that terrorists are the only threats to security. Any number of present situations, from finance to food safety, are at least discursively addressed by "security," which has emerged as less a concept than a horizon for certain kinds of thought and institutional action. The immediate topic of this book, the violence of terrorism and of counterterrorism, is extreme, dramatic, and worth careful consideration, but concerns for security of all sorts suffuse the contemporary moment. We ask, what does "modern" mean under these circumstances, and what might we do to help?

Part I

Security Between the Profession and the Public

Chapter 1

Introduction
A Sense of the Modern

Air travel is a by now traditional symbol and expression of whatever it is that "modern" means. Early in the last century, Gertrude Stein (1938: 76) elegantly conflated her first flight, Cubism, and the sense that there had been a rupture in history itself:

> ... yes I saw and once more I knew that a creator is contemporary, he understands what is contemporary when the contemporaries do not yet know it, but he is contemporary and as the twentieth century is a century which sees the earth as no-one has ever seen it, the earth has a splendor that it never has had, and as everything destroys itself in the twentieth century and nothing continues, so then the twentieth century has a splendor which is its own.

Like much else considered modern, air travel is a mass-produced phenomenon. Millions upon millions of individuals fly every year, many of them repeatedly. Commercial travel has been made available to an astonishing degree. One may speak of the traveling public, and what "public" means – the ways in which it makes sense to think about security in democratic terms, or does not – is one of the central concerns of this book. To flip from public to private, airports also are places where the law-abiding bourgeoisie routinely submit to restrictions on their movements, searches of their belongings and more or less intrusive screens of their bodies, i.e., relatively invasive security, generally backed by visible weaponry. In airports, members of the public are objects (one recalls prisons, camps, and other places where force organizes how people can move in space) as well as consuming subjects, buyers of flights. For now, we presume that anyone likely to read this book will be familiar with air travel, and to our purposes, will have "gone through security" many times.

Air travel is modern not least in its schizophrenia, itself a modern complaint. Air travel encapsulates many of the incommensurables and even contraries of life today, from the extraordinary engineering needed to transport people from London to Lagos at 38,000 feet; to the environmental price of a "cheap" flight; to the class structures of seating and staffing; to various worries about bad things happening, some prosaic (a heart attack), some dramatic (a marauding terrorist attack) – all somehow vaguely understood in terms of "security"; to the fine dining and luxury goods available in any terminal worth its lounges. The schizophrenic character of air travel is expressed in the nervous systems of aviation and visible in the design of airports. Moreover, as passenger numbers increase so too do the pressures on infrastructure, which must accommodate shopping and yet more staff and, and, and … Housing all this, especially the capricious gods of speed, retail sales and security, makes it hard to achieve tranquillity, which the institutions of air travel have traditionally sought for their patrons, perhaps like the spas late nineteenth century members of the European haute bourgeoisie sought for their nerves. No doubt there is something fundamentally unsettling even if no longer statistically dangerous about being miles above the ground, where failure equals death.

Such questions of (in)security have been technically/bureaucratically/legalistically addressed. In response to the dangers of flight, and through another notably modern process, a UN body emerged during the 1940s to govern the "general security" of aerial life: the International Civil Aviation Organization (ICAO). Year after year, through a process of regulatory accretion, the surface of the earth was divided into navigable regions, and once local practices were standardized. Social order, that Hobbes imagined as a monstrous Leviathan, is sometimes achieved through endless meetings, tedious negotiations among technocrats. This painstaking work played a key role in giving the world the now familiar experience of international commercial flight. Today, Nairobi learns from bombings at Brussels, and few people pause to ask how this huge achievement of global modernity is possible at all. So, for all of these reasons, what the novelist Walter Kirn (2009) called "airworld" is a plausible place to begin our inquiry into what it might mean to be modern under a regime of counterterrorism, and perhaps more broadly.

Important historical figures tend to draw their own dark shadows, and this same modernity has long been admired by terrorists of various sorts. During the late 1960s, the frequency of airline hijackings in the USA reached two per month. Since then, a deadly game of castles and cannons has been played, with airports displaying many of the traits of cities under siege, guarding against terrorists believed to be "out there." And sometimes the terrorists do in fact emerge, and people die, occasionally in unprecedented ways. In response, the airports change their tactics. ("Has this bag been in your possession since you packed it?"). "And so it goes", as novelist Kurt Vonnegut said of the Dresden firebombing in World War II, itself an aeronautic expression of the imbricated insanities and rationalities that constitute the contemporary.

For an example of this tactical evolution, airport security traditionally has erected static checkpoints in order to filter entrants to the "airside" zone, i.e., airport security sought to protect the planes and their passengers from hijacking. But recent terrorist attacks – Frankfurt, Brussels, Istanbul, Orly – have occurred "landside," i.e., the terrorists ignored the heavily protected planes. Instead, for such attacks the planes and the airport were an occasion and a place when and where people gather, making themselves likely targets. Although those minding the castles have ways to respond, as noted in the Prologue with regard to measures taken at Nairobi, it has not been easy to close the security gap presented by landside attacks in airports designed to protect planes. Some airports are next to cities, some are in cities, while others are crowded cities in themselves. "Landside" thus names places where the high-tech airport of today meets not only the progressive ideals of the early twentieth century but also the *polis* of old, i.e., where concerns for security and willingness to cooperate engage fundamental political commitments, often expressed in the quotidian terms of local government. But who is the public here? And who is "the terrorist" that would shatter the public's more or less fragile accommodations? Such questions, vast as they are, are familiar yet striking examples of a constellation of problems that may be summarized as the issue of what modernity, not least under a counterterrorism regime, means.

One way to make such questions tractable, which will be explored further on p. 00, is to consider an airport to be an artifact, that is, to understand security architecturally. To start simply, a building is inscribed by the concerns of its builders, concerns that in the case of airports inescapably include security. So, airports, from their very remote parking to their distanced baggage checking to their concrete potted plants to their trains to otherwise unreachable gates and so forth can be seen as artifacts, maps or traces of imaginaries of what might happen, and what might be hindered if security professionals do their jobs well. That is, the airport is a present expression of articulated, and in that sense past, anxieties about the future.

Ephemera, including the intentions, fears, and general views of the world that informed the construction of an airport, are by definition not fixed – they can shift very quickly. This instability of meanings is one of the significances of "landside." Until the Brussels attack, airports, at least for security purposes, were generally considered in airside terms. No longer. Similarly, after the 9/11 attacks, airlines armored their cockpit doors, so that a terrorist would have difficulty getting to the pilot and taking over control of the plane. In 2015, a Lufthansa pilot locked the door, and flew a Airbus 320 carrying 144 passengers and six crew into a French mountainside. What was first intended to be a door was reimagined as a wall against terrorists, and then was reimagined again, as a barricade against would-be rescuers.

So how do we think about airports? Or trains? Or shopping malls? Or churches, mosques, synagogues? Note that this is not exclusively, or even primarily, a matter for expertise. The experts who designed, for example, airside security systems to keep explosives off planes were not wrong.

The engineers and technicians who hardened the cockpit doors so that a terrorist could not seize control of the plane and use it as a giant bomb, as in the 9/11 attacks, were not stupid. But as any writer knows, creators have limited control. The designers of chemical detection systems or cockpit doors could not control the meanings that could be made of their creations by an adversary, especially not over time.

In the same vein, what might be said about the people and practices devoted to protecting such sites? Stated in the abstract, this would seem to be a preeminently anthropological question. Moreover, the experts upon whose shoulders the work of security falls see cultural challenges everywhere, especially where tacit knowledge meets the realm of explicit standardization or where near-future threats must be anticipated. Although the passenger experience has been tightly choreographed for decades now, efforts to understand public behavior in actual emergencies presently are inchoate and isolated from the traditional academy. What do people – members of the traveling public, especially under attack – do? In short, the airport offers an ethnographic site par excellence, which has been the subject of Mark's work for years.

Ethnography has had difficulty getting through security, as it were. Oftentimes, "security" has been engaged derivatively, as the expression of a hegemonic state, i.e., the construction of the discipline has meant that security itself is rather under-studied. But suppose we take security seriously, as the Prologue was meant to suggest, and on its own terms? This book attempts to show that airports, and security generally, provide opportunities to ask more general questions about the nature of the contemporary, especially how we understand the bureaucratic state, and about what politics might be available at the present time. Might these shadowy spaces be made, if not democratic, at least more legible?

In *Navigators of the Contemporary*, David argued that a growing number of projects were exploring the experimental ethos found in the very structure of the contemporary, projects that foregrounded the role played by the expert as a "paraethnographic" counterpart. Scientists, central bankers, and even security experts are open to dialogue, especially if the conversation takes place under conditions of trust. ("I wouldn't be talking to you at all, but M_____ said you were a friend of his.") And what has emerged from such conversations? In key ways official power, i.e., power over modern life, is both quantitatively less and qualitatively different from what is often assumed in the social sciences. Security ethnography prompts us to reconsider central aspects of the social imaginary widely articulated through Max Weber's phrasing, perhaps with some damage to Weber's thought. To caricature: the Weberian imagination is of a powerful state composed by rational bureaucrats, who organize social life so that it becomes completely logical but also utterly without charm, disenchanted. In the security context, however, we find bureaucrats – often with considerable human anguish — struggling with their consciousness of their own uncertainty, despite all their data. Their jurisdictions are confused; their resources limited; their agency constrained. They have to deal with people, with all the messiness, pathos, hope, and so forth that entails. Adrift in seas of data, the future is terrifyingly uncertain. But the past is not clear, either, which matters, because understandings of the past inform policy and so the direction of agencies, not least their budgets. Where Weber posited an overweening state, we see great vulnerability. Where he focused on the inexorable victory of bureaucratic logic, we see the considerable constraints, widespread failure, and often very human emotions of official practice. The picture of "bureaucracy" that emerges is far less rigidly rational, and far more human, than social scientists in bleak moods often imagine — and there is hope in that.

Bureaucracy is presently receiving a fair amount of attention from anthropologists. For examples, consider Matthew Hull's *Government of Paper* (2012), Nayanika Mathur's *Paper Tiger* (2016), and Bernardo Zacka's *When the State Meets the Street* (2017). The emphasis in such books is on materiality, and the scale is the everyday. From a disciplinary perspective, this mode of writing is convenient because longstanding concerns — the nature of power and the (modern) state — may be addressed without substantially refunctioning ethnography. Everyday experience gives life to the cold monster of Nietzsche's imagination, and thus the possibility of academic critique and proposals for reform.

Rather than decry a cold monster from afar, we have tried to talk to the people who do the work that we collectively call state action, and to consider their predicaments, virtues and failings, seriously. So, most dramatically, Weber famously defined the state in terms of the monopoly over legitimate force. Terrorism and counterterrorism, in both principle and practice, make a mockery of this elegant definition. Force is exercised in myriad ways during a terrorist event, and less obviously, at other times, too. By extension, actual states are complex and contested, more open textured than often thought, allowing more scope of action. There is hope here too. Consideration of "security" suggests that the modern condition, and in particular the bureaucracies of the modern state, can be more human than is often assumed, for good and ill. The very failures of bureaucracy, at least if "failure" means not realizing the ideal-typical terms we have from Weber, at least open the door to more democratic politics, and perhaps help to ameliorate our alienation — a mood not disconnected from terrorism, or from broader discontents. The bars on the iron cage are a little rusty; the lock can be picked sometimes.

Contrary to belief widespread in the critical social sciences, the key task does not seem to be speaking "truth" (understood as something to which the scholar has exclusive access) to "power" (understood as a morally immature yet immensely capable sovereign, an impetuous princeling). For much of political life, the better and harder questions concern what might be imagined, and how such things might get done, with what consequences? In particular, the relatively amateurish position of the ethnographer provides the opportunity for a public (as opposed to professional) view, and just maybe, a public understanding if perhaps not a democracy. Consequently, the ethnographer may be able and even obliged to move from *Wissenschaft* to *praxis*.

To recapitulate in the interest of clarity, this book aims to do three things. First, in traditional fashion, we tell many stories, make a host of observations, and perhaps irrepressibly suggest any number of questions about security. Taken together, these efforts should shed some light upon a world that is in some sense familiar to anyone in the global contemporary, yet obscure to most of us. More deeply, we hope to have provided a grammar for thinking about security, if not a full-throated philosophy.

Second, and again rather classically, we use our discussion of this world, the familiar yet mysterious securityscape through which all of us move, to make a broader argument. We wish to humanize the bureaucratic state by describing bureaucracies teleologically, as places with noble purposes, at least on good days. Bureaucracies are institutions through which society may work together to try and bring about a future better than would otherwise come for us. Moreover, work in bureaucracies is done by people, not machines, with the expected human all too human weaknesses, but also virtues. The dismal image of bureaucracy that we have inherited from literature – Melville's Bartleby to Adams' Dilbert, say – is not completely untrue, but it is hardly the whole truth. Without bureaucracies, modern society would not exist, and so it is a specifically modern task to engage bureaucratic life. Simply dismissing bureaucracy as soul-destroying, or, as Arendt (1958) has it, rule by noman, does not suffice for a serious engagement. Little better is "speaking truth to power," which often amounts to little more than dismissing the truth of the people doing the work.

Third, we hope that this book makes a suggestion, perhaps to be more extensively developed elsewhere. Ethnography, whether or not conducted by academically titled anthropologists, can be especially useful to finding a more humane politics in contemporary present situations. Expert bureaucracies are intrinsic to our world, and therefore unavoidable, and have been since the birth (or a birth) of the modern in the Napoleonic era. If one aspect of "the modern" is the mass society embodied by the *Grande Armée*, its converse is the specialized expert with some degree of official power, embodied by the Prussian General Staff. As is familiar and discussed on p. 00, experts in the military and elsewhere are beset by the intellectual and organizational costs of substantive specialization and limited jurisdictions. In this context, the ethnographer can mediate, and indeed synthesize. What the ethnographer synthesizes, and represents both to the experts within a given situation, and ideally also back to the academy and/or society at large, is some notion of "the public" that official experts serve, but cannot see in the round, due to their specializations and often competitions. The ethnographer of the contemporary, we suggest, stands in relation to the public in a way not unlike the traditional anthropologist stood in relation to native culture.

But there is a vital difference. In situations of anticipation, such as security and indeed most "policy" enterprises, the understanding of the public moving forward into the future is emergent. The public is the intended beneficiary and often the object of official action. Most obviously, money is spent. The airport gets built; the weapons are purchased. So, ethnography engaged in the articulation of conceivable futures and the forging of an actionable vision has moved from the acquisition of descriptive knowledge, *Wissenschaft*, the utilization of such knowledges, to bureaucratic *praxis*. Thus, the anthropologist who has "a seat at the table" is also complicit, which poses problems worth discussing.

In exploring how bureaucracy may be humanized and suggesting how ethnography can move from *Wissenschaft* to *praxis*, this book uses experiences in security, in airports, and in other settings to begin recasting some significant aspects of contemporary experience, especially in public spaces. Concepts in play include security, bureaucratic rationality, the public, the state, and the modern in some of its senses. One obvious subject is largely missing: the terrorist. Like Nairobi and every other airport, we presume the threat of terrorism, but do not say much of anything directly about the terrorist. The book does not discuss: the backgrounds of terrorists; processes of radicalization; the similarities and differences among different terrorists; the relationship between terrorism and various policies (neoliberalism, oil, Israel, etc.); or the religious (economic, ideological, etc.) aspects of terrorism; the punishment of terrorism; the construction and durability of terrorist networks; the relationship between terrorism and the internet in various guises; and many other things. Plenty of ink has been spilled already on each of these topics, and any number of other books could have been written.

That said, "terror" plays an indispensable role in the construction of the contemporary. It is too much to accord killers the status of prophets of the contemporary that Gertrude Stein gave to artists. (Not that it has not been tried.) Many terrorists are buffoons, which is bad theater but true. And surely other sorts of people, not least citizens, have done much to construct what we recognize as the modern world. Those things said, terror, at least as it draws our interest, requires actions by society as embodied in the state and otherwise. Collectively, such actions in fact do comprise much of the contemporary order, symbolized by our experience of moving through an airport. We live in a world "of terrorists," not because we are or should be particularly afraid, but because without terror, our world would have emerged differently.

Instead of focusing on the terrorists, this book focuses on the set of responses comprised by "security," whether or not labelled "counter-terrorism." This book tells stories about attacks and about the defenders, those who guard the castle. There is convenience here. From an operational perspective, security often does not rely, cannot rely, on much understanding of the attackers. Terrorists rarely present their references, and often lie on their CVs. And we are skeptical that there will ever be a comprehensive and actionable theory of "terrorism," that we will ever know, for example, who will be radicalized and why, with sufficient confidence to do much in advance. That is, even the relatively simple sorts of security, mostly physical, that we expect in airports are unlikely to be positively defined. Simply put, a new adversary is always possible.

New adversaries are likely to be called forth by the dialectics of modernity itself. The failure to define terrorism means that it is not entirely clear what sorts of violence "count" in discussions of terrorism, when societies decide that their commitment to security has been insulted and action must be taken. Some conflicts are between nations, tête-à-tête as it were, but the great game has been played for a long time, not always in daylight. School shooters, church shooters, synagogue shooters may or may not have a rhetoric. Bombers may target people of another race, citizens of an occupying power, a tyrannical government, opponents of the caliphate, etc. Drug lords adopt ideologies; ideologues move drugs. Governments may respond legally, through police and courts, for example, or extra-legally by various means, e.g., drones, intelligence agencies, or the catch-all "contractors," especially in those areas of the world where nobody takes the local government very seriously. Special forces, bodyguards of various sorts, and killers for hire stalk the earth and fly through the air.

Is there an end in sight? In many ways, the world has grown more peaceable. Perhaps it might be hoped that the world will outgrow both terrorism and counterterrorism, fear and security, but we are skeptical, not least because the sorts of violence suggested above feel so modern. While we offer no theory of terrorism, from our vantage castles and cannons seem to be tactical expressions of cultural truths recognized by not only Weber but Freud and above all Nietzsche, in which the price of culture is rebellion. Be the long term as it may, for now and the foreseeable future the specter of the terrorist occasions the building of walls in which we must live. The castle has been constructed around us, as Kafka surely would have appreciated, and we must do what we can with that reality.

References

Arendt, Hannah. 1958. *The Human Condition.* Chicago: University of Chicago Press.
Hull, Matthew. 2012. *Government of Paper: The Materiality of Bureaucracy in Urban Pakistan.* Berkeley: University of California Press.

Kirn, Walter. 2009. *Up in the Air*. New York: John Murray Press.

Mathur, Nayanika. 2016. *Paper Tiger: Law, Bureaucracy, and the Developmental State in Himalayan India*. Cambridge: Cambridge University Press.

Stein, Gertrude. 1938. *Picasso*. London: BT Batsford.

Zacka, Bernardo. 2017. *When the State Meets the Street: Public Service and Moral Agency*. Cambridge, MA: Harvard University Press.

Chapter 2

The Horizon of Fear

"Security" (dis)orients contemporary thought across a range of present situations, much like the unattainable horizon nonetheless encompasses a sailor. This book addresses security in the familiar and perhaps paradigmatic sense of the physical security of individuals in public places, like airports, but also schools, houses of worship, shopping malls, trains, and bridges in London, that operate under the specter of armed attack. The concept of "armed attack" is also vague but familiar, encompassing forms of violence often called "terrorism" and casually distinguishable from both "wars" and "crimes." Protecting public spaces from armed attack, however, is hardly the only enterprise structured by some notion of security.

Consider computer security, another sort of critical infrastructure. While historically recent, and ideologically legitimated by a rosy future (innovation!), the process of digitizing operations is now several human, and many more machine, generations old. Code, meanwhile, has become a space of innocence circled by threats. Flash crashes happen, and sometimes airplanes crash, too. Perhaps unsurprisingly for a digital era, the perennial conflicts among nations, between institutions, and over property are now also conducted online. Efforts to ensure digital security have grown apace, and many of the more philosophical aspects of this book could equally well have been situated in the adversarial evolution in cyberspace rather than the games of castles and cannons played in airports.

Or finance: way back in the 1970s, Herstatt, a fairly obscure German private bank, suddenly stopped settling its transactions. Only then did it emerge that much larger and better known financial institutions in several different countries were exposed to Herstatt in the relatively short term, and were unable to cover their own positions. Due to the opacity of the matter, these same institutions were temporarily denied credit, and were at risk of collapse. Similar things had happened before, for example the failure of the Knickerbocker Trust and the ensuing Panic of 1907, and would happen again, for example the implosion of Long Term Capital Management in 1998, but until the Global Financial Crisis "Herstatt Risk" remained an arcane worry. Now we speak more broadly of systemically significant institutions, argue over past causes, and worry if, when and how such a risk might emerge next, like an iceberg out of the fog of proprietary and often instantaneous transactions, and titanic institutions have no time to turn.

Or one day there is an outbreak of something odd, frequently a new strain of something common, a statistically implausible number of people in a seemingly random "hotspot" sicken and some die, and the hunt is on for a pathogen and its vectors of distribution, beating a path back through the bewildering network of global food production, with grain, meat, fruits and vegetables shipped from one continent to another, and distributed through a tangled web ... but maybe it is not food contaminated by the runoff from a feedlot, but instead an errant traveler who picked up a disease somewhere, perhaps at a wet market, and brought it somewhere else, and so on, and there may be no drugs, or the drugs do not work, now that microbes the world over are fed a steady diet of once efficacious antibiotics.

Such stories are literally true, but they also serve as parables for a global society, or a constellation of societies if that seems better, where networks almost always function just fine, albeit under continuous threat of dramatic disturbance, with potentially catastrophic losses in blood and treasure. As always, poor people in general suffer more, and some socially minded scholars and activists speak of the "global precariat," people whose insecure status evidently defines them. One might go on, but there is no need: the point is that narratives of security run through present situations, based on the specific facts of different settings, resulting in variances of thought and action, but nonetheless recognizable as species of the same genus.

It would be nice to define the genus, at least. But the concept of "security" mocks the rationalist impulse to order a disquisition by first defining terms. From a historical perspective, security has denoted different things during different eras. In ancient times, it referred to the philosophical search for inner serenity. Specifically, in ancient Rome, the term security meant *securitas*, the spiritual state of not caring despite the chaos around. For Stoics a/the purpose of philosophy was to find such serenity. Later, there was security in the sense of *pax*, the peace of Empire on earth before the end of days. Then came security brought by the state. Hobbes, Locke and later Weber described this. We still live in this normative world, Weber's "monopoly of the legitimate use of force upon a territory," but today we also have the explosion of the use of the term security – today everything must have security, from airports to the milk supply – and now security is the leitmotif of the contemporary. "Security" has become a preferred term when discussing a multitude of important global issues, even in settings where other terms were used in the recent past. "Security" addresses, without specifying, a range of concerns endemic to bureaucracies of various sorts, as "excellence" also seems to do.

Writing in the closing years of the Cold War, scholars observed the rise of elusive security discourses and practices as the international and institutional order flexed in response to an increasingly interconnected world. They foresaw security attaching itself to the concerns of governments, populations and individual persons, gaining bio-political strength from life itself. But it would be naïve to ask what this security was, on its own terms. The search for a theory of security, according to the founders of Security Studies, is the search for an "essentially contested concept," (Buzan 1983) which should be left capaciously vague. Like art, justice, freedom, or even consciousness, security is always contested because it involves value judgment without an agreed measure for either "value" or "judgment". One person's human security is another person's oppressive state apparatus. Seen ethnographically, however, words like "security" are not so much essentially contested concepts as scenes of discourse. "Security" does a lot of work in many present situations. For the ethnographer, then, security presents a problem in the sense of intellectual challenge, task or even opportunity, rather than obstacle. So, without aspiring to rigorous definition, what do people mean, in general, when they talk about security?

As "scene" suggests, "security" entails a context, which can be a physical space like an airport, or a set of connected financial institutions, or a computer network, or the habitat of a microbe. Regardless of how it is constructed, security characterizes a "space," wherein inhabitants expect to operate peaceably, ordinarily, with little thought of danger – but such expectations may be violently disrupted. The bomb may go off; the bank may fail; the virus could spread. The space may no longer be safe, and that quality known as "security" may be lost.

Space need not be secure. Across medieval Europe, over many centuries, the idea and eventually custom emerged that peace was the norm, as in King's Peace, *Landfrieden*, or the various truces said to be ordained by God, whether or not there was a king in power. Kings began by decreeing a peace in their immediate vicinity, and in other areas of particular importance to the Crown, e.g., highways. In England, for a few centuries, the King's Peace died with him, to be redeclared, or not, by his successor. But by their very declaration, such peace expressed their limited scope and even novelty. Peace was ensured by effective authority; such authority was hardly omnipresent. Outside the realm of the King's Peace, one had no reason to expect security. One might rely on one's own prowess, or the morality of others, and much was in God's hands. Those things said, this world was not presumed to be, in the nature of things, safe. The King's Peace was safe, as a matter of law at least, in this area for this time, and only because the King so decreed.

Gradually, the notion of peace was expanded in both time and space. In England, for example, Edward I made the King's Peace perpetual; "justices of the peace" were established by Parliament in 1327. Similar developments occurred throughout the continent, under royal or church auspices. Peace may thus be seen as concomitant with the rise of the state, and law in the sense we use it today. Put differently, it is not so far from the idea of the King's Peace to Weber's famous definition of the state as the entity which has a monopoly of legitimate force upon a territory, which we discuss on p. 00. For now, however, it suffices to note that the idea of security also entails the idea of a ruler. Someone must assert sovereignty, must govern the space, whether it is a bank regulator or a webmaster. That is, security is a good which is provided, not merely the absence of harm. An analogy might be made to health care. In modern societies, fostering health, e.g., through sanitation and vaccination, and ameliorating ill health, are understood to be obligations of the state. Being sick is a failure of government, not merely bad fortune. By the same token, a breach of security is a failure of authority to be effective, even an insult to the sovereign, a proposition to which we shall return.

Since the Enlightenment, government styles itself as rational, and operates through bureaucracy. In most contexts, "security" is a bureaucratic responsibility, though the bureaucracy need not formally be part of the state and need not be publicly legitimated. Financial institutions employ any number of compliance officers; data security is part of every company's business. In the course of this book, "officials" may be elected, career government service, military, supranational, contractors, corporate ... Leviathan in the coat of many colors. But regardless of the precise legal status, the suicide bomber, or the propagating virus, is always also an official failure. Combining the fear of failure with bureaucratic rationality, we see official efforts to control spaces, to regulate movement, and above all, to surveil – to dictate the patterns of interaction within the space, so that nothing can go wrong. We see CCTV on every corner; data monitoring; metal detectors here and yon.

Fear has political uses. Enemies, Carl Schmitt famously overstates in *The Concept of the Political*, are the *a priori* of politics. And security is better than a named enemy. "Security" is a horizon. There is no end to security concerns, no end to the enemies that might be imagined. Which is not to say that there are no enemies, but is to say that the logic of security is in principle totalitarian – one need only recall the Red Scare, McCarthyism, and "The Paranoid Style." The recent Gulf War was fought on the pretext of weapons of mass destruction held by Saddam Hussein, who indeed wanted them. The presumption of such weapons by both heads of state justified violence. Saddam appears to have been so fearsome that his own lieutenants deceived him about their failure to acquire such weapons; totalizing logics wrapped about one another like snakes. Thus the fear – real or merely paranoid – of the state can lead to the overextension of the state beyond the bounds of human decency, one way to read *Macbeth*, and much of twentieth-century history.

In this light, it makes some sense for individuals to confront the state with fear, perhaps the intense and disabling fear that in normal circumstances would be diagnosed as paranoia. But what are normal circumstances?

How far are "we" (in the United States, in the United Kingdom, in China, even in Ecuador) from the surveillance state imagined by Orwell in *1984*? Insofar as this or that contemporary state is not in fact totalitarian, to what extent is that the result of its incompetence rather than virtuous intentions or sound institutions? As Walter Kirn more recently suggested, the paranoia that ranges across the US West is a sort of folklore response, a report from the *Zeitgeist*, to a state whose powers are enormous and unaccountable, indeed only suspected. Perhaps the black helicopters will not come, but look at what has happened so far.

Fear may be justified. The Soviet Union did in fact slaughter millions of its own, preach world domination, and arm itself with horrific weapons. The United States adopted policies of assassination and torture. States have become totalitarian in deed and sometimes even in word. The Twin Towers actually fell, which presumably many other people doubted in odd moments, as one momentarily disbelieves the loss of a loved one. Marauding shooters go to the mall, or kill in schools. There is no need to multiply examples, and it bears remembering that statistically speaking, individuals are dying at historically low rates.

Security thus presents an epistemological problem: on the one hand, the state's fear of some adversary, or the citizen's fear of the state, may be more or less justified in a given case, but on the other, the logic of security has a life of its own, and can lead to the paranoia of both governments and citizens. The US government may invade Iraq in the name of freedom and our way of life even as wealthy, mostly liberal, Californians acquire safe rooms and missile silos converted to swank bunkers, buy motorcycles to escape the gridlock of the panic, and stockpile ammunition. All of this may be wrong, even crazy, but it has its own logic – "paranoia within reason" (Marcus 1999). In this book, we consider the paranoia within reason of those who must manage security in public spaces and, come the day, respond to violence. And do it again, under different circumstances (how different?), tomorrow, and the day after … the horizon recedes.

Studying the security of public spaces requires a degree of sympathy for the devil, that is, the state. At least as a theoretical possibility, one might understand the state to be the greatest repressive entity in human affairs, Nietzsche's coldest of all cold monsters. Critique, in this view, would involve unmasking the nefarious workings of power by documenting the impact of some state action on the poor and suffering, and/or "theorizing," i.e., renaming the state's activity in the critical, post-structural language of certain precincts of the academy. From this unsympathetic stance, however, it would be difficult to do fieldwork. Measures undertaken in the name of "security" would be understood as ritual expressions used to solidify power and hence concretize the state itself. The job of the critic would be to call such things out for what they are, that is, to oppose the state. Not incidentially, such opposition provides a role for the scholar, who is no longer a scholar of security as such. After all, the project proceeds on the assumption that the concept of "security" has already been unmasked, revealed to be something else, viz., a rhetorical device for the machinations of the state. Thus the critic presents as a sort of political actor common in the academy. While speaking truth to power might be praised as exemplary critique, critical thinking about security as such – by which we mean knowing how security unfolds in a given scene; staking out a position accordingly – would be retarded, if not abandoned altogether.

Here we offer a more sympathetic if by no means completely forgiving view of how security is pursued in critical infrastructure. Perhaps unsurprisingly, "security" work is volumetric, layered, future-oriented, with multiple overlapping meanings, many of which address core understandings of the contemporary itself. No doubt officials have their prejudices and other failings, but they often also confront real problems. As a society we justifiably expect, and officials also expect of themselves, that the state (more precisely, various aspects of the social with capabilities and authority) will do something about threats, not merely put on a show.

Perhaps this expectation is somewhat old-fashioned. Maybe security is a rather coastal, bourgeois concept, already beginning to fade from the scene. Security is very expensive, and taxes are high. Public spaces have not always been safe; in much of the world the state makes few pretensions at being effective. Even societies in which states claim great responsibility for social welfare (Norway, France, Japan) suffer terrorist attacks. People who really want security usually buy it for themselves and their friends and family. Gate the neighborhood, fortify the compound, harden the car. Even in the developed world, those with real power seem to be abdicating, no longer flying commercial among their far-flung enclaves. Manhattan's new condominiums resemble those in Dubai, turned inward on themselves, away from the street with its less high net worth, and potentially dangerous people. Soon enough the rich may give up on the idea of civic, as opposed to private, space altogether. Government's obligation to provide security to the people is hardly a natural law, just the opposite in fact. Maybe social scientists ought to be sympathetic, at least sometimes, to those who quaintly try to protect the lowly citizen.

But all the sympathy in the world, to say nothing of the data collected from CCTV and internet snooping and the like, will not solve the epistemological problem at the heart of paranoia within reason. While the official incentive to collect data is understandable, and much may be prevented, "security" writ large resists solution. Security is often treated as a problem that the powers that be are expected to solve, but this is a category mistake. Security cannot be solved, any more than management or education can be solved.

Why? Security is both very general and yet requires specification, and hence imagination of a threat. Subsequent chapters will provide more detail, but for present purposes, let us start from the proposition that security is a negative and rather abstract notion: we expect security, violence to not break out. But it is difficult to prove a negative. We cannot apprehend "security" as such. We may hope, assume and even think that no violence is about to erupt, that the killer is not pulling up to the door, but killers often arrive unannounced. Places are safe until they are not. Is the nearest airport safe, right now? If there is an attack in the next few hours, then we shall come to know that the airport was not safe. Even if a security expert could find flaws in an airport's protective systems, chinks in its armor, the attack mostly does not come, and we might just deem the airport safe, until such time as disaster happens. That is, security, like education or management, includes the future in the present. But the future is uncertain. Security thus entails uncertainty; security cannot be fully known, or solved.

While security is a general and collective notion (of an ill-defined set of bad possibilities, none will happen), risk is a far more specific concept (the odds of specific event x happening within y timeframe are z). Attempting to provide security writ large tends to slide into the more tractable problem of assessing and responding to specified risks. To say that "this place" is safe implicitly answers prior, often unstated, questions about specific futures. Safe for what? Safe from what? For how long? For example, security professionals are currently worried about "active shooters" and "landside security" in airports. Active shooters are a sensible concern, but since the future has not happened yet, such specific worries are more or less speculative. Security is a placeholder, a floating signifier, filled from time to time and place to place with anxieties about what might happen. Facts are indispensable, but security ultimately happens on the terrain of imagination, and many things may be imagined.

Many things can be imagined for the simple reason that they have happened, at another time and usually another place. There was a terrorist who did this, and there might be another. What can be done to prevent or neutralize this, now specified, threat? As is often said, a great deal of security work consists of closing the barn door after the horse has left. But the barn is dark inside, and perhaps there are other horses. People and especially institutions would be foolish not to learn from history.

Attention to past disasters, however, teaches an even darker lesson. The participants did not imagine the crisis in advance, or else the danger would have been avoided, or at least addressed differently. Instead, the participants understood belatedly, if at all, as the crisis unfolded, or after the fact, and perhaps even now do not understand. Looking to our own security, how do we know what lies just over the horizon? The 9/11 Report (2004) spoke of a failure of imagination, which is true, but like many truths, easily oversimplified. Neither individuals nor institutions are omniscient, have any real sense of all they do not know, what is yet to be invented. The question is what should have been anticipated. Unimagined things – unknown unknowns – sometimes happen anyway.

Security failures are obvious in the event, but whether or not something is secure — really secure? — cannot be known. It is impossible to think "security" as such, full stop. Failures may be ameliorated and analyzed, and specific risks may be hypothesized and planned for, but these are partial approaches to security, not security itself. Thus security is not definable not just because it is a contested concept, as discussed on p. 00. Even were various users of "security" somehow to reach consensus upon the values at stake, and to agree on how to judge the complexities that arise in virtually any security situation, the uncertainty of the future, of the threat not yet imagined, much less executed, would remain. The wisdom of a crowd in agreement is not the truth. The obligation to provide security thus becomes a horizon, an infinite regress, an invitation to ceaseless anxious thought. Such paranoia within reason is both psychologically and institutionally almost unbearable, and both individuals and organizations turn to tactics, hence the "Secret College" discussed in the next chapter.

References

Buzan, Barry. 1983. *People, States & Fear: The National Security Problem in International Relations*. Chapel Hill, NC: University of North Carolina Press.

Kirn, Walter. 2015. "If You're Not Paranoid, You're Crazy." *The Atlantic*, November.

Marcus, George. 1999. *Paranoia Within Reason: A Casebook on Conspiracy as Explanation*. Chicago: University of Chicago Press.

National Commission on Terrorist Attacks Upon the United States. 2004. *The 9/11 Commission Report*. Washington, DC: US Government Printing Office.

Orwell, George. 1949. *1984*. London: Secker & Warburg.

Chapter 3

The Secret College

Entering an airport's security checkpoint, the demarcation between landside and airside, passengers are asked to remove their shoes. Unless they are not. Liquids were once unregulated, but now may be carried onto planes in a maximum of three small see-through containers. Anecdotally, toothpaste seems to be a borderline case, not quite liquid and rarely in transparent packaging, and the three ounce rule is often ignored. Less noticeable protocols abound, for instance regarding when vehicles first enter surveillance as they approach the airport, which itself preferably sits at the end of its own highway on a wind-blasted steppe, like outside Denver. Potted plants are made of reinforced concrete; posts are bollards. Parking is tightly if fairly discretely administered, occasioning complex new constructions, because vehicles may contain weapons, or themselves be bombs, as under New York City's World Trade Center in 1993, the Alfred P. Murrah Federal Building in Oklahoma City in 1995, or the Marine Barracks in Beirut back in 1983 and admittedly in hostile territory.

Like places, individuals are protected under a multitude of more or less opaque rules and procedures. Not all floors of a hotel are equal; some lobbies and windows are suspect; schedules and routes change suddenly and unannounced. People are vetted. There may be helicopters (expensive and high visibility) or hardened cars with follow cars (ubiquitous in some places) or soft cars maybe alone (less noticed). Drivers are highly trained to evade; passengers to duck. Somebody watches, usually unobtrusively. "It is like an onion, with layers. As you get closer to the person being protected, security tightens," the head of a firm that provides "close protection" said, as if that were an explanation in and of itself.

Who knows such things? Who creates such protocols, makes such rules? More subtly, how do they know or even guess what the rules should be? For what are these people training, and why train in this way, as opposed to training for something else, or in a different fashion? What do the people responsible for such things know they do not know, that is, what do they discuss amongst themselves, en route to promulgating rules for the rest of us? The visible practices of security, along with the rest of the iceberg suggested by what is visible, imply a body of knowledge, expertise, areas of professional consensus and therefore also disagreement. Security, including counterterrorism, is an expert enterprise.

An expert discourse does not exist without experts, people with status as well as knowledge. Some people are authorized to speak, and are listened to, accorded respect within the discourse. Joining in a security discourse requires one to be somehow accredited, in the first instance usually by successful service in some organization, a military service or a police force, for example. But joining a service provides only entry level status; the ladder stretches far higher. When one thinks of the career path for those in counter-terrorism, one immediately thinks of service as an agent, or more likely an analyst, with an intelligence agency. But, especially since 9/11, police forces around the world expanded their counterterrorism capability with new and older but swollen units. At the tip of the spear one finds various SWAT teams and, of course, the black-clad special combat forces. Elite ("Tier 1") special forces units, such as the SAS or the Navy Seals, have especially rigorous admissions criteria and intense, prolonged, training regimens. Combinations are possible, and as careers develop, prominent experience comes to be expected, in addition to affiliation with prestigious institutions. The cv (and there is a cv) should include items like "Chief of Security at _____" and/or "Combat Service in _____." All of which is to say that security is professional, and is in that sense modern.

Most professionals, paradigmatically medicine and law, are creatures of the university. Would be professionals are trained according to some curriculum, and if successful, are legally eligible to stand for full accreditation to the profession, to practice. While security experts may be university trained (intelligence officers commonly are), security as such is not an academic field, and is indeed secret, as discussed on p. 00. And while universities may be elite and exclusionary, they are anything but secret. So, the professional question becomes, which affiliations and what experiences mean what, to those in the know? Rephrased, how are reputations gained and careers defined? In a multi-jurisdictional and international context, without a central authority, discussion of relative reputation is endless.

Authority thus established, individuals may become plausible candidates for responsible positions that must be filled, as in other arenas. Consider the judiciary, or a corporate board, or a hospital, or even a university administration: ambitious and capable people show themselves fit to hold official, not incidentally prestigious, positions. Conversely and symbiotically, security institutions need officials. Personal ambition and organizational imperative are reciprocal drives, impelling the motor of bureaucratic rationalization forward. Which is a more complex way of saying that security is a modern enterprise, the bureaucratic rationalization of violence, Weber at the margins of civil society. Such people in such contexts are, of course, this book's "subjects."

From outside it is tempting but no real answer to dismiss security measures as mere "security theater," signifying nothing, and thereby dismissing security professionals tout court (cf. Schneier 2006). We think otherwise. Most obviously, sometimes security works. Attacks are prevented, foiled, contained. Threats are neutralized. These things happen. At the same time, it is true enough and an operating assumption of this book that governments especially must be seen to do something after an attack, and nowadays, with a view to imaginable attacks. Security is politically inevitable, and for the same reason, security measures have a public face. Displays of force are not least displays, and so there is indeed an element of the theatrical about much security. But taking the "theater" in "security theater" seriously, the question of what knowledge, held by whom, and with what authority, reemerges. Theater entails the play of meanings, both expressed and received. Who authors such meanings in such fashion as to be effective? Staging plays is a complex business, and hardly costless. Security measures are frequently inconvenient, slowing travelers, for instance. So how is "what to do" decided, according to what values and metrics? Even supposing it to be pure security theater (albeit with actual violent interventions), is it worthwhile for Her Majesty's Government to keep a helicopter filled with SAS commandoes aloft over London at all times, for random dramatic example? Mark asked a senior special forces operator, a legendary figure, about the UK's policy to deploy the SAS on a permanent basis over the capital. The operator thought that his government's policy was a ridiculous move, tactically ignorant, but he was really baffled at the lack of public outcry: "This is a country that fought the Nazis and didn't sell its liberties!" he declared. "You see, he said, we are a tool shed, and every country worth its salt has a tool shed. They need us. But you don't want to leave the shed door open."

Return to the Demo described in the Prologue. Security professionals from several different sorts of agency (military, intelligence, police, even some medical responders) and from various European countries, as well as politicians, corporate suppliers and the occasional academic or other scholar, gathered to watch a demonstration of how a counterterrorism operation might work under certain plausible circumstances, and with what loss of life. This was indeed theater, intentionally staged, albeit as realistically as possible. The show was designed to be persuasive, to make arguments about threats and preparedness, about prowess and funding, and so on. That is, the staging dramatized certain aspects of security practice in Europe at the present time, not least sociological and professional aspects.

For present purposes, thinking about security as a field of ethnographic inquiry, "security culture" for want of a better term, the Demo highlighted ways in which security is a nervous and reactive milieu, in the castles and cannons fashion of military knowledge, responding to real and imagined moves by enemies. The milieu spans institutional and professional boundaries, i.e., these are not isolated institutions, nor structured networks, nor even Deleuzian assemblages (c.f. Samimian-Darash and Stalcup 2017). In peculiar fashion, security seems to be a contemporary version of late-medieval Europe's secret colleges. Experts of various sorts gather, discuss, argue. Worry. Debate relative reputations. Decide, tacitly or not. We call this the secret college.

Secrecy is an obvious difference between security and other professional discourses. (Another is violence, discussed on p. 00.) To be sure, security has no monopoly on secrecy. For medical doctors and lawyers, patient and client information is generally secret. In any number of businesses, information may be proprietary, and trading on it a crime. But these are secret aspects of businesses carried on in broad daylight. In contrast, by hypothesis, security information poses some danger, could be used by adversaries. Secrecy is at the core of security; the words are even etymologically related. "Secret" comes from Latin words for separation, sifting, keeping from knowledge or view. "Security" comes from the same Latin for separation, from care, fear, or anxiety. Both words hark back to the Greek for idiot, person in a private station, without reputation, even a fool. To be free from care, then, requires keeping things hidden, out of public view, private, secret. Descartes the former soldier said "Je m'avance caché," I go forward hidden.

This is more than philological fun; this is how security works. Schedules change without notice and unannounced. Counterterrorists fight in balaclavas. In the UK, disclosure of information about violent interventions is generally banned under the Official Secrets Act. Claims are made and neither confirmed nor denied. And so forth.

The importance of secrecy, not just as a matter of professional ethics but for people's safety, raises interesting questions for the ethnographer. One frequently must be cautious about releasing potentially sensitive information. Consequences of the publication of information, seen and unforeseen, could be dire. On the other hand, and to be simple minded, secrecy poses great potential for abuse. More positively, much can be learned from thinking and talking seriously about the security regimes under which we live – hence this book. In an effort to balance such considerations, we have written in broad and discrete terms, and this text has been vetted in several quarters.

Although secrecy is central to security, there are more gray areas than one might expect. What is said and what is decided is more or less secret, sometimes more, sometimes less. Indeed, security cannot be completely secret. The secret college generates a great deal of knowledge, and even more policy and practice, founded on the professional consensus of the day. As with any other professional discourse, much of this learning is really only understandable to those with the experience, skills, or professional history to make sense of it. Such learning, however, must eventually be applied to places or people, and so become at least somewhat visible. Security professionals must address others, not least in order to tell them what to do, establish protocols, regulate the building of airports and the placement of bollards, and so forth and so on. In our research, under the right circumstances, we have found people quite willing to talk. Professionalism also carries with it professional pride, and curiosity. The highly secretive US Joint Special Operations Command (JSOC), running several more or less covert wars, even publishes books.

If one understands the world of security as a secret college, then one should not be surprised to find different faculties. In late 2011, Mark joined a counterterrorism training program at a major international airport. This is an extract from his ethnographic notes on his first day of training:

> I turned up an hour early, which was fortunate, because I spent that entire period of time trying to find a "seminar room" on the lower level of the airport. Eventually, I found a doorway with several large men standing outside – business suits, close cropped hair – chatting with an air of impatience. Someone asked for my name and waved me into a room with a folder on every chair. I picked up a dossier and sat down. Seconds later, a man in a dark suit strode to the front of the room, rippling the atmosphere as he walked past. Suddenly the room was full, silent and intense. "Right," he said, "We're here to talk about yesterday's incident." He paused for emphasis. My pulse shot up, and I scanned the documents in the folder for clues. "This could have been serious," he continued. "A known threat, three airports, and no one flagged it." Apparently, the exact nature of the threat was none of my business. I was in the wrong room. A very large individual removed the folder from my hand and escorted me out of the conference.
>
> After about five minutes in the hallway, which seemed like an eternity, the large individual (who, I abruptly realized, was guarding me) stopped glaring, turned his back, and answered his mobile phone. The world of security is hierarchical and internally partitioned. My guard's milieu was policing protocols and compliance with aviation regulation. Another door, further down the corridor, led to a different room that was used by an operational counterterrorism unit, a very different world. Actual counterterrorism was, literally, none of his business. The phone call came from that room, and it had an immediate impact on his body: he tensed up, even more so, and turned to face me. "Sorry," he said. "Sorry," he said again, more loudly, in the direction of a young man walking down the corridor towards us. The rather scruffy young man approached with, "Don't worry about this lot. Glad to meet you." He escorted me away. During the seconds-long journey to the end of the corridor, and seemingly without any effort, he extracted most of my life history. Then he paused, and put a hand on the back of my

elbow. "If you don't mind," he said, "I've just one request: just don't contradict me in front of the lads, even if you think what I'm saying is bullshit, yeah? This is my first day running the course."

Much as a university comprises faculties, security includes various organizations, and each has a different function and history. The broad intelligence community stretches from backroom analysis to frontline operations in war zones, including "targeted killing," and other forms of "direct action." Domestic "homeland" security reaches out to overseas military intelligence activities, but also works with specialist police units. Police work itself may entail everything from community approaches to reducing gang involvement to counterterrorism teams. Depending on the scene of the emergency, various armed responders may be authorized to engage. Medical professionals concern themselves with virtually battlefield scenarios. Security hardware is a huge business, with specialized engineers. In the Demo with which this book began, various "faculties" of the secret college came together for training against a marauding attack.

★★★

Counterterrorism. Sometimes security fails, and the secret college reveals itself in other ways, more cultural and less institutional in character. To focus on the violent culture (no other word will do) of counterterrorism specifically, consider the following stories. On September 21, 2013, members of al-Shabaab entered the affluent Westgate shopping mall and office building in Nairobi, Kenya, and started shooting. Almost immediately, the news circulated among security professionals on social media. L_____ worked for a company that provided security to corporate executives, including some with offices in the complex. L_____ is a Western European professional soldier, a "Tier 1 operator" with extensive experience in Iraq and Afghanistan under various commands. When he heard about the attacks on an operators' WhatsApp chat, he and his colleague immediately drove to Westgate to extract their clients. He gained entry through a loading deck, unarmed, evaded the marauding shooters, and successfully extracted the executive and his wife. He went back in, repeatedly, and by discovering overlooked doors and passages, managed to shepherd many dozens of members of the public to safety. A citizen gave L_____ his personal weapon, so he was able to return fire.

CCTV footage of the first moments of the al-Shabaab attack on Westgate Mall is utterly disturbing. Civilians ran, hid, were hunted down and murdered; dozens fell where they stood, while others bled to death slowly next to their hidden relatives. Occasionally one sees a terrified security guard. Later private security and police attempt rescues, crouched down and peering around walls. Little wonder: they were facing a small army

live-streaming a massacre. But the fleeting appearances made by L_____
on the silent horror show suggest a different kind of security. He com-
mandeers a weapon and immediately checks the action and ammunition.
He moves differently. This is his profession. The horror show continued for
four days, and many of the particulars are disputed.

Six years later, on January 15, 2019, members of al-Shabaab entered the
DusitD2 complex. DusitD2 was also in the Westlands neighborhood of
Nairobi, just a few miles from Westgate. During a recent research trip to
Nairobi, former "operators" guided us around the hotel and shopping
complex, an utterly contemporary space in that it looks like the backdrop to
a violent video game, with various expensive yet characterless buildings
joined by walkways and bridges, apparently housing unexceptional activities. We stood on the lawn where a suicide bomber blew himself
up. Perhaps his loud death was a signal for the shooting to begin? Our
guides explained the al-Shabaab tactics, and their own reaction on hearing
the first reports. Local police often befriend ex-patriate operators – it pays to
know where such professionals are. Our guides then described what happened when word reached C_____, a relatively young but high-ranking
special forces operator. C_____, they told us, was shopping nearby, driving
in his own car, with his "kit" safely tucked away in the trunk. He drove to
the site to inspect the security cordon and found none to speak of, not any
effective effort to halt the massacre. Coincidentally, C_____ and L_____
had served in the same European "Tier 1" unit. C_____ fought his way
through the complex, some eighteen hours of combat, mostly alone. Hour
after hour he emerged with the civilians he rescued, "pounded" a bottle of
water, and then returned to his own frontline. Local police, for the most
part, let this professional be. Proof of kill pictures showing al-Shabaab
weapons and bodies were circulated on restricted social media. This is a
world.

There will be some people who are willing to turn from such violence,
thankful that such events are rare and over there. Others will be troubled by
the presence of dangerous professionals in a land not theirs. But the problem
of the secret college is not to be dismissed on the basis of distance. Around
the world, serious crime and terrorism are met with tactical response from
so-called SWAT (Special Weapons And Tactics) teams. In the US from
1972 to 2018, paramilitary-style drug raids, carried out by similarly equip-
ped and dressed SWAT teams, increased by 26,665%. Moreover, the so-
called "Pentagon pipeline" funnels significant quantities of military equipment to civilian law enforcement. Striking examples include the purchase
by Kennett, Missouri, population 10,932, of an MRAP mine resistant
vehicle (the leading cause of unnatural death in Kennett is drowning in a
swimming pool when drunk).

SWAT policing is actually a rather old model, and hardly purely American. Much of the essence of SWAT policing was invented in colonial

laboratories like turn-of-the-century Ireland (the Auxiliary Division with its cohort of ex-WWI heroes) and 1920s and 1930s Shanghai, where modern SWAT techniques were perfected by British Lt. Col. William E. "Dan" Fairbairn – a man who inserted himself into no fewer than 666 shooting incidents – and Eric Sykes, a professional hunter, arms salesman and police sniper. During WWII, Fairbairn and Sykes operated a secret college where they revolutionized the close quarters combat used by allied secret intelligence services and special forces, and after the war they left an influential legacy in manuals such as the US Marine Corps' *Kill or be Killed* (1943). Their legacy was also hugely influential in Los Angeles following the Watts Riots in 1965, the event that led to the Special Weapons and Tactics teams that we know today, teams that were originally a counterinsurgency force. In 1969, SWAT officers became embroiled in a four-hour shootout with members of the Black Panthers, and in 1974 they engaged the Symbionese Liberation Army on Compton Avenue. In the ten years after the Watts riots, the number of SWAT teams in the United States increased from one to five hundred. Soon every town wanted one.

Today, most US cities have a SWAT team, even Middleburg, Pennsylvania, with a population of just over 1,300 persons and very little crime. In Fairplay, county seat of Park County, Colorado, a town of less than 1,000 people, David overheard a SWAT team commander talking shop with a fellow policeman over breakfast. This might seem a little surreal, and is. But Colorado is where the influential Columbine high school shooting happened, in 1999. "Columbine," a stunningly beautiful alpine flower, came to mean something else, left fifteen dead, and popularized not only tactics but also a style of violent performance. A few years later, up the road in Aurora, Colorado, PhD candidate James Holmes interrupted the screening of a Batman movie, *The Dark Knight Rises*, by standing on stage and firing into the audience. It was reported that, when arrested, Holmes claimed to be "The Joker," a claim made plausible by the fact that Holmes had died his hair to match that of the Batman character. This claim was later disputed. In Park County itself, the Platte County High School suffered a hostage crisis, in which seven female students were taken hostage and sexually assaulted. One of the hostages was murdered; the assailant shot and killed himself; members of the SWAT team also shot the assailant. During the drafting of this chapter, a young woman travelled to Colorado, purchasing a weapon and advertising her intention to commemorate the twentieth anniversary of Columbine. Schools were closed. She shot herself in the mountains to the west of the Denver without killing anyone else. A few weeks later, a pair of students entered a school in Jefferson County, Colorado, a few miles from Columbine, and shot nine students, killing one.

Such stories can be read in many ways. From some perspectives and with some denominators, these stories are anomalies, for all their horror. For example, the Federal Uniform Crime Reports are clear that from the 1970s onwards the number of police officers feloniously killed in the United States has declined by 80%. One may find other statistics indicating the outbreak of peacefulness. Over roughly the same time, however, SWAT deployments have increased by over 900%, and 80% of all such deployments are to execute warrants. On the other hand, in Park County (according to the 2010 census, population 16,206), the sheriff department's effort to execute an eviction notice in the winter of 2016 resulted in a gun battle which left one sheriff's deputy dead and two others wounded, one critically. The tenant was killed. Perhaps such things are mere expressions of America's violent culture. Maybe there is something about Colorado, "almost heaven" it seems. But again, this is a nervous, reflexive milieu, which can be and is understood in many ways. At any rate, one of the things that has happened is the adoption of SWAT policing.

America is less exceptional in this regard than Europeans might assume. SWAT is a policing hammer, and the whole world is filled with nails. Terrorism in 1970s Europe amplified a trend towards specialist policing, and the same is true for most major cities around the world. SWAT tactics can be tools of political repression. For example, in 2015, Brazilian anti-corruption police swooped to arrest members of BOPE, Rio de Janeiro's famed Special Police Operations Battalion as part of "Operation Black Evil." Several senior officers who enjoyed the status of heroes thanks to a series of hit "Elite Squad" movies were charged with offences ranging from distribution of narcotics and weapons to extrajudicial murder. Lines grow fuzzy when one wears a balaclava to work.

Even a relatively benevolent sovereign, however, might find itself acquiring hitherto wartime special forces capacities for "ordinary" domestic use. If the "worst case" happened, and there was no SWAT team, no explanation would suffice. That said, the seemingly inexorable rise of SWAT-style teams internationally is hard to explain satisfactorily. Key drivers seem to include the risk aversion of mainstream police authorities, competition between authorities and governments, and the dense networks that exist, especially in the realm of counterterrorism's secret colleges, urging "best" practices, i.e., enhanced capabilities. As a result, many countries have counterterror teams drawn from police close quarters combat groups and military special forces. For present purposes, the point is that it is now normal to be able to deploy military grade force at very short notice in the supposedly civilian heart of the societies that regard themselves as most advanced, somehow beyond violence.

Maybe precisely because these societies are so advanced, their violence is generally highly professionalized, hence the secret college. Developing countries, however, may present a different picture. Despite numerous devastating attacks by al-Shabaab, Kenya's ability to respond to terrorist events has been repeatedly criticized as not just ineffective, but "unprofessional," not least by the Kenyans themselves. To extend the analogy slightly too far, contemporary security practice recapitulates the medieval and modern story in which the university creates a professional caste. The extent to which a society could afford a good university, and consequently sophisticated professionals, was (and is) a point of national pride. In the same vein, our praetorian guards have, if not degrees in kinetic force, at least elaborate credentials, meaningful to those in the know.

Which is not to say that security professionals are uniform; quite the opposite is the case. As noted above, "security" comprises dozens of different jobs. Even within the relatively specialized domain of counterterrorism, operatives are trained and serve in different units, in various countries, and though elite, are nonetheless a fraction of security forces. Security forces more broadly are of various types, and all must function in broader public, political, economic contexts, each with their own authorities. As one would expect of any group comprising members of different professions (guilds or castes or other elites), there are endless discussions of prestige, priority, what forms of respect are owed to whom, which house or fraternity is "better" or, sometimes importantly, in operational control.

In an actual event, much depends on the particular configuration of services in that jurisdiction. For example, an attack in London would trigger an alert to nearby police. But depending on the severity of the incident, the alert might also elicit a response from nearby armed officers or from the highly trained counterterror officers of SO-19. In the most severe cases, the response might come from above, literally, if control is yielded to the black-clad troops in the Special Air Service (SAS) helicopter that keeps a permanent watch over the city. In Paris, a vertical line can also be traced, from unarmed municipal police on the ground to RAID, the elite tactical unit that has a rather fiendish-looking black panther as its logo.

Mordant humor aside, around the world, men and a few women (very few in this overwhelmingly male workplace) talk daily about events that have happened, and train to intervene in events that have not yet happened. The milieu is composed of adjacent specialists, shadowy government and intelligence officials arrayed against terrorists, who are somewhere out there, plotting atrocity. Formally independent high-level international counterterrorism units exist in a dense professional world. Units train with one another. Neighboring military units, such as the SAS and Irish Rangers, have longstanding agreements for staff exchange. Police close quarters combat groups, such as GSG-9 in Germany, SO19 in London, and France's RAID, regularly participate in each other's training, sharing "best practices." They even have their own special forces Olympics. Personnel may on occasion move from one unit to another in a different capacity – ex-SAS operators, for example, are in high demand, and retired operators may take on consultancy roles, hiring others for overseas corporate contracts, sometimes working for arms and equipment companies (though this is not high in prestige, but rather categorized as profitable "sales" work), some of which is sold back to state purchasers – the circular flow of security. Over the course of a career, talented individuals may serve in more than one nominally national military, either directly, or as "contractors" of various sorts. To speak of "guilds" would be to go too far, yet attendance at secret college events is for members only (Bigo 2016). There units share knowledge, people, events, memories, and expertise.

★★★

Professional learning comprises and informs some set of practices, "law" or "medicine" or, we argue, "security," indeed makes those practices, understood as professions, possible. The secret college shapes all sorts of work, but is more dramatically realized as one approaches the "tip of the spear," among those whose job it is to use lethal force, from close combat teams to special forces, the elite graduates, as it were. Unsurprisingly, they drink together. European operators might be overheard describing some historical mass shooting event in serious tones, before nudging an American colleague with, "I suppose you'd call that an average Tuesday." These jokes work because the world described here is one where comparison is everything. Tactics are compared, training, every potential move and counter move; every detail is considered, debated and discussed – as the ancient Roman historian Josephus used to say of the legions, "Their training is bloodless battles, battles are bloody training." In the summer of 2015, the "great debate" in a training center bar was where to place three rounds in a "hostile." The North Americans favored, "Two in the chest, one in the head." The Europeans scoffed: "Always put one in the groin ... work your way up, they'll have bled out by the time you hit their head." One year later, a large group gathered angrily at the same bar to discuss how to respond to a central European instructor who described moving a hostage rescue unit down the aisle of an aircraft "side on" to increase speed. "Fool", one of the operators declared in ear-shot of the instructor, "Now, we need body armor for our arm pits!"

All of that said, many aspects of the culture are cosmopolitan and, frankly, refined. Individuals expect one another to have sophisticated opinions on current and past security events, peppered with a distain for lowbrow xenophobia or racism – biases which suggest no real effort to understand the professional issues at hand. Conversations almost always slide back to tactical matters. Indeed, this is the realm of tactics, and one can imagine counterterrorism training as contemporary martial arts mastery, a diasporic world of secret colleges in which people train constantly with one eye on the style and techniques of rival masters.

To be clear, this enterprise is about "the delivery of kinetic force," more colloquially called killing. Comfort with confrontation and violence separates the secret college from society at large, and further separates counterterrorism forces from those positioned lower down the ladder. Within counterterrorism and special operations more generally, what separates the tiers is cognitive speed and physical prowess. A former SAS trooper put it this way, "It's not just about hours putting down rounds at the range. Lots of people do that. My business is killing, so when I shoot, I'll kill you, every time. I never miss."

"Comfort with" or even "preparedness for" violence subtly mis-characterizes the stance of counterterrorism operators, the sort of people that one former special forces soldier called "capable individuals." "Pro-grammed" is too mechanistic. Studies have shown, for example, that police officers with combat experience are less likely to fire their weapons than policemen who have no military service. That said, the point of all the training is to make fighting almost automatic. Professional responses to armed attacks exhibit very little of the confusion and variety that char-acterize the public under attack: no hesitancy about what to do, no gath-ering of courage, no deciding rather unpredictably on doing this or that. Extensive training allows prior tactical thinking (done in the secret college and instilled through practice) to become reflex, second nature, so that it can be executed without much thought. Even in training, a Tier 1 operator has faced intense conflict and physical aggression. If he has seen actual combat, so much the better – the well-trained veteran is as certain as one can be of responding to violence with fortitude and skill. Actions like the Westgate and Dusit2 interventions – by individuals with extensive special forces training and combat experience – exhibit great courage and prowess, no doubt, the exercise of which takes a profound toll. In the event, how-ever, violent performances are largely on autodrive, second nature, the fruit of years of intensive practice and even actual experience, as well as innate aptitude.

In a fight, Tier 1 operators have more time to think than other people, because they need to think or worry about less. They know what to do, and they are confident (proud, arrogant) in their will and ability to do so – the bravado of the warrior remarked since the dawn of literature. Maybe short to medium term decisions must be made, perhaps analogous to a driver deciding where to go, but little or no thought is required about what to do *right now*, or how to do it, much like an experienced driver does not think about the act of driving. Asked what made men like him different, one former paratrooper said "I have a reset button. When things are going crazy, I can stop and think about what needs to be done."

This point must not be overstated. As noted, violence often takes a ser-ious toll even on those who are very good at it. The US military in recent years has lost more personnel to suicide than to its adversaries. Here is David's account of a first meeting with a Tier 1 operator after combat.

It was not long after the terrorist attack, and the devastating counter-attack mounted by B_____, who was now even more renowned.

There were concerns about international ramifications. Members of the secret college made calls on our behalf. B_____ agreed to meet us in the lounge bar of a very exclusive and remarkably dark hotel. Shadows and expensive wood, the sort of place that guests who did not want to be seen and did not mind paying would go. Apart from the barman, and then later some guys that were in town selling arms, and some women who seemed to be prostitutes, we appeared to be the only guests.

B_____ was there when we arrived, sitting in a corner. He was of average height and build, that is, smaller than I expected. He moved comfortably and was obviously fit, but he was not particularly imposing. It was strange, as a once very athletic man not yet old, knowing that the fellow shaking your hand and standing a little close, maybe, could kill you so quickly, no question. B_____ introduced himself politely, and we sat down. I asked what he was drinking; the local cocktail, with honey; I ordered one. He was anxious, tired. Very, very tired. Preoccupied. Quick little movements, a touch disconcerting.

B_____ talked a bit with another Tier 1 operator, one of our liaisons, sitting across. They talked about his fighting gear. Back to tactics. The standard (for urban combat?) kit should be leaner, B_____ seemed to be maintaining, although he had obviously been sufficiently lethal with the tools he had. I was not quite sure what B_____ wanted more or less of, but I did not want to interrupt for clarification. And why would I care, apart from idle or slightly morbid curiosity, about the details of a fighter's gear? For that matter, what did I want to know? How they died? How he felt? What he thought about the strategic or social context? Here it was, the chance to talk to the tip of the spear, and there was very little to say. So, I just sat there next to him, in the deep chairs in the corner of the shadowy lounge, drank my exotic drink, and listened, keeping an eye on the others.

And then, two things happened, both strange. Gradually, B_____ started talking, quietly. As we were sitting side by side, his head was less than three feet from mine. We knew who he was, or roughly what he had done, but who were we? What were we doing? He seemed genuinely interested, but also wary, understandably. The general situation, and his personal and professional situation, was delicate. He had been assured that we were cool, discrete, not journalists or anything. So, he had agreed to meet us in the first place. I told him what we were about, about this book, in effect. You can't con an honest man. As Mark noticed, he wanted to talk. To me. Gradually, he began to talk some about his experiences, general aspects of his service in various parts of the world, his background, what Kipling would call "The Regiment" that was, in some deep way, his home, now.

The second thing that happened, even stranger, was that I felt oddly protective of B_____. Obviously not physically, but somehow existentially. Even dangerous people, maybe especially dangerous people, need ...

B_____ left relatively early, nervously, without being melodramatic, yet somehow bothered. We drank till quite late with the arms dealers and other security types who had wandered in or come with us. But B_____ and I would talk more, at other bars, in lighter moods, elaborate song/toasts, or over email, mediated through the secret college. Security concerns abound, and we live in very different worlds. I cannot say that B____ and I are friends, but in other circumstances, we might be.

When asked what sets Tier 1 operators apart, one said "we don't stop." Dogged will, even more than skill or strength or bravery in the ordinary sense, seems to typify elite fighters. B_____ did not say this, but the description certainly fits him. Short of killing such a man, putting his name on the tower, as the SAS say of their fallen, there is little way to stop him. But "dogged" expenditures of energy are, in some deep literal sense, exhausting. They deplete the resources, drain the well on which they draw, leaving the man nervous, empty, tired.

We professors can talk like this in part because we are older. Also, it is not our fight: we are not only excused from fighting but are generally expected to denounce such things. The operators' stories (usually involving death) are laden with non-judgments to the effect of "good, bad or indifferent," so as not to interrupt the flow of the narrative, or perhaps to avoid casting moral doubt on themselves, friends, or comrades. These are stories driven by action, often as a way of demonstrating character and even virtue, especially bravery and skill. Sometimes even the bravery and skill of guys on the other side, like the professional Chechen sniper who would have his clients set up a nest in advance in a high rise, preferably under construction, with his weapon and a forensic suit. He would enter the building unarmed, take the elevator to the room, put on the suit, kill, take off the suit, and exit, leaving no trace, free to travel from country to country, clean at the borders. Or so it was said. "Big balls" in this extremely male world.

In such stories, purpose, motive, justification, are not so much abstracted away as merely presumed. From the counterterrorist perspective, that sniper's job is to kill our guys. Our job is to kill him and other bad guys. It is not our job to consider whether the adversaries are actually bad guys, whether we are any better, what other options might exist ... the only questions are tactical and almost aesthetic. What actions, what people, are worthy of admiration? Like any professionals, security professionals must presume the virtues of their profession, to which they have committed so much. Within the more limited domain of counterterrorism, where the enterprise is violence, the culture is not only professional but heroic in a Homeric sense. Achilles spent little time worrying about the Greek cause. He cared about his honor, even more than his life.

The politics of their world, at least as operators will say when asked, are simple. Their world exists to shelter our world. "We protect you while you sleep." Their "we" exists relationally, then, with evil people active in the shadows on one side and with "you," the rest of us, in innocent slumber on the other side. At present, serious concerns about militarization, radicalization and mass intrusions into privacy, to say nothing of the meaning of citizenship, bureaucracy, and governance, are justified. In this light, how the twilight realm of security operates vis-à-vis the public, and their empathetic distance from one another, should matter to all. But what is "the public" for purposes of this discussion? To that question we now turn.

References

Bigo, Didier. 2016. "The Sociology of Transnational Guilds." *International Political Sociology*, 10 (4), 398–416.

Samimian-Darash, Limor and Meg Stalcup. 2017. "Anthropology of Security and Security in Anthropology: Cases of Counterterrorism in the United States." *Anthropological Theory*, 17 (1), 60–87.

Schneier, Bruce. 2006. *Beyond Fear: Thinking Sensibly about Security in an Uncertain World*. New York: Springer Verlag.

Chapter 4

The Mysterious Public

Grammar. The idea that counterterrorism, and security generally, exists to protect the public is not only the view from within the secret college. At least in the United States, government action, such as funding the Department of Homeland Security, must be taken for some "articulable public purpose," or else it is unconstitutional. Statutes therefore generally begin with a statement of public purpose. "Public" here is mostly a gesture. To survive constitutional review, Congress must only articulate some public purpose, that is, here "public" basically means "not private." Congress cannot take money from people via taxation, or more directly, and simply give it to individuals in their private capacities. Which is not to say that individuals cannot benefit, and others suffer some harm, from government action – almost any regulation shifts wealth. In shifting wealth, however, Congress must provide some sort of public justification. So here, the concept of "public" can be understood only vis-à-vis its opposite, "private," i.e., neither "public" nor "private" has much content. The public to whom laws are dedicated, that the security community serves, like "security" itself, is a horizon for thought, understandable in conjunction with other abstractions, and as instantiated in particular settings.

Ambivalent dualities abound; ironies immediately arise. In the very public act of establishing Homeland Security, Congress created a realm of secrets, protected information. But, turning back around, the very notion of "secret" logically implies the countervailing idea of the public, those from whom the secret is kept. As discussed in the preceding chapter, secrets are a form of knowledge, hence secret college.

At the same time, we also speak of public knowledge. Things that are public are known, or at least knowable. Indeed, shared knowledge, at least knowledge of a place or other context, is part of what constitutes a public. But what if the shared knowledge is of the existence of secrets, that is, awareness of not-knowing? After terrorism, and after governments publicly create agencies that operate in secret, people know that they do not know, that they are all passengers on some airship of fools. In "Humiliation," a song about targeted killing by drone, *The National* captures the mood: "The surprise of the week; is that I never heard the sound."

Awareness of non-knowledge inspires conspiracy as explanation. While it is tempting to dismiss conspiracy thinking as delusional, sometimes conspiracies indeed exist. Somebody knows, plans, spies, and at some point, acts. Terrorism requires planning, preparation, and so does interdiction. Some wars are conducted in secret. Such people must be among us, waiting for their opportunities, or just picking up this and that at the store on the way home to Bethesda. Too much thinking about conspiracy, however, erodes the very notion of "public knowledge," which converges on "official account," not too far from "party line," unbelieved. Public knowledge comes to be regarded as tactical rhetoric, with the approximate candor of press releases and advertisements. In a spooky time, the public square becomes a hall of mirrors, and the truth is widely suspected to be "out there," held by others.

None of this is entirely new; conspiracy is as old as politics. That said, there is no reason to think that suspicion is constant across time and place, and we seem to be living in a particularly suspicious moment. History matters, and this seems to be a particularly fragile time for the *res publica*, the things that we hold in common. No doubt many social dynamics are at play. Surely, for example, the radical rise in material inequality in all developed countries, which has more than a little to do with the development of new technologies, tears at the sense that we share public spaces. While there are no doubt other reasons for the current state of "public," however, changing notions of "security" are part of the story.

As already noted, "security" has been understood in different ways over the centuries. With the end of the Cold War, the word began to spread through the archipelago of contemporary social life, and was used to describe all sorts of problems, not just the protection of airports and other critical infrastructure from armed attack. But as already suggested, "security" does not exist in conceptual isolation. As the foregoing few chapters demonstrate, security implicates other notions, often dyadic, like secret/public, known/anticipated, risk/uncertainty, and so forth. Taken together, such concepts constitute a conceptual grammar, or, to change images slightly, a matrix of thought. Changing the meaning of one word in the matrix affects the meanings of others.

Some such changes are inevitable, even if the nature of the change might not be obvious in advance. The conceptual grammar with which security is thought is responsive to circumstance, and therefore articulated in different ways at different times. Changing notions of security thus imply changing notions of the public. As a result, what may superficially seem simple, such as the idea of the "public" that the secret college serves and for which the US Congress legislates, turns out to be quite mysterious, shifting.

Unsurprisingly, the evolution of the conceptual grammar seems somewhat clearer in hindsight. Here is an interpretation of the recent past that might be helpful. Like "globalization," "security" evidently gestures effectively if vaguely toward something important about the times. The connection between the words is more intimate than it appears to be at first blush. In the years between the fall of the Berlin Wall and 9/11, much attention was paid to connections amongst things until then separated from one another and thought separately, too. The world seemed to be knitting together, and there was much talk of networks, assemblages, neoliberal markets, and the like. Old particularities would be relegated to the dustbin of history ... it was a moment.

New awareness of connections, whether or not new in fact, brought new anxieties. What was lost? What if such channels, upon which we evidently depended, suddenly stopped? In particular, what if bad things flowed? Rapacious capitalism, migrant criminals, calls for genocide or terror, data breaches, strange diseases or contaminated food, carbon dioxide from coal plants thousands of miles away, financial contagion? And soon enough, events confirmed and specified fears: 9/11, the Global Financial Crisis (including the European Debt Crisis), migrant crises, the poisoning of social media, the brooding omnipresence of climate change and mass extinction – all this before the COVID-19 pandemic that broke out as this text was being finalized. Networks connected us, but sometimes to carry out terrorist attacks; to ship drugs, arms, or slaves; to steal data, elections, and perhaps our sense of self. The nation, indeed vehement nationalism, came roaring back, now also organized as a network. The moment, the honeymoon, was over. The contemporary was seen to be global and for that very reason insecure, vulnerability to dangers arriving unexpectedly. Here again, airports serve both as familiar instantiation and as metaphor.

A revealing moment occurred in the wake of the 2016 New York and New Jersey bombings. London Mayor Sadiq Khan was visiting New York at the time of the bombings and, perhaps feeling less pressure than usual while overseas (as a liberal and a Muslim, Khan attracts more than his fair share of negative attention), he blundered into a political minefield when he suggested that counterterror preparedness is "part and parcel of living in a great global city." His critics, including keen tweeter US President Donald Trump, pounced, while his defenders muttered defensively about context. And context certainly does matter: that same year the EU experienced 142 failed, foiled or completed terrorist attacks, with the largest proportion occurring in the UK. Indeed, Khan's own city experienced a narrow miss when two would-be suicide bombers were apprehended after they asked Twitter followers to help them pick from the final shortlist of targets.

By way of contrast, recall older notions of security centered around wars among independent nation states. Through the Cold War, the purpose of the military was to provide security against foreign adversaries, albeit sometimes abetted by spies. In the darkening of the "new world order" epitomized by 9/11, it became clear to the security community that the enemy was not just within the walls. Terrorists were members of the public, our own people. The public had become a mystery, containing secrets. This sense of the enemy among us was not unprecedented; few things are. Irish terrorists struck in England from time to time; anarchists killed a US president. But that was Ireland, in the one case, and that was a long time ago, in the other. September 11th changed everything, it was said over and over again, and a lot did in fact change, but September 11th was the deadliest event in a long string of bombings, shootings, trucks run amuck in urban centers. In consequence, the security community received more powers to surveil and control.

As a result, the public became, if not exactly the enemy, both the object of inquiry and the terrain on which security was achieved or not, all the while remaining the *raison d'être* of security in the first place. Every contemporary discussion of an attack touches on whether or not the perpetrators were known to security services. Public surveillance, the gathering of information that might prove to be useful, or that might suggest some threat, has come to be expected. The secret college serves the public by watching, guarding over, monitoring. Worries about government overreach in the name of security were voiced immediately after 9/11, and have hardly subsided. The public's relation to the secret college grew even more ambivalent in the literal sense of simultaneously contradictory: security seems to have metastasized, and anxiety about security measures has kept pace.

To recapitulate:

- the practice of security raises questions about "the public" that the security community serves;
- "public" is understood in terms of "private" (and vice-versa);
- "public" is also understood in contrast to "secret" (even if not strictly private) information; which mirrors earlier discussion of "secret" as akin to "security"
- but a society riven by secrets is hardly to be understood on "public" terms; conspiracy and spookiness seem more apt descriptions;
- globalization provides networks for the transmission of unexpected dangers in the heart of the social order;
- the metastasis of security thinking: the understanding that danger is internal to the social order (terrorists within the walls);
- making the public the terrain and object of security;
- raising public fears about the security apparatus.

All of which is intended to demonstrate how abstractions like "security" or "public" provide a grammar, but only a grammar, with which to think and discuss shifting circumstances. In what follows, we turn to circumstances and discuss two settings in which "the public" was instantiated. First, the public is the terrain of the counterterrorism/policing practice known as behavioral detection. Second, when an attack begins, what does the public – the people actually there at the time – do? How do such instantiations help us to think about the sorts of public we might wish to be?

***

Behavioral Detection. As the 9/11 attacks conclusively demonstrated, numerous terrorists could not only hide in crowds, they could coordinate, and ultimately carry out complex attacks. For the secret college, a key practical question was how were terrorists to be detected and interdicted before the attacks actually began? An experimental ethos arose in airport security, and behavioral detection was an innovation. "Behavioral detection" refers to a collection of tools and techniques that, used properly, enable operators to identify and so respond to abnormal and potentially dangerous activities in critical infrastructure sites like airports. A particular policing unit in the UK was widely regarded as having cracked the code and devised a comprehensive methodology for the detection of terrorists hiding in the murky waters of the crowd. Like alchemy, their methodology was (and is) a secret, but their results, as evidenced by arrest records, were pure gold. Senior policing and security figures were keen to know what worked and why. In due course, Mark was invited to join their training program.

Behavioral detection is conducted alongside the use of a variety of standardized tools, including so-called first-generation biometrics, notably fingerprinting and facial recognition. Second generation biometrics are already here: ATM-like machines that can ostensibly detect lies are already being tested; the near-future promises smart corridors filled with sensors to detect abnormal bodily signals. Much behavioral detection, however, is low-tech and high-touch, i.e., humans observing other humans in order to detect suspicious behaviors. Such behavioral detection relies on culturally situated understandings of what is ordinary, and what is not, and deserves further investigation. The US Department of Homeland Security's Transport Security Administration (TSA) alone spends over one billion dollars per annum observing human behavior. Most European countries, and all major European airports, now operate detection programs of variable quality. International airports have become technical universities in which a narrow ethnographic gaze is being trained on crowds each and every day.

The training Mark received was in the Behavioral Detection Screening System (BASS), which began life in Boston's Logan Airport and quickly spread around the world. (Richard Reid, the shoe bomber, was taken into custody at Logan.) Done right, BASS is a counterterrorist policing system that does far more than watch the public in an airport. Highly skilled officers assess an airport's behavioral environment in order to make subtle adjustments that will "disrupt the baseline behaviors," so as to elicit responses that can then be interdicted. Rather than passively wait for something suspicious to happen (one hopes, before the attack begins), BASS creates circumstances to which people must react. The underlying premise is that those with malicious intent (and weapons) will react to such circumstances in discernibly different ways, thereby giving themselves away.

The US Homeland Security approach is a watered-down version of BASS, and the approach taken in several European airports is also a low-cost version, in which poorly paid former baggage screeners are promoted to monitor crowds. Such watered-down versions may be worth little. The US Government Accountability Office assessed the TSA's system in 2011 and concluded that the results were "the same as or slightly better than chance" (Maguire and Fussey 2016). In contrast, BASS policing, in the UK at least, produces outstanding arrest results. As discussed in Chapter 8, the reason for using a watered-down system when a better one is available is explained by the airport police maxim, "We don't make money; we cost money."

While it would be irresponsible to discuss sensitive operational matters, it is possible to give a feel for behavioral detection. In the course of one afternoon during training, the team with which Mark was on operational deployment encountered, inter alia, a young man carrying a significant quantity of cocaine. The team altered the crowd baseline, and the young man betrayed himself with the exaggerated bodily reactions of a 1920s silent movie actor. The team also stopped a man carrying a vast amount of cash while disguised as a priest. Later on, they identified and assisted a young woman who was traveling with an abusive partner, under duress. These are the kinds of cases, and a fraction of the number, that a major airport deals with every day (see Maguire 2014).

But then things got really interesting: the team encountered a convicted terrorist, who had been released under the Good Friday Agreement. The following is from the notes Mark took during a quiet moment later that day:

> I walked out of the conference room in the bowels of a regional British airport with the twelve other trainees. "Now for a bit of fun," said the senior trainer. ... "We'll chat on level 1," he said. "And if any one says boo to you, say, 'I'm with him, I'm carrying a firearm, and the rest is none of your business!'"
>
> I held the door. ... The armed "uniforms" adjusted their protective jackets and weapons and followed us. They generally stayed quiet; the hierarchy was clear.
>
> The officers used personal mobile phones rather than radios. The more junior trainer came up to me, pointed at an information screen while saying, "You hear that? 'He's coming up in two minutes'. I don't know where you stand on this, but to me this man is a convicted murderer, and he's walking about like he never saw explosives in his life. You know there'll be trouble if we stop him – he's a citizen now, it's all in the past. You ... you don't even think of staring." Out of

habit, however, I looked at the gaze of my opposite number across the hall, and when he redirected his gaze I involuntarily looked at the tall, thin, pale man. He glared at each member of the "covert" team in turn, smiled at us, and walked on. No one spoke. We reassembled behind a secure door. "It often happens," said the junior trainer. "They can see you, and you think you're hunting them!" "It's usually an ex-service man or special forces – he was a terrorist!"

(quoted in Maguire and Fussey 2016: 37–38)

★★★

The Public Under Attack. What happens to the public during a terrorist attack? What do they do? What should they do? Starting para-ethnographically with the Demo described in the prologue, since 2015 Mark has been exploring public behavior during terror attacks. He reconstructed a series of marauding terrorist attacks ("MTAs"): Milltown in Belfast, 1988; Glasgow Airport 2007; the Westgate Mall in Nairobi, 2013; the Charlie Hebdo, and Thalys Train attacks in 2015, London Bridge and Borough Market in 2017, DusitD2 in Nairobi in 2019. On one level, this is a practical project about how to make spaces like airports safer; and there is significant media interest in how "we", the public as constituted by media, behave in extraordinary situations. But paraethnography also opens the possibility of critique. Recall the Demo: "ten minutes" of running, hiding, bleeding and dying; it would take time for the Leviathan to arrive. The modern security bureaucracy cannot tolerate this. Force must be brought to bear and order must be restored. But bureaucracy, with its formal processes and procedures, lacks the agility. Therefore, it keeps people on retainer to handle such matters. Helicopters filled with black clad specialists. Individuals who say things like "My business is killing." In those ten minutes, and for just a little while longer, a lifeworld is revealed, and then hidden once more.

Mark's research began with a study of emergency first responders. Ambulance crews with direct experience of terrorist atrocities described encountering scenes that overwhelmed their senses and exceeded their training and experience – in short, terrorist attacks produced "battlefield conditions." Their kit was lacking in the basic equipment carried by military medics, yet, suddenly, medics in a battlefield is what they were. After the 2015 Bataclan theater massacre, for example, hospital workers received ambulance after ambulance filled with badly wounded victims. Their sense of horror only intensified when they saw that la brigade des sapeurs-pompiers de Paris crews were using their own belts as tourniquets to stop victims from bleeding out. Members of the combat group RAID also described a sense of shock and professional inadequacy. As they attempted to clear the Bataclan in the dark, they wondered if the fire sprinklers had been triggered at some point, only to realize that it was not water but several centimeters of blood that covered the theater floor. As they pressed forward under heavy fire, civilians grabbed at their legs, pleading for help, and slowing their progress. It was hell.

In Mark's project, first responders and combat groups have agreed that a greater emphasis on the public was needed as a first step in delivering aid and understanding behavioral environments. Responders want to train for better evacuation and work with special forces to learn about battlefield medicine. For their part, police special forces argue that if they better knew normal public behaviors, then they would be better placed to detect abnormal behaviors. At a deeper level, however, their training distanced them from the public. One special forces soldier who later went on to a policing role explained the problem bluntly. "You see," he said, "to us, at that moment, you are sheep. You are innocent, and in the way, and our job is to herd you out of harm's way. The other side, their job, if they know what they're doing, is also to herd you, so they can slaughter you." At present, in these circles, the public is an object, to be moved, triaged, treated, protected or eliminated. But this is an oversimplification. The public can do, or not do, many things, some better, some worse.

Discussing the public during a terrorist attack, however, is a little like talking about the public in an airport. Who exactly do we have in mind? Are "members of the public" researchable communities or just individuals and groups thrown together momentarily in a society of strangers? Moreover, how can one possibly compare an event in Northern Ireland with one in Kenya, or an event in an airport with one in a small urban enclave? On the other hand, while differences exist, media reporting often sounds the same notes: crowds, apparently, panic, and raw human emotions are exposed by sudden violence. Maybe the journalists are not wrong; maybe broader lessons may be learned. What role do instincts play here, and how variable are human reactions along the lines of culture, gender, class, and age, for starters?

Months of conversation with counterparts resulted in a list of case examples. Mark's research includes relatively recent events in a variety of spaces and regions to elicit the universal and particular in reactions, together with a sample of failed, foiled and successful attacks. From the extraordinary marauding attack on Milltown Cemetery, Belfast 1988, forever captured by BBC cameras, to the massacre inside Nairobi's Westgate Mall, each case offers different points of interest, from the composition of "the crowd" to the aims of the attackers and the weapons deployed. Significantly, the time scale of each attack also varies considerably, from a few minutes in the case of Thalys to many hours, even days, in the case of Westgate Mall.

Why focus on the first ten minutes, such a precise time? In emergency medicine, there is a temporal concept called the "golden hour," which refers to the period following traumatic injury during which medical intervention stands the greatest chance of saving a life. Emergency services also speak of the "platinum ten minutes," during which a crew assesses the event and implements their plan. All of this is to say that it is common to break up an event into moments when best practices can be implemented. Time matters, especially in emergencies.

For counterterrorist armed response teams, time also matters. The ideal scenario is to be on site already or at least close. For example, when the 2015 San Bernardino attack occurred, a SWAT team, as luck would have it, was training nearby. The 2019 Dayton, Ohio, attack was over in less than a minute, as nearby police officers shot the shooter. In the usual case, however, the counterterrorist team is not on site, and must travel to the scene. Transport takes time. The hope is that sufficient kinetic force can be delivered within a matter of minutes, but this is often optimistic. Once there, the armed counterterrorist response team must clear the area, "neutralizing all threats," before emergency medical aid can be delivered. This also takes time. The window for the treatment of victims may close.

The nature of wounds also must be considered. During recent marauding attacks the assailants came prepared. The Kouachi brothers, who attacked the Charlie Hebdo office, carried a submachine gun, a shotgun, and M70 assault rifles. The M70 fires a 7.62mm round, ammunition that is designed specifically to devastate a human body. One graphic description, from one of several tier-1 soldiers who had witnessed the effects of such munitions: "Think about you and a friend working on a tree, and you fall backwards off the ladder and land for a wee while on your mate's chainsaw. Something like that, except worse." The efficacy of such weapons shortens the time the victims have to get stabilized. The description is important, because emergency medical teams in Europe rarely deal with gunshot wounds, and certainly not large numbers of victims who were hit by 7.62mm rounds. In short, the nature of a marauding attack, the weapons used, and the structure of armed and medical response suggest a reasonably clear period of time, about ten minutes, during which time the public cannot rely on professional aid, and may act in more or less effective ways. During that time, the public will be alone with attackers, and even basic interventions, from evacuation to medical kits, can save lives.

The Anthropology of Ten Minutes is an ongoing research project. While much has been learned already, conclusions will not be final – how could they be? The public comprises people with many differences, some alluded to above. There is no "baseline" MTA. Moreover, people learn, and therefore, public responses may change. In the attack at the STEM School Highlands Ranch, in suburban Denver (2019), for example, students fought, slowing the attackers, and packed the wounds of victims until medics arrived. The death toll was much lower than in some similar attacks, involving very similar populations, perhaps at least partially for these reasons. Columbine was 20 years earlier, and a few miles away. School shootings with battlefield style wounds are quite thinkable in Denver, and people responded accordingly.

To what extent should institutions and organizations anticipate such events? Should people be trained for them? In an MTA, most deaths result from bleeding. In the United States there is a movement to train students, teachers, and other civilian bystanders how to respond to an MTA, and in particular, how to stem bleeding until help arrives. What might such "second aid" training entail?

Military institutions have the most experience of battlefield-style injuries. Therefore, over a two-year period, Mark interviewed members of US, Irish, UK and French special forces units on the subject of battlefield medical care. The lessons were clear. In the first minutes (literally minutes) of a marauding terrorist attack, one needs to connect bleeding victims with full medical trauma care. Failing that, time can be bought for bleeding victims with three things: tourniquets, blood clotting agents, and "packing" (the latter two can be combined in hemostatic dressing that both mechanically "packs" and delivers a chemical clotting agent). To work, tourniquets, blood clotting agents, and packing materials must be applied correctly. Perhaps surprisingly, there are few practical obstacles here. The materials are quite inexpensive. A kit retails at about €5, with some new technologies coming online for the application of hemostatic agents. It is also quite possible to teach people without medical training how to deal with bleed trauma. Military forces do it all the time and are happy to teach others, training the trainers.

One might imagine a future in which such "Second Aid" was taught in schools and in suitable voluntary agencies. Second Aid kits could be located in airports, transport hubs, stadiums, critical infrastructure sites, and at public gatherings, much like defibrillators. A Europe-wide campaign could install and "map" Second Aid kits, like the recent campaign to map defibrillators, which has proved itself to be a life-saving measure. Who could possibly disagree?

★★★

Public/Culture/Ethnography. As mentioned, from the perspective of the counterterrorism combat teams, the public are sheep, to be evacuated from the scene of the attack, and then kept out while the professionals neutralize the threat. Among the many failings of the Westgate Mall attack were the reciprocal failures to get people out and to establish a secure perimeter containing the attack. Hours into the attack, the mall could be and was entered and exited in various ways. In contrast, from the perspective of the medical teams, the public are primarily trauma victims, to be stabilized on the spot and transported to hospital as expeditiously as possible.

Both perspectives on the public are important, valuable, and true in their way. Certain perspectives are integral to the performance of certain jobs. Counterterrorist operators need to get innocent people out of the way;

emergency medicine treats people as victims. "Sheep" and "victim" bespeak expertise, the purposes (telos) that define very different enterprises. But "the public" is obviously much more than either sheep or victims. The truth of the expert is by definition partial, at most a view on the public, but hardly a rounded understanding. While experts are also, outside of their jobs, members of the public, that understanding is idiosyncratic and casual. Everyone has an opinion. Professionally, experts know that the public is something more than sheep or victims, but what? Experts, and bureaucracies comprising experts, and taking jurisdiction over public life, confront the public as a mystery.

Here the social sciences, and ethnography in particular, can help. Without quibbling over semantics, representing "the public" is much like representing "a culture" – the traditional task of anthropology. Ethnography addresses the public and bureaucracies in many ways, discussed in the course of this book, but experts tend to have rather pragmatic demands. How, they tend to ask, can your presently abstract knowledge be translated into something I can use to help me do my job? Security experts of various sorts, ranging from unarmed airport police to counterterrorism teams want to know more about what is "normal" behavior, or perhaps abnormal but harmless, and what signals that something more dangerous is afoot. Emergency personnel want to know what can be taught. School students in the United States are now routinely drilled in lockdown procedures, and taught to prioritize their responses (run, hide, fight) in ways that the secret college determines will maximize their chances. In short, experts tend to treat the public as an object, and scholarship as a resource that might help them achieve their objectives.

Asking ethnography to help improve security practices – necessarily implicating violence – raises any number of intellectual and political problems. Any effort to bring scholarship (philosophy) to the aid of politics (especially violence) is problematic, and has been at least since Plato went to Syracuse to help the king. At this point in this text, however, it is worth articulating two thoughts to be developed.

First, in any number of present situations, the structure of expert discourses creates limited views of the public. The public, both in the physical sense of actual crowds in places, and the broader sense of the social space betwixt and among the "silos," evades articulation by experts, precisely because they are experts. We argue, however, that this public is not only a key space for contemporary anthropology, it offers the possibility of a sort of democratic politics. Getting there will require us to offer something of a theory of bureaucracy, and to suggest new roles for ethnography, whether or not understood as an academic enterprise.

Second, the sorts of interventions that expert discourses request change the environment in which we live, and are therefore at bottom public and political, and not expert, questions. During the Cold War, schoolchildren were told to duck and cover under their desks. This was ridiculed but now they are taught much the same thing, and also how to pack a wound to stanch internal bleeding. Few of these children will confront an MTA. In the United States, however, MTAs are increasingly woven into the social fabric. In what may or may not be denial, the response to the threat of MTAs in Europe has so far been much more muted. The more general question, however, is at what point do the demands of security experts, or any other experts, become excessive? As argued in Chapter 2, the logic of paranoia within reason has no end point. Ethnography can help us step "outside" the security discourse, and ask after public values.

We are quite aware that extensions of state power are commonly understood in the academy as efforts to achieve the dark dream at the heart of the state, total supremacy. As discussed on p. 00, the logic of paranoia within reason is totalitarian. The practice may not be, i.e., organizations and individuals generally do not follow their logics to their often bitter ends. That said, totalitarianism certainly must be feared today. It also bears remembering, however, that the extensions of state power discussed here happened in the wake of 9/11, that is, the state extended its power in response to massive failure. To the question of failure, we now turn.

References

Maguire, Mark. 2014. "Counterterrorism in European Airports." In Maguire, Mark, Catarina Frois and Nils Zurawski (eds.), *The Anthropology of Security: Perspectives from the Frontline of Policing, Counterterrorism and Border Control*, 118–138. London: Pluto Press.

Maguire, Mark, and Fussey, Peter. 2016. "Sensing Evil: Counterterrorism, Techno-science and the Cultural Reproduction of Security." *Focaal*, 75 (3), 31–45.

Chapter 5

Knowledgeable Uncertainty and the Specter of Failure

Failure structures the world of security. A successful day in this world is one during which nothing happens. If an event does occur and is successfully brought under control without much damage, it is expected that the work of the professionals involved should not be publicly remarked. No need to frighten people unnecessarily, it will be said. There's no need to give attention to the perpetrators, which might inspire other attacks, it will also be said. On the other hand, a successful attack is noisy, costly and potentially career ruining. Following a terrorist attack, motivations must be uncovered and blame must be apportioned. It is easy to blame anonymous institutions, so police, emergency services and others are often charged with failure.

From a certain contemporary vantage, these institutions indeed did fail. Syllogistically: security professionals were expected to keep the peace; the peace was broken; security professionals failed. QED. The major premise, the idea that a collection of bureaucracies is responsible for something as nebulous as "security," deserves special attention. Security has meant different things over the ages, but today, security has been literally institutionalized. Not just institutionalized, security has been professionalized, resting on a body of knowledge and a program of training by a dedicated elite – hence "secret college." In this imaginary, whatever an attack might mean, it is also an institutional failure. Conversely, from the institutional perspective, the possibility of failure is a spectral presence that hovers over all decisions and interactions, and over careers, too. And there is something deeper, a sense of impossible responsibility:

> As an ethnographer, aware of the limits of my technical knowledge, I spent long hours in the company of police who needed to concretize their roles by thinking about what could go wrong. They were searching not just for solutions but also for deeper answers. One day, as I sat in a patrol SUV driving around the airport perimeter with a seasoned officer, we intercepted some children playing on restricted property. A faux interrogation was greeted with comments about the

officer's inability to effectively pursue them on foot. But after he let the children go with a friendly warning, he pointed out the window to the back of one of the terminals, which was just visible on the horizon, beyond a dual carriageway off ramp choked with cars, coaches and public busses. "I can't protect this. How could I?" he said, before driving away.

The possibility of future horror, maybe soon, makes the present inchoately anxious.

Still, one must carry on. How are such bad futures (which futures?) to be avoided? Making institutions, and therefore individuals, responsible for security concretizes and specifies these questions. In the contemporary moment, at least, fear of what harms an evildoer might inflict is a bureaucratic task. Security organizations imagine, worry, anticipate. Perhaps potential terrorists can be identified? Plots uncovered? Recall, from Chapter 2, the concept of paranoia within reason, the logical multiplication of fears of what might be, with no end in sight. If security is a bureaucratic task, then paranoia within reason means that the institutional appetite for information is insatiable. CCTVs bloom like weeds.

It is unclear how successful such intelligence efforts are, or even how to think about what would constitute success. In some circles it is argued that this is not the golden age of terrorism, and that violence in general has declined in historical terms. It is also argued that the interconnection of sensationalist media highlights awareness of terrorism. Many terrorist attacks are foiled. One might argue that the security community is doing a good job, that the glass is more than half full. There is much to be said about the details of each of these arguments, but not here. For present purposes, even assuming that these arguments are more or less true, they miss a fundamental point. Surely attacks have not ceased. It is always possible that worse things await. Paranoia within reason remains, not just as intellectual possibility but as institutional reality, even if the glass is half full. Nobody expects that "security" will be declared accomplished, barriers taken down, teams let go to find other work, perhaps in the hospitality industries.

By the same token, the security community will continue to collect massive amounts of information, will try to anticipate the next attack. None of which is to say that the secret college's thirst for data should go unchallenged. (Similar things might be said about the thirst for data in the private sector.) It is to say that the understanding of "security" as, in large part, a question of knowledge, appears to be very durable. (Hence the emphasis we have placed on knowing.) But it is not clear what the secret college has learned from all of its information, or to put it differently, it is not clear how data informs the practice of security. Some failures are notable.

One of the most quoted lines from the "Report of the National Commission on Terrorist Attacks Upon the United States," the official name for the 9/11 Commission Report, is that US security agencies suffered from a "failure of the imagination." Without devoting much time to thinking, this analysis seems commonsensical, satisfying even. After all, since Pearl Harbor and throughout the Cold War, the United States devoted massive intellectual and physical resources to preventing surprise attacks, from the analytical efforts of game theorists and code breakers to the early-warning stations arrayed like giant ears pricked for sounds made by Soviets. How could all of these efforts have failed so spectacularly? Perhaps, behind all the secrecy and swagger, security professionals simply lack imagination? This is why the 9/11 Commission's analysis delivers such a satisfying answer: therein the security apparatus appears to be useless and those working within it to be dullards.

A more careful reading of the Commission's analysis suggests that things are more complicated. Before the 9/11 attacks, various agencies certainly played out scenarios and exercises that pointed to the precise vulnerabilities that were later exposed, and in retrospect, the terrorists themselves seemed to be offering helpful pointers. In 1993, Ramzi Yousef attacked the World Trade Center with a car bomb. Later Yousef joined with Khalid Sheikh Mohammed in the 1995 Bojinka plot, an extraordinary effort to simultaneously bring down 11 airliners on route to the United States. So, one man was involved with both target, the World Trade Center, and method, planes. Yousef was arrested in 1995 in Islamabad, convicted in US district court, and remains in ADX Florence, a "supermax" prison in Colorado. Yousef's comrade, Khalid Sheikh Mohammed went on to confess (under torture) to being the mastermind behind 9/11. The pattern seems clear, but, apparently, the imagination needed to appreciate the pattern was lacking. Another danger sign, the full significance of which was missed at the time: August 2001, the "suspicious behavior" of Zacarias Moussaoui at a Minnesota flight school led to his arrest. A report went to the intelligence community titled, "Islamic Extremist Learns to Fly." One is tempted to ask: just how much imagination was required?

Those charged with foresight are always partially blind, while hindsight blesses one with accurate vision. Roberta Wohlstetter's celebrated study, *Pearl Harbor* casts the problem thus:

> It is much easier after the event to sort the relevant from the irrelevant signals. After an event, of course, a signal is always crystal clear. We can now see what disaster it was signaling since the disaster has occurred, but before the event it is obscure and pregnant with conflicting meanings.

> (Wohlstetter 1962: 387)

This, of course, is a broad problem for humanity, as nature gives all societies the intellectual resources to imagine wrongly, guaranteeing regular failure.

This problem is especially sharp, however, for those modern bureaucracies charged with keeping populations safe from harm. The 9/11 Commission echoes Wohlstetter's careful analysis:

> The methods for detecting and then warning of surprise attack that the US government has so painstakingly developed in the decades after Pearl Harbor did not fail; instead, they were not really tried. They were not employed to analyze the enemy that, as the twentieth century closed, was most likely to launch a surprise attack directly against the United States.
>
> (*9/11 Commission Report* 2004: 347–348)

"Failure of imagination" is at best a shorthand. As an intellectual matter, the attacks could have been imagined, and indeed were, notably by the attackers themselves. But could the security community, comprised of different organizations, have been expected to come together over speculation about this specific danger, as opposed to others? That is, "imagination" here is collective, not the individual imagination romantically associated with artistic endeavors. Imagining the 9/11 attacks and then stopping them would have required institutional coordination that did not take place. The information was out there. As an intellectual matter, as a matter of abstract thought, recognizing and foiling the 9/11 plot is not that hard, especially in hindsight. But bureaucracies inscribe thoughts into institutions and careers, raising organizational problems. On September 11th, those problems were fatal, and the 9/11 report spends much of its 585 pages attempting to think through an organizational architecture that would be less vulnerable.

Fortunately, most terrorist acts are also failures. Attacks are usually fumbled, foiled and often farcical from beginning to end. The "first" suicide bombing in history, the anarchist attack on Alexander II, was most likely never intended to be fatal for the attacker. The Fenians also had their share of disasters: the plot to murder Queen Victoria during her Jubilee failed because the assassins missed the boat, literally, to England. During the twentieth century, each wave of terrorism – nationalist, fascist, Marxist-Leninist or religious – came as tragedy and reappeared as farce. In 2016, to give just one striking example, an al-Shabaab radical detonated a bomb concealed in a laptop on Daallo Airlines 159, 14,000 feet over Somalia, blowing a small hole in the fuselage. He was immediately sucked out and fell to his death, the only casualty.

The list of errors in judgement, insufficient technical knowledge, and poor tactics seems endless. Some plots are foiled before they ever take shape, sometimes with the assistance of the security services. On other occasions the lack of basic technical knowledge held by the attackers is staggering: physics, the 24-hour clock, doors that open outwards, these are all the natural enemies of the would-be terrorist. Moreover, failure compounds. Anxiety in the face of suicidal action is alleviated with narcotics, the effects of which are hard to factor into planning; and poor planning leads to panic in the face of unanticipated events. Indeed, this is often the best argument in favor of theatrical security performances – the sight of security is often sufficient to alter the outcome of a terrorist attack. And even in cases in which the attackers were "professional," extraordinary errors do occur. The 1995 Bojinka plot, which aimed to take 10,000 lives by downing 11 aircraft, failed because a terrorist accidentally started a chemical fire in his apartment. He was arrested after he tripped over a tree root while attempting to flee.

Relying on the failure of others, however, is no more sensible for a defender than relying on the assurance of academics that, from a sufficient altitude, violence is decreasing. Sometimes, attackers succeed. They might even get better, in the sense of grow more dangerous. Security services in Europe, North America and elsewhere fear the day that they will meet their match in the form of trained killers. A curious dynamic is at play in counterterrorism: one must train to respond successfully to enemies who have not yet appeared, but who might, but they also may never even exist. The oddity of this dynamic is expressed in innumerable military histories. As Cohen and Goosh (1990: 237) summarize:

> The job of anticipation is often thought ... to have the task of fore-telling an enemy's actions. ... It is difficult enough for an intelligence organization to grasp the enemy's current state, to include his methods of operation and tactical preferences. The task of predicting the future – as opposed to issuing a warning – is a wholly unreasonable one. Moreover, effective anticipation involves not only estimating the enemy's likely actions but comparing them to one's own ways of war.

For the defender, nightmarish possibilities haunt the waking world. The fact that terrorists are on average rather poor at their jobs brings little comfort. An attack might succeed because of blind luck, or attackers may learn enough about their target to expose a vulnerability. Worse, security professionals may have to respond to trained attackers or never-before-seen weapons. In such a case, their methods and systems may work and yet the attack will still succeed because the adversary is just that good. In such a case, the security professional will stand accused of a failure of the imagination, of not seeing it coming. Many, perhaps most, senior security experts know by heart the text of the chilling IRA note to the British government following the failed assassination attempt on Prime Minister Margaret Thatcher: "Today we were unlucky, but remember we only have to be lucky once. You will have to be lucky always" (Taylor 2001: 265).

Needless to say, the secret college is not always lucky.

★★★

Recall also from Chapter 2 the epistemological problem at the heart of security: much may be imagined, and things happen which have not been imagined. "Security" is thus a horizon of thought, an infinite regress. In principle, the problem of security cannot be solved, but only managed. Now that such ideas have been bureaucratically concretized, the regress plays out in the institutions comprising the secret college:

- Information is necessary; there can never be too much; acquire as much as possible.
- Information is never enough. Uncertainty remains. The regress is infinite.
- As the number of players and the quanta of data multiply, interpretation and coordination problems arise, and the needle in the haystack is often missed.

Such contradictions foster a robust, if anxious, institutional structure. More information is needed, but the problem cannot be solved. There is always more work to be done.

Attention should be paid to the phrase "cannot be solved." This is meant quite literally. In confronting the uncertainty inherent in the future, no bureaucracy can be sure of itself. Security is decided all the time, but is in principle undecidable. A better effort may provide better answers, but such answers nonetheless will be incomplete, at least in the world of imaginable (and unimagined) possibilities. Security practice is therefore fundamentally compromised by the bureaucracy's knowledge (or suppression) of its own limitations. The infinite regress is not an empirical question having to do with the competence or lack thereof of any given bureaucracy at any specific place and time. This is not a "problem" to be solved by a better bureaucracy, some advance in expertise or technology. Struggling to cross the horizon of fear is the essential work of security, whatever specific measures may be demanded by context. To quip, confronting the always uncertain future is the never done business of security, the rest is tactics. Indeed, any bureaucracy that tries to answer for an uncertain future is in a similar situation, only less dramatically so.

To understand security in terms of a theory of knowledge, an essential reality independent of material circumstance, is a very Weberian thing to do. For Max Weber, the point of the interpretative social sciences was *verstehen*, to understand, which meant to see the facts of the world through the interpretive lens of some general idea. Famous examples include the idea of bureaucratic rationalization, or of the state as the holder of a monopoly of legitimate force upon a territory, both of which are preoccupations of this book. A similar approach, perhaps familiar, is taken by Carl Schmitt in defining politics in terms of the willingness to fight against an enemy, and then later, in terms of the state of exception. Clausewitz's definition of war as "politics by other means" is another example.

Weber, and indeed a great deal of the German intellectual tradition, operates through *Kritik*, which manages to be both empirically sensitive and philosophically powerful at the same time. Facts are understood in terms of ideas. Conversely, ideas inform facts, and especially, for Weber, social reality. Weber, like any educated German, self-consciously understood *Kritik* vis-à-vis Kant's domination of the German, and indeed much of the Enlightenment, imagination, the echoes of which can be heard clearly in contemporary public discourse. A more patient scholar might trace *Kritik* back further, through Kant's Pietist upbringing to Luther's criticism of Catholicism in terms of fundamental tenets of Christianity. Weber's engagement with Luther is explicit, e.g., the notion of vocation, and the ultimately existential stance of the scholar, for whom facts themselves can never lead to understanding, and so he must at some point say, "here I stand." One might go back still further, through Luther's Augustinian education and subsequent scholarship to Augustine himself, and from there, to Plato ... a thought, which, due to the brevity of life, will not be substantiated here. What is critical for present purposes is that Weber's work leads to understandings and articulations of society that are central to the interpretive social sciences, and indeed to public discourse. Weber, like Shakespeare, is full of clichés. In particular, when we discuss bureaucracy and the administrative state, the state and the use of force, and modernity itself, we cannot help but echo Weber.

Yet *Kritik* must always be done anew, as circumstances present themselves and must be understood, coped with by humans, including intellectuals. Weber said that the point of the social sciences is not truth as such, but the final truth we are able to achieve, that is, existential struggle: "to see how long we can stand it." One of the demands of our day is to understand what "security" means, what it means to live under a realm of security, especially including counterterrorism. Ethnographic research, reflected back upon itself, a portrait of the security official and especially his typical problem, the infinite regress, has emerged. This portrait is at some angle to Weber's picture of the bureaucrat, especially as it has come down to us. To simplify, Weber understood bureaucracy in terms of rules, rationality, clarity. We see security in terms of uncertainty. Reframing bureaucracy has consequences for how we understand the state, and the contemporary itself. A Weberian approach thus has led us to conceptions at some variance with Weber's, and indeed, with regnant assumptions in the social sciences.

Our reckoning with such large questions must wait, because our portrait of the secret college and its world is far from complete. Having just discussed the uncertain future, it is time to turn our attention to the contested past.

References

9/11 Commission Report. National Commission on Terrorist Attacks Upon the United States. 2004. Washington, DC: US Government Printing Office.

Cohen, Eliot A. and John Gooch. 1990. *Military Misfortunes: The Anatomy of Failure in War*. New York: Free Press.

Taylor, Peter. 2001. *Brits: The War against the IRA*. London: Bloomsbury.

Wohlstetter, Roberta. 1962. *Pearl Harbour: Warning and Decision*. Stanford, CA: Stanford University Press.

Part II

A View From the Profession

Chapter 6

Learning from Experience, or Not

Seeing Horses. Security professionals and bureaucratic administrators generally are often criticized for acting after the fact, shutting the barn door after the horse has escaped. The counterargument to this nostrum is that bureaucracies, like people, learn from experience. The archetypal bureaucrat might admit, in a candid moment, that yes, that horse has left the barn, but now we have seen a horse, and we know what to do about horses, or something to that effect. The secret college learns, on good days. Sometimes the traces of attacks can be seen while getting through security in an airport, for example when taking off shoes that, Richard Reid taught, could contain a bomb. While horrors no doubt await, who believes that an attack operationally like that of September 11th will happen again? That door has been closed, or so one must hope.

★★★

The Past is Contested. If experience is key to learning and thus the evolution of security practice, then it matters that the past is so often contested. "What happened?" often turns out to be a surprisingly difficult question. "What does it mean?" and "what, therefore, should we do?" are worse. The fog of war, to echo Clausewitz, was rarely if ever thicker than during and after the 2013 Westgate Mall terrorist attack in Nairobi.

Westgate Mall is an upmarket shopping mall with associated offices in the Westlands neighborhood of Nairobi. Shortly after noon on September 21st, some number of terrorists entered the mall by at least three entrances, and began attacking mallgoers with automatic weapons and hand grenades. Subsequent CCTV footage showed four terrorists talking together; four is the official number of terrorists. Two terrorists crossed over onto the rooftop level of an adjacent parking deck, and began executing people under the sky, while press helicopters circled overhead. The terrorists on the roof of the parking deck announced that they were al-Shabaab, the Somali group linked to al Qaeda. Their intention was to kill Kenyans, in retaliation for Kenya's armed presence in Somalia.

As noted in Chapter 3, former special forces soldiers and security operatives, white Europeans, helped shepherd hundreds of people to safety, with some help from a few individuals employed by mall security. The parking deck was evacuated, eventually, with the aid of emergency medical services. For most of the first day, Kenyan security services established no cordon, and had no effective command and control. Progress against the terrorists was very slow. Admittedly underequipped, the Kenyan special forces did little to engage and fell back under fire. CCTV showed some looting by soldiers. Strikingly, the parking deck was not taken, despite multiple entrances and the possibility of landing helicopters on the roof.

The Kenyan government repeatedly announced that the incident was over and the building cleared, only to be contradicted by the escape of more civilians, renewed gunfire, or explosions. Days into the incident, the entire concrete parking deck and some of the mall was destroyed by what was officially described as "a fire" but is widely believed to have been a car bomb. The death toll has been listed as 71, although there is evidence that this is low. The names and nationalities of the terrorists were never confirmed, nor were the bodies ever identified. Nonetheless it has been asserted that there were four terrorists and they were killed. There is an eyewitness account that one was shot and believed killed. Due to the lack of bodies and a security cordon, however, there is widespread speculation that some or all the terrorists at some point put down their weapons, exited the building, and disappeared into the Nairobi street. In subsequent media coverage, the valor of Kenyan security services was extolled, the contribution of (white) expatriates ignored.

Soon afterward, however, the Kenyan government was immediately pilloried in the national press for their handling of the situation. A number of reports were done, by institutions inside and outside of Kenya, which unsurprisingly produced different accounts. Interviews with witnesses produced still more differences, again unsurprisingly. This is not the place to detail operational failings, point out tactical opportunities not taken, or to cast aspersions beyond this: on the rooftop of the parking deck that day, a cooking event for children was held. Many of the children were killed or wounded while Kenyan security services failed to engage. Those children that were saved were rescued by volunteers.

Today, Westgate is thriving again. The Israeli owners have rebuilt the mall, and have made some improvements to its security architecture, judged fairly superficial by the professionals. There is no memorial. The past is suppressed, contested, unclear. Probably not much, but maybe some things have been learned. Six years later, al-Shabaab terrorists attacked the DusitD2 complex, also in the Westlands, not far from Westgate Mall. Again, a European special forces soldier responded, and was given *de facto* operational discretion within a cordon. The terrorists were neutralized, and deaths mostly confirmed. The death toll was lower, too, with 21 civilians and 5 attackers killed.

It is tempting and not wrong to say that Kenya is a developing country with limited resources. Besides, this event was embarrassing and, frankly, repugnant. Children died because nobody was willing to engage. Detailing what actually happened can only cause controversy. And the site was destroyed, somehow but in fact. Underneath such facts lurk questions concerning the structure of Kenyan society. Perhaps the state is mostly about a paycheck, and if opportunity arises, other benefits. In this view, the state is not something worth dying for, and certainly not some entity with a monopoly on the use of force, not even the legitimate use of force.

Sometimes circumstances simply are difficult. To be fair, the terrorists at Westgate were well organized, well-armed, and by all accounts fairly methodical. As the event ended, much of the site was destroyed. In the wake of the 9/11 attacks, the US government, with its immense resources and in this instance concentrated political will, went to great lengths to determine what happened, and to establish an authoritative narrative. But there were no survivors of the four planes involved. Some of the evidence was obtained by torture. Authoritative narratives are hard to come by, even when the facts are agreed and resources vast. And even agreed facts may suggest many different things about the world.

★★★

Paranoia Within Reason. At 08:49 on July 7, 2005, Islamic terrorists detonated Improvised Explosive Devices (IEDs) on three London Underground trains. There was supposed to be a fourth train bombing. Eighteen-year old Hasib Hussain arrived at the Northern Line at the appointed time, only to find that the service had been cancelled. Hussain left the train station and attempted to phone his friends for guidance. They were probably already dead. CCTV picked Hussain up wandering about, but he did not attract police attention. He was a "clean skin": he had no police record beyond youthful shoplifting, and he was not on any terrorist watch list. At 09:47, his mind made up, Hussain boarded a double-decker bus in Tavistock Square and detonated his IED. He killed himself and 14 innocent civilians, and he maimed dozens more. The official death toll from the 7/7 attacks was 56, with 784 injured.

London went into lockdown. The 24-hour cable news channels began their exhausting coverage. "Experts" appeared on the news to give their assessment of every possible element of the unfolding tragedy, and conspiracy theories mushroomed wherever there was a gap in knowledge. The mysterious workings of the security sector seemed to add to the sense of paranoia and performance. Counterterror police units alluded to a shoot-to-kill policy in the event of any future attack, while the terrorists, who the Intelligence Services somehow missed, were perhaps the first wave of a larger attack. And who were the attackers, really? "Home grown" terrorists radicalized because of poverty, reacting to UK interventions overseas? Was Britain, in truth, to blame for the tragedy that befell it? The sense of paranoia and performance deepened with every mention of "Israelis." CBS News reported that, apparently, British intelligence warned the Israeli embassy of the impending attack minutes before it occurred. Of course, even conspiracy theorists are prepared to accept that mundane, undifferentiated intelligence briefings probably go to at-risk embassies in major capitals. But how to explain a simulation training exercise in which bombs explode in the London Underground on the very morning of 7/7, including the presence of mysterious counterterrorism "agents"?

During an academic conference in 2007, a well-known academic mentioned this training exercise, telling the large audience with great confidence that the exercise was run by MI5 with assistance from Israeli Mossad agents.

A simple search would have revealed a different truth. On the morning of July 7, 2005, Visor Consultants was running a scenario-based exercise for the publishing company, Reed Elsevier, to enhance crisis management for 1,000-plus office staff. Outside the window, actual bombs went off. Crisis management is now a routine aspect of life in many large, risk adverse corporations and public bodies. The world of crisis management is populated by various experts with careers in the military, police, and sometimes even the intelligence community. Security is now stitched into the infrastructure of the contemporary, making conspiracy – the search for "explanation" to stabilize existing worldviews – a matter for academics and the general public, too. Paranoia within reason for everyone.

★★★

The Art of Interpretation. As variously established commentators struggled to react to the events of July 2005, the actual terrorists had already crafted their explanation. One of the attackers, Mohammad Sidique Khan, left a video tape that opens with him denouncing "spin" and insisting that he will address his audience in such a way as to avoid any confusion:

> I and thousands like me are forsaking everything for what we believe. Our drive and motivation doesn't come from tangible commodities that this world has to offer. Our religion is Islam obedience to the one true God and following the footsteps of the final prophet messenger. Your democratically-elected governments continuously perpetuate atrocities against my people all over the world. And your support of them makes you directly responsible, just as I am directly responsible for protecting and avenging my Muslim brothers and sisters. Until we feel security you will be our targets and until you stop the bombing gassing, imprisonment and torture of my people we will not stop thi

fight. We are at war and I am a soldier. Now you too will taste the reality of this situation.

(BBC 2005)

Mohammad Sidique Khan could not have been clearer about his motivations: he was at war with the world protected by security agencies, indeed with the modern world *in toto*. He attacked ordinary politics twice, once by murdering people, and then by telling the world why he did it. One is tempted to think of contemporary terrorism as propaganda by violent expression, occasioning struggles over interpretation (see also Contee 2019). Right-wing terrorists share this obsession with clarity of expression – Anders Breivik left an enormous 1,500-word manifesto for the dark web dwellers; and in New Zealand it is a crime to possess a copy of Christchurch terrorist Brenton Tarrant's reference-heavy manifesto. Terrorism, it is clear, assaults politics and occasions political expression too.

Academics, including anthropologists, offer their own readings of such events, because that is what they do. Examples comprise a literature, but one will suffice for present purposes. A decade ago, anthropologist Pnina Werbner penned a curious, wistful yet imperious, essay in which she reflected on her fieldwork experience during major global events, including terrorism, and noted that the ethnographic became redundant as a source of material for intervention into the "realm of public affairs," because *"the ordinary cannot explain the extraordinary!"* (Werbner 2010: 199 [original emphasis]). She continues,

> We need ... to reflect on our main task as anthropologists. Is it to speak out on "terror," broadly defined, and attempt to "explain" its causes and consequences? If so, what might such explanations consist of? Or is it rather to study the predicaments of vulnerable minorities suspected or accused of harboring terrorists? The first option would lead us to highlight Islamic violent militancy – in Britain the so-called radicalization or fanaticism that persuades apparently ordinary young British-born Pakistanis to become suicide bombers. The alternative aim would lead more modestly to a reflection on the impact that widespread securitization and wars in the Middle East and Pakistan have had on local diasporic lives.

This short quotation is saturated with meaning. The anthropologist is presented with two options, only one of which is (morally) correct, so we are actually presented with an injunction. The first option is to acknowledge the "public" in public affairs, perhaps conceding that religious violence and radicalism fascinates and seduces, perhaps even offering articulation if not complete explanation, and maybe helping the public respond. Unthinkable. We are instructed to turn from the public to (diasporic) locality as counter-public, so as to offer modest reflections on the impacts felt there. Membership of the loyal opposition to power has its advantages. This is thinkable.

> These days, anthropologists increasingly study people who are the victims of violent and humanitarian crises, of civil war, incurable disease, and the fall-out from global or state terror. Our conceptual tools have had to be stretched beyond their limits to comprehend such events. Our ethnographic mediations necessarily start from the bottom – from the small places where we do our ordinary, quotidian research.
>
> (Werbner 2010: 206)

A passion for the ordinary and paucity of flexible conceptual tools puts one in a bad position to say much about security policy, or any policy. And if one finds oneself in a corner, paint brush in-hand, surely questions must be asked? Perhaps one's passion for "small places" is a problem? From our perspective, it is possible and would be good for ethnographers to do far more to help public affairs, including security. Be that as it may, for now it suffices to note that academics, like governments, the media, and terrorists themselves, insist on their version of events.

★★★

Chapter 5 argued that danger cannot, finally, be anticipated. This Chapter 6 has argued that the past is unlikely to be well-known, and certainly not agreed upon, making learning and deciding what to do difficult. But if danger cannot be anticipated or even understood from experience, perhaps danger can be prevented or precluded? Perhaps we can build a castle so robust that our ignorance, the scope of which we cannot know, is irrelevant?

References

BBC. 2005. "London Bomber: Text in Full."September 1. Available at http://news.bbc.co.uk/2/hi/uk/4206800.stm [accessed April 7, 2020].

Contee, Simon. 2019. *ISIS and the Pornography of Violence*. London: Anthem Press.

Werbner, Pnina. 2010. "Notes from a Small Place: Anthropological Blues in the Face of Global Terror." *Current Anthropology*, 51 (2), 193–221.

Chapter 7

Security by Design

Introduction. One way to try and make the vague yet pervasive problem of security tractable is to understand it architecturally. Rebuilding after truck bomb attacks such as the Oklahoma City Bombing or the US Embassy bombings in Dar es-Salaam and Nairobi in 1998, an obvious concern is to ensure that explosive laden trucks not be allowed so close to buildings. The general problem of security, then, can be and is specified if not exhausted by the far more tractable problem of managing truck traffic. There are things that can be bought, that can be built, that keep trucks away from buildings. In a process sometimes called "target hardening," security imperatives inform reconstruction. US embassies all over the world have been rebuilt as fortresses, or replaced by new, more defensible, buildings, often farther from the center of the city.

From rebuilding after an attack to attempting to achieve security by design *ex ante* is but a short step. "Design" here covers a large range of intentional enterprises, from international negotiations to technical blue-prints for a specific building. As noted in Chapter 1, the International Civil Aviation Organization (ICAO) governs the general security of international aerial life. Institutionally, ICAO measures, and more generally, evolving senses of best practices, are transposed by the Airports Council International (ACI) into guidelines for specific airports, i.e., the range of authorities where such airports are located, for practical realization. If not, there is a risk that planes do not land. Through such not entirely soft law practices, airport security practices are standardized, if not perfectly, worldwide. The entire process is a remarkable example of an efficacious international jurisgenerative practice. A couple of brief excerpts provide the flavor:

> This advisory bulletin is addressed to ACI members and identifies a number of options and best practices airports can use to protect landside spaces. Not all of the measures identified would be the responsibility of the airport; in many instances airports own the real estate landside but the responsibility for public spaces lies with local law enforcement. However, the measures below can be used in discussion with local

authorities and national regulators when determining the risk level and appropriate actions. The top priority should be to agree responsibility and accountability for measures between the airport and the regulator.

...

Building design

- Consider infrastructure and airport design features to mitigate the threat from attack. These might include:

    - blast proofing;
    - the use of materials to minimize damage (such as shatterproof glass);
    - bollards, flowerpots and other structures to prevent drive-in attacks;
    - the separation of vehicle drop-off and pickup points from the terminal entrance through use of a concourse or other pedestrianized area; and
    - management of space to reduce gatherings of people.

- Reduce access to areas (such as terraces) where an active shooter or bomber might have access to crowded public areas.
- Reduce areas where items can be hidden, such as opaque rubbish bins or concealed corners.
- When new buildings are planned near the airport, engage with local planning authorities to ensure that security considerations are taken into account, such as balconies, terraces or windows that open, close to the terminal building.
- When designing new terminal buildings, ensure that security considerations are taken into account; retrofitting is more expensive.

(ACI 2017: 1–3 passim)

And so forth. To generalize, a new embassy, airport, or even a less high value target like a park or a streetscape, is inscribed by the interests of its builders, including security. As noted in the introductory chapter, airports and other critical infrastructure reflect and express fears of events that might be prevented or at least contained, if the castle is built correctly. From this perspective, construction is a collective present expression of articulated anxieties about the future.

★★★

Castles and Cannons. Jan and Margaret (not their real names) are white South African ex pats. They live in Kenya, where they run a company that design security systems for private and commercial use, sells the hardware, and manages the installations. Jan has the curious but effective habit of telling stories in dialogue.

"So I always tell people, when people say, 'I was in just in Nairobi.'

'Well did you go to Bar X?'

'No.'

'Then you haven't been to Nairobi.'"

Obviously, we went to Bar X, along with various friends of Jan, and perhaps we met some more there. Almost everyone we met, then and on other occasions in our fieldwork, had something to do with security. This was a recurring pattern. There was rarely any, "Oh, she manages a bank, and he's got a construction company," although at Bar X we were joined by at least one politician. In general, however, the secret college drinks together. Often and heavily. Bar X is an indoor/outdoor bar, open astonishingly late, a place for "one more" drink for locals, black and white, and people passing through for whatever reason. Security loitering outside, but far too close to the street, the professionals scoffed, and far too easy to lob a grenade onto the patio where we were sitting. Why not put up some netting, for inexpensive starters? Perhaps this was for our benefit. Mark was there studying terrorist attacks, after all, with David looking over his shoulder and wondering what it all meant in the scheme of the contemporary. Perhaps not. Security was what these people did for a living, and what they shared.

Somehow, conversation turned to how the security design business worked. David, rarely afraid to look ignorant, simply may have asked. Jan started a parlor game on the back of a sheet of paper that appeared from somewhere. "Suppose you have a compound." In Nairobi, as in many parts of the world, that is a pretty normal thing to say, but it bears reflection. The security industry is enormous, worldwide, including in the most developed countries. But in more developed countries, security is often pushed to the back of the mind, some sort of institutional responsibility, like the supply of electricity or meat. Security is vaguely the responsibility of the government. Or of some large corporation, or whoever runs the gated community … it's the sort of thing that is best done discretely, like slaughtering animals. In the United States and Europe, for example, weapons detectors in civic buildings are still somewhat disturbing. In Kenya and much of the developing world, however, such things tend to be more out in the open. Just like chickens might die out back, homes and even small businesses have armed guards, and so acquiring security, including weapons, is a fairly middle-class activity.

"You have this compound," Jan says, "and you want to protect it, so you come to us. You've got some amount of money, let's say, and you can buy security cameras, or bollards, or maybe hire one of those guards in a little house." Maybe weapons were an option. In the course of the evening, there were many weapons discussions, some involving knives in kitchens, and a good deal of spousal teasing. At any rate, we went for the cameras.

"Where are you going to put those cameras?" We pointed on the drawing to where we thought they should be placed, getting it wrong, of course, leading to clucking from most of the table. Academics. You can take them out, but … This led to a long discussion about camera placement, the vulnerabilities of cameras, maintenance, and the like.

"Now," Jan says, "you've got some cameras, but they aren't very good. So let's say you can spend a little more money." He then laid out a list of options. We weren't taking notes, so this is a loose reconstruction from memory. "You can upgrade the cameras so they see in the dark. Or you can add lights. Or you can add backups, maybe with motion detectors."

Perhaps we chose motion detectors, and then learned how hard it was to keep motion detectors from going off accidentally. Monkeys. Birds. People stopped checking, if they ever were checking, like the townspeople stopped coming when the boy cried wolf. None of which means, of course, that there might not be intruders, or wolves. So maybe we chose lights that might at least frighten casual burglars away.

At some point, probably David but somebody said, suppose somebody does not care about being seen? They just want into the house, to kill you. This led to a discussion of bars, and steel doors, and entry systems, and their problems. In South Africa, reputedly, more people die from being unable to escape their burning houses due to the bars than are saved by the bars themselves. Entry systems, various forms of ID for various levels of access, constituted a huge part of Jan and Margaret's business, especially on the commercial side, but they had their weaknesses, too …

"OK, but suppose somebody really wants you dead? They drive up to the house, ram their way into the house." Jan increased our budget again. Choices were offered. How about rerouting the driveway? That would at the very least be inconvenient, and depending on the site maybe impossible. Also, for a commercial site, it was probably infeasible, maybe illegal. Delivery and perhaps emergency vehicles had to be able to get to the building. So maybe we should buy a security gate, perhaps with those bollards that disappear when somebody presses a button.

Perhaps we could require cars to stop some distance from the house, route traffic in such a way that it could be observed before it entered the compound, and security deployed accordingly? More cameras. Perhaps searched? More staff. And if they cut power to the house? This led to a discussion of power back-ups, and communication of both data and images via satellite communication. And if they nonetheless breached? Internal barriers. Weapons. Knife fights in kitchens, and tales of personal prowess. Safe rooms.

As the White Cap flowed and the game went on, both the threats and the defenses become more and more elaborate, expensive, almost baroque. For every threat, Jan offered a technical solution, at a price. Every solution, however, had a weakness, or could be evaded by a change in the attacker's tactics. David and sometimes Mark would guess. The rest of the table, including Jan and often Mark, knew better answers and corrected. Eventually, a team of commandoes in armored vehicles is imagined to be smashing its way into a compound. The guards flee or are killed, but the commandoes meet with heavily armed defenders. Deep within the bowels of the house, in a modern day analogue to the medieval castle's keep, the fabulously wealthy recluse huddles in his or her safe room, signaling the outside world, pleading for reinforcements.

A number of points are salient, i.e., stick out like the angle of a fortification. First, such games of castles and cannons have no endpoint. Given resources and interest, there is always a next move, for either the attackers or the defenders. This is the architectural version of the infinite regress introduced in Chapter 2, and bureaucratized in Chapter 5. To put it epistemologically, the concept of security – the effort to make the uncertain future certain in the present – is self-contradictory, logically impossible. Efforts to square the circle lead to the infinite regress.

Second, as we have seen already, one role for the ethnographer is to step outside the professional logic and speak from the perspective of the public. At some point, the game is over, or should be, and the logic of the game should be suspended. The compound is secure enough.

Third, the fact that there is always another move does not mean that the players have much liberty. In particular, the defenders end up imprisoned by their own defenses, locked in their safe rooms. "If all that Americans want is security, they can go to prison," Dwight D. Eisenhower is reported to have said. "They'll have enough to eat, a bed and a roof over their heads." Eisenhower provides a nice counterpoint to the perspective often associated with Foucault's rereading of Bentham's panopticon, in which the state erects security measures, and reduces the freedom of its citizens, in an effort to secure its own power. The actor, in this story, is the state, not the "docile" individual. But that is not the only way to look at things. In Bar X, and as Eisenhower suggests, citizens might seek to be secure even at the cost of their own freedom. For obvious example, people often use electronic conveniences that spy on them, i.e., build their own panopticon and give it to others, and just hope that laws are strong enough to prevent painful abuses. In one of the little ironies of the contemporary, many people who start out worrying about the state end up relying on it heavily indeed.

Fourth, and sticking with Eisenhower, the evolution of security tends to restrict the freedom of the defenders, which makes the attackers attractive. We may construct the jail, build the castle's walls around us, but we are still trapped within the castle. Modernity, as Kafka understood, feels like prison. The game starts out as defending the compound, or the airport, from evil-doers. But the defenders find themselves first thinking like the attackers – what will they do next? But such thinking almost requires imagination, dreaming – what would I do next? Everybody at the table becomes, in their minds, an attacker. Attack is where freedom, and so creativity and a certain kind of joy, lie. Knowing this, citizens may forgo security, may even seek to undermine it. Old ideas about the *acte gratuit* resurface; terrorism may be proof of some individual agency.

Fifth, this is why it is so important to be able to stop the game, as already mentioned in the second point above. The game must be stopped before it becomes nauseating, before violence comes as a sort of relief, or even becomes attractive because at least there one senses freedom.

★★★

Landside and the Problem of Definition. Jan simplified the game in his favor, at least the early stages, simply by drawing a box on a piece of paper. The box subtly redefined physical security as an essentially spatial concept. Protect the space, that is, the compound, and you protect the people within it. The design problem, then, is not to provide security (whatever that is) but to organize a space (that we understand) with the intention of making the space safe. Security emerges as a consequence of good design. Good design requires answers to practical, not easy but tractable questions. Where do the trucks go? What about some planters, that also serve as bollards, here?

Such spatial thinking runs through airport security, which as noted on p. 00, traditionally has established a cordon around the planes and their passengers, i.e., sought to secure the compound. This is not a question of airport design per se. Airports are high value and familiar targets, and so easy places to observe architecture responding to recent attacks and expressing the latest thinking. As already suggested, however, in any number of critical sites, measures are taken in response to threats, and as imagination prompts. Collectively, such measures inflect environments. After a while, the accumulation of such sites creates a securitized, even militarized, built space. The following is taken from a doctoral dissertation, with all that implies.

Because the levels of security zone restrictions vary from zone to zone, a simple and objective set of criteria is used to distinguish and classify security zones and security landscapes based on their overall level of restriction and or the presence and intensity of certain benchmarks.

These benchmark variables will be access restrictions, behavioral controls, and surveillance. Access restrictions will include: bollards, Jersey barriers, gates, or fences located at entrance and exit points to a space or building. Behavioral controls include posted signs prohibiting activities such as photography or loitering, or physical features that discourage sitting or gathering in small or large groups. Surveillance measures will include security guards/police officers and other human surveillance. Closed circuit television (CCTV) video surveillance cameras are also included under surveillance.

Indeed. From the perspective of many in the social sciences, and many citizens, the creation of such spaces is unfortunate or worse. But for a manager, the box has a subtly seductive quality. If only these issues can be contained, maybe even solved, then my job will be done.

But it turns out to be harder to construct the right boxes than one might think. For decades of airport construction, the bounds of the compound were taken to be rather self-evident. The places are called airports, after all – surely the planes define the relevant space? One significance of landside attacks was that this seemingly self-evident proposition was forcibly denied.

In Europe, there is a strong desire to create seamless and "smart" corridors to connect the different forms of transportation. Ideally, one should be able to deplane in Amsterdam's Schiphol Airport and board the Thalys Train for Paris, or take the link from Brussels Zaventem Airport and join the Thalys Train in Gare Central. The contemporary airport is a high-tech castle built to protect those within its walls, but this is a very extended landside zone. What of all of these transportation links? This near-future vulnerability was already known before 2015, but after the Thalys Train Attack the pressure increased to close any and all gaps. Since then, train companies, bus companies and transportation agencies have moved front and center in airport security. Trains and busses are not traditionally seen as part of airports, for obvious reasons, but new thinking was required in the wake of the 2015 attack.

On August 21, Thalys 9364 crossed the Belgian border bound for Paris with 554 passengers onboard. At 17:45 CEST Ayoub El Khazzani emerged from the WC on carriage 12, stripped to the waist and carrying an AK-M assault rifle; he wore a rucksack on his chest which contained nine ammunition magazines and a container of petrol. He also carried a Luger pistol and a box-cutter knife. A Frenchman, known only as "Damien A" attempted to grapple with El Khazzani but was overpowered. Fifty-one years old, Mark Moogalian stepped away from his wife to intervene, and managed to wrest the assault rifle from the terrorist. Unfortunately, El Khazzani shot him with his pistol. With Moogalian and "Damien A" down, El Khazzani moved towards the main part of the carriage with the clear intention of murdering the passengers onboard the train. But, after a rocky start, things only got worse for our shooter, fast. The modified assault rifle jammed. Ten meters away, Anthony Sadler sat with his best friends, Airman First Class Spencer Stone and Specialist Alek Skarlatos. As further discussed in Chapter 11, the unarmed Stone and Skarlatos would overpower the heavily armed terrorist, with aid from others, and a massacre would be avoided.

Quite apart from the bravery of the young men, from the point of view of systems design, when Ayoub El Khazzani emerged from the restroom, stripped to the waist and armed, the system had already failed. He was not carrying any identification. The passengers who boarded from Amsterdam and Brussels airports had passed through layers of security, but at some point they crossed an invisible border into the unsecured landside. The security "gap" here is the wide-open door of internal European travel, open also to dangerous individuals. El Khazzani was not unknown. He had been flagged by the French, Spanish, German and Belgian security services – he kept company with radical jihadists and was rumored to have travelled to Syria. Although he had been flagged, he was not followed, because the resources do not exist to follow every threat or protect every potential victim.

Ayoub El Khazzani represents a peculiar type of terrorist then. He is an internal threat, in some ways like the IRA in the UK or the Red Army Faction in West Germany. But his goals seem less focused, and his connections and cells appear much more diffuse, and he therefore sends less of a clear signal. It seems that he spent time with Abdelhamid Abaaoud, the leader of the 2015 Paris attacks, but the ties are weak. From the point of view of the intelligence community, El Khazzani is one of many, a somewhat radicalized individual who has not yet committed an act of terrorism. Moreover, if one nation alerts another as to the presence of an individual such as El Khazzani, it is not clear if or how the information will be treated. Downstream from the world of intelligence, counterterrorism combat teams only learned of this individual after the fact of his attack. Counterterrorism, as a professional matter, did not happen.

To many counterterrorism experts, it seems clear that El Khazzani failed because he had very bad luck. Unusually resilient individuals happened to be onboard carriage 12 on the day he chose to attack. Even then, he could still have succeeded but for a series of smaller failures, jammed weapons and the like. Had it not been for chance, resilience and failure, the Thalys Train attack would likely have resulted in a massacre. The security structures had failed. Once you open the box, anything can happen.

★★★

Reinterpretation. As demonstrated by the *ACI Bulletin* quoted above, and by the discussion of the Thalys attack, the meaning of "airport," for the purposes of airport security, has changed. What appeared to be a stable concept turned out to be labile. Similarly, during the 9/11 attacks, terrorists forced their way into the cockpits of four planes, overpowered the pilots, and took control of at least three planes, which were flown into their targets. (The fourth plane was evidently the scene of a battle, and crashed in a field in Pennsylvania.) In the aftermath of the attacks, airlines armored their cockpit doors, so that a terrorist would have difficulty getting to the pilot and taking over the plane's flight controls. As noted in Chapter 1, in the Germanwings/Lufthansa disaster, a pilot waited until his copilot was out of the cockpit, locked the door, and flew the plane into a mountainside. What was first intended to be a fairly simple door was reimagined as a wall against terrorists, and then was reimagined again, as a barricade against rescuers. The general point here is that terrorism is an act of reinterpretation. At the simplest level, airports, or trains or planes, or shopping malls, churches, mosques, synagogues all have peaceable social functions, implying activities like travel, commerce, education, worship – the terrorist changes all that.

Whatever such places normally mean, or were intended to mean, in consequence of mass violence, they become slaughterhouses. Oftentimes, after the fact, such reinterpretation is buried, unacknowledged. Reconstructed sites often make little or no acknowledgment of terrorist attacks. And there is something eerie about visiting a place, now returned to "normal," and knowing.

Reinterpretation extends to the realm of tactics, hence the game of castles and cannons. Returning to the 9/11 attacks, one of the reasons the attacks were so successful is that well into the morning of September 11th, airport security professionals "understood" hijacking, or thought they did, and for good reasons. Airports have long been admired by terrorists, and hijackings were common in the US and elsewhere in the 1960s and 1970s. If hijackers succeeded in gaining control of a plane, a hostage situation ensued. The professional consensus was to negotiate, in an effort to secure the safety of the passengers and also the plane. People were (and are) trained for hostage negotiations. Even if negotiations were unsuccessful, the process gave teams time to plan an intervention. For their part, hijackers usually had a list of demands, including such things as release of political prisoners, money, and safe passage. Security had control of the airport and if necessary the airspace, but the hijackers had leverage, too, the passengers and plane. Sometimes hijackings were violently resolved, as at Uganda's Entebbe airport, sometimes negotiations prevented killing, but both sides expected to negotiate. There was a process.

The attacks on 9/11, in contrast, followed a different script altogether. The passengers on the planes were not seen by the terrorists as hostages with which to bargain. The passengers were seen as casualties. This was Bin Laden's war, and the point of the operation was to inflict losses upon the enemy (see Westbrook 2015). By the same token, the planes were not bargaining chips, either, nor even modes of transportation. They were cruise missiles, with their fuel tanks taking the place of the explosive charge conventional in a purpose-built missile. The security community did not realize, until it was too late, that the script had been flipped.

Again, as suggested in the Introduction, these questions of meaning are not exclusively, nor even primarily, a matter for expertise. The experts who attempt to provide security by design are not necessarily proven wrong when security fails. The best of castle walls crumbles before a new cannon. The structures and flows of any civil society, the movements of people, are always vulnerable to dark hearted reinterpretation.

The intentions of the designers may be ignored, subverted, and their creations put to other ends.

★★★

The Future is Poison. In 2017, Mark was invited to present ongoing research on public behavior during terrorist attacks to an invitation-only event in the UK. The three-day meeting was held in an ex-air force base in rural England to facilitate the discreet demonstration of new counterterror equipment. This was the second meeting of a loose network of European and international emergency responders, police and various former or active members of elite military branches. The network organized a panel of speakers for the first day, mainly populated by senior police officers. The opening speaker described the organizational dimensions of the police response to the London Bridge and Borough Market attacks. Mark described public behaviour during the Glasgow and Thalys terrorist attacks based on his interviews with survivors and those who intervened, such as the Thalys Train heroes.

Members of France's famous RAID began a well-rehearsed analysis of the Charlie Hebdo massacre and the subsequent hostage situations. Two days after the massacre, ISIS sympathizer Amedy Coulibaly murdered a number of Jewish customers at a kosher supermarket in Port de Vincennes and was killed by RAID members. Meanwhile, 35 kilometers away, Saïd Kouachi and Chérif Kouachi impersonated police officers in order to gain entry to the offices of a signage company in Dammartin-en-Goële. The brothers held people at gun-point for many hours until police forced them out of the building with explosives and shot them both dead. RAID too uses "boxes." They conceptualize terrorist situations with concentric "boxes," with the innermost box containing the terrorists and sometimes, unfortunately, civilians. The innermost box is essentially a kill zone, with its occupants – including the hostages – presumed "already dead." Negotiation is not really the point.

By the end of the presentations, the audience had numerous questions about hostage situations and sieges. As noted, the secret college is the realm of tactics. It was as if the ambiguous and disorderly complexity that is a terrorist attack could be ordered into a number of precise technical matters. Indeed, there was enough material presented that morning to keep people talking all day – and for the rest of that day and into the night, they talked and talked, about lasers and locked doors, surveillance cameras and exterior walls, explosives and poison. The conversation really started on the way to lunch. Mark asked a question about the explosives used during the Dammartin-en-Goële siege. In order to explain the effect of flashbang grenades, a Dutch fire officer tried to explain the broader approach to "breeching" buildings, i.e. how to force entry into a building or room so as to maximize the delivery of kinetic force and minimize risk to your own forces. At some point during the conversation he lost all interest in explosives. "Lasers," he said, over and over again, were the way forward.

It turned out that there are several schools of thought, however, and each school of thought seemed to have a representative present at this event. The lunch table included a former British army officer working as a consultant, an ex-counterterror police officer, a member of a secretive military unit, the Dutch fireman who loved lasers, a member of the German federal police, and a medical doctor from Belgium. As lunch was served, each person at the table, with the exception of the doctor, reflected on the Dammartin-en-Goële hostage crisis and the best options from their perspective. The atmosphere around the table was akin to that of a serious boardroom meeting.

The ex-counterterror police officer, for example, noted that the siege had lasted for over eight hours, pointing to the protocols for hostage rescue that must be observed, even in the case of two terror suspects armed with, among other weapons, a rocket launcher. "But that's time to gather intelligence," the former army officer pointed out. "If they're talking, you never know," said another. The conversation continued along this line, with everyone present agreeing that negotiation was a matter for negotiators, but while the talking was happening their attack plan was already going into operation. The goal was to have the best plan, or series of plans, ready for a green light. We were back in the realm of tactics. "Lasers!" said the Dutch fire officer, "It's the future for going through doors, and walls even."

Due to the gravity of the topic, everyone thought it best to skip the next session and discuss the merits of lasers. The hours rolled by. A senior officer in RAID joined the discussion at one point to advocate on behalf of explosives and helicopter-based interventions, but withdrew quickly, blaming his poor English language skills. By late afternoon, the former British army officer was leading the discussion. A charming individual with an Oxbridge manner and the attire of a wealthy farmer, he now operated a successful consultancy company that carried out "risk assessments" for multinational corporate infrastructure, focusing on the Middle East and South East Asia. He did not, however, push a corporate line during the debate. Rather, he was adamant that sufficient technology was already available for any situation. The key, he believed, was just well-trained people. To support this position, he recalled incidents in Northern Ireland, Iraq and Afghanistan. The more that the former officer described places and events, however, the less frequently he used impersonal language, instead describing how he and "the lads" ran operations in various parts of the world. But eventually he ran out of steam, because the mysterious realm in which he operated was still a quasi-military one, and the tactics and technology required in a place like Paris plainly would be different.

Pretty soon, the group had begun to arrange a mental table-top exercise in which a suburban door had to be breeched and some civilians rescued from two terrorists. It was decided, unanimously, to run the table-top in the bar in the officers' mess. At some point that evening, Mark realized that he had been elected as the judge in this fiercely competitive battle of tactics. Mark stood at the bar in the ex-military base with three men standing in front of him, forming an inner circle.

The former British army officer tried his best to offer a human-centered strategy for how to neutralize the imagined threat and rescue the hostages. But this approach was too loose for another of the men in the inner circle, a German policeman with an engineering background. His thesis, which was hard to dispute, was that effective use of breeching charges and flashbangs could put you into the building immediately. "Lasers!" the Dutch fire officer said in response to every claim. A number of years earlier, the policeman had begun to experiment at home, inventing a whole package of hyper-specialized devices for removing structural barriers, from locks to fences and from reinforced doors to external walls. He combined several devices until he had a "kit bag" of bizarre medieval-looking equipment. Soon, he was known internationally as one of the leading international experts in the field of breaking into buildings. Famously, according to others present that day, he ended a hostage situation (a violent domestic dispute) in an attic by predicting when the hostage taker was maximally distant from his victims, and then triggering a charge to undermine the floor beneath him. Nonetheless, by early evening, the Dutch fire officer's absolute faith in lasers seemed to be winning over the crowd.

Then, to everyone's surprise, the Belgian doctor intervened. "Remember the Moscow theatre siege?" he said. "Well, I invented the poison gas used to knock everyone out."

In 2002, dozens of armed men attacked Moscow's Dubrovka Theatre and took hundreds of people hostage, demanding the withdrawal of Russian forces from Chechnya. Because of the difficulty of storming the theatre and because of where the terrorists positioned the explosives, Russian special forces and intelligence officers elected to pump the building full of a toxic substance. The threats were neutralized and hundreds of hostages were rescued, but several hundred people also died from a variety of causes associated with the assault. Having only vague memories of the incident, Mark asked the Belgian doctor for more details.

He described his work as a medical examiner during the 1990s, and his growing sense that terrorism was likely to be a major challenge for Europe following 9/11. Why, he wondered while watching a popular espionage film one day, had nobody ever perfected a "sleeping gas"? He began experiments in his garage at home. "My wife found me twice unconscious on the floor," he recalled. But then he got somewhere. He approached a German colleague in a university biochemistry lab to assist with the empirical work, but was rejected. Eventually he found a Russian colleague who could help. "And what about all those people who died?" Mark asked.

The doctor patiently explained that most of the fatalities in Dubrovka Theatre occurred either when people fell unconscious in seats and their airways closed, tongue prolapse, or when emergency workers piled them on their backs on the pavement outside. "The gas worked," he said, not without pride. Everyone else had gone quiet. Secret colleges have informal codes, invisible lines, taboos even. "Well," the doctor said with a shrug, before taking his leave, "the future is poison."

★★★

Attempting to achieve safety by design is an inevitable response to danger, as old as piling rocks in front of a cave. In principle, however, authorities that attempt to design safe spaces confront three ultimately insoluble problems:

- Infinite regress, in the design context often called "castles and cannons."
- Definition, spatial or otherwise. As the landside problem illustrates, danger may elude managerial definition, fall outside the jurisdiction.
- Reinterpretation. Terrorism contests peaceable understandings.

Contemporary social and political discourse commonly positions policy and the agencies that attempt to effectuate them as, at least in principle, rational. Weber's disenchantment with modern life stems from the gradual replacement of organic social life with coldly rational structures. Someday, everything will be subject to rules, and there will be no joy. Bureaucracy, and Weber, will be addressed in more sustained fashion later on, but so far, this book has painted a different picture of bureaucratic existence.

Expert bureaucrats cannot know the public they are meant to serve; indeed, relations with the public are downright spooky (Chapter 4). Bureaucrats acknowledge the insufficiency of their knowledge, and their inability to handle the knowledge they do possess, and are generally haunted by the specter of failure (Chapter 5). Their efforts to learn are hindered by ignorance over what happened, and where the facts are reasonably certain, radical differences of interpretation (Chapter 6). More distressingly still, the effort to encompass and organize the social at the core of the bureaucratic enterprise, to design a safe airport, say, is beset by fundamental problems (Chapter 7). Rather than rational expressions of the will of the state, the enterprise of bureaucracy – the rationalization of the social – might better be seen as in principle impossible, but the effort is required nonetheless. The practice of bureaucracy is Sisyphean.

Should we sympathize with Sisyphus? To some extent, certainly – he is not the cold monster that the social sciences have grown so comfortable hating. Sisyphus, too, is imprisoned by his circumstances, with few options.

Yet pursuit of security in the teeth of the problems endemic to bureaucracy is not only both necessary (what else could be done?) and endless, but also strangely disturbing, even nauseating. Poisonous. The logics of expertise extend indefinitely. Followed to their bitter end, experts will in fact create something akin to what Weber called the iron cage, an insufferable modernity. It is small comfort that, as Kant understood but Weber sometimes forgot, logics are rarely followed to their bitter end, and the better sort of person may buy their way around the most onerous aspects of the contemporary. Modernity nonetheless often becomes dreary. Sometimes rebellion becomes an object of fantasy, not least in the secret college itself. Sometimes violence erupts. As will be developed further below, the vital question is when have things become "modern" enough, and it is time to stop?

References

ACI – Airports Council International. 2017. *ACI Bulletin*. Montreal,July 20. Available at https://aci.aero/Media/6ba36069-433b-4eec-9709-fa3b5d7af9de/Nka2Ew/About%20ACI/Priorities/Security/Smart%20Security/ACI%20Advisory%20Bulletin%20on%20Landside%20Security%20Update%20July%202017%20(002).pdf [accessedMarch 8, 2020].

Westbrook, David A. 2015. *Deploying Ourselves: Islamist Violence, Globalization, and the Responsible Projection of U.S. Force*. London and New York: Routledge.

Chapter 8

Constraints
Conflicted Domains, Scarce Resources, Limited Agency

Conflicted Domains. This book began with the Brussels airport attack of 2016 largely for symbolic reasons. As the epicenter of the European project, Brussels epitomizes an integrated contemporary, in which social authority is both fragmented and collected in complicated ways. Who has authority, and with what room to maneuver, are complicated questions, but especially obviously complicated in Brussels. It is not wrong to say the Belgian state, but Belgian statehood must be understood both in the context of the European Union and the almost national (whatever national means) powers of Flanders and Walloonia (Zaventem is in Flanders). The local commune also matters. The North Atlantic Treaty Organization is headquartered a few miles away in downtown Brussels; Supreme Headquarters Allied Powers Europe is just down the road in Mons. NATO and SHAPE care about airspace management. The airport itself is owned by a consortium of investors including not only the Belgian government but the Ontario teachers' pension fund (OTPP), Queensland Investment Corporation (QIC), APG Asset Management (a Dutch pension fund), and Swiss Life, an insurer. The airport responds to "advice" from the international aviation community formalized as the ICAO, a UN organization dominated by the United States, the EU and other leading providers of planes and service, and consequently regulatory best practices. The regulatory space cannot be assigned to a single entity. In the lucid prose of the Airports Council International:

> Aviation-specific security regulations focus on the airside spaces (non-public spaces of airports accessible only to air passengers who hold a valid boarding pass and to security cleared staff). These regulations are designed to prevent unlawful interference with air transport. Landside spaces (airport spaces accessible to the general public) are subject to general security regulations enacted by national authorities. It is therefore up to these national authorities to review and coordinate with airports to identify the appropriate measures that match their specific threat scenario.

> (ACI 2017)

During the height of globalization's fashionableness, roughly between the fall of the Berlin Wall in 1989 and September 11, 2001, there was much loose talk about the end of the state. Obviously, states still matter, in airport security and otherwise. But just as obviously, to speak of "the state" as a Leviathan, a body with a single will, from which politics issues like speech, is a radical oversimplification. This book uses notions like the secret college and the ethnographic representation of the public as ways of talking about the political without resorting to a Leviathan with an imperious will. Something much more complicated, hopeful and yes, still dangerous, is what we must engage.

Yet the simplification continues; it has its uses. Sherry Ortner (2016) recently argued that a "dark anthropology" has long been in vogue, characterized by a focus on suffering and a political righteousness aimed at powerful actors (see also Westbrook 2008). Many ethnographies of security surely fit into this mold. Phrasing the problem of politics to be confronting Leviathan posits a holder of power, a sovereign with (im)moral agency. In our times, when power is in many hands with many relations, the idea of a unitary sovereign is implausible, does not square with ordinary experience, and so Leviathan has become an ideology, in some circles often called "neoliberalism." In this imaginary, the role of the academic (especially the progressive and engaged academic, as all academics must be) is to speak truth to power.

The world of security is actually far more complex, less Manichean. Leviathan comprises diverse agencies, and the men and women who run such operations are trying to do many things at once, with imperfect information and no doubt impure hearts. But to get a feel for the actual regimes of security under which we all live (has any reader of this book not boarded a plane?), we must actually talk to the humans who operate our security systems. The questions are familiar, at least from a reasonably privileged middle-aged perspective. How do the relatively senior figures in which we are primarily interested locate their authority, specify their jurisdictions, do their work, within a common contemporary, albeit one that is fractured or separated into "silos"? How do they organize their activity vis-à-vis other institutions; what relations do they have to manage? Who are the clients, consumers, or competitors? To whom do they ultimately answer? An old Army joke: a bright young captain is giving a briefing about recent actions and presumed intentions of "the enemy." A colonel curtly reminds him: "the Vietnamese, sir, are the adversary. The Air Force is the enemy." (Services may be changed to fit the occasion.) Or, to put the matter in perhaps familiar terms: how much of the work of the University is neither research (about truth), nor teaching (about the young), nor even "service" (whatever that might be felt to be), but struggles for advancement within the University itself?

Politics almost everyplace is simpler than it is in Brussels, but even where there is consensus on the state, the scope of official agency is often quite narrow in practice, much narrower than implied by words like "state," "government" or even "law." Such words are abstract, unspecified, and hence unconstrained, implying freedom of action, room to maneuver. Actual officials, however, are specified in countless ways, hemmed in, their options limited. On the ground, officials never see the freedom promised by the abstract "state." True enough, evil can be banal, bureaucratic in the worst sense. Arendt was not wrong. But conversely, if we wish to achieve good, we must also work through organizations, bureaucracy, but "Banality of Good" is not so pressing, or did not seem so then. Today, people urgently require ways to make some peace with the contemporary, what was once called "the Establishment" or even better, "The Man." Until we confront bureaucracy as it operates, we will not be able to discern, much less judge, and we will understand ourselves bitterly, merely as ruled. Understand power, and then speak whatever truth you believe you possess.

★★★

Scarce Resources. In order to keep doing what they are doing at all, officials generally must struggle for resources. In airports, the gods are speed, sales and security, but security is very much the lesser deity: the airport is a facilitator of important activities like getting people to distant places, and making money off them en route, and when all goes well, what use is security? Which is another way of saying that security is not always welcome. Actually, the position of security is even more parlous. By its nature, airport security raises concerns about privacy (they feel you if they want to), invidious discrimination, and an overweening state, to say nothing of the simple cost. A seasoned police instructor captured it well by saying, "We don't make money; we cost money."

In the wake of the 9/11 attacks, terminals swelled with the presence of conspicuous, muscular, and intrusive security. It is not too difficult to calculate the costs of such security, at least the direct costs of hiring people and buying materiel. (Putting a price on a changed milieu is a fool's errand.) Calculating the benefits, however, is immeasurably harder. Terrorist attacks are rare and unevenly distributed, so the efficacy of security measures is hard to measure. What is the worth of security at a place that is not attacked? Security itself might become a target, as with the attack on military personnel at Orly Airport, France in 2017, and surely the point of security was not to give more targets to terrorists?

Security measures may come to be seen as disingenuous. After an attack, the powers that be need to be seen as having taken action against an acknowledged threat. If – heaven forefend – another attack occurs, at least they will have tried. Conversely, if the powers that be do nothing, and an attack happens, they will have no leg to stand upon. So the powers buy something visible; whether or not the purchase actually reduces danger is a distinct question. Many people are skeptical that they are made any safer by "security." It is tempting to discount security measures as theater, specifically, government efforts to cover their own asses.

Without arguing that any particular government agents are pure as the driven snow, there is more to be said. The visible presence of security may deter attacks, although it is admittedly difficult to assess that which did not happen. Moreover, visible security may instill confidence in the peace-loving public, and that would seem to be a good thing. Even understanding security measures as essentially theater, then, it is unclear what such theater means, and to whom. And sometimes security does in fact work. People with the intent to kill are stopped before they do so, and killers are neutralized before the body count escalates.

Stepping from "security as theater" and actual attacks into the mundane world of everyday security operations against threats that can been named but rarely appear, the unpleasant queues and questionable military-style policing are both part of the peculiar calculative reasoning in counter-terrorism: there's always too much security, but when things go wrong there's never enough. It is only when things go wrong *and* the system contains the danger that a security system proves its worth. Until such events, the erosion of the institution's justification and hence its funding is the order of the day.

Various shortfalls have been mentioned *en passant* throughout this text. The BASS security system, for example, is only in place in a few airports. Although not expensive in and of itself, training and retaining personnel sophisticated enough to make the system function as designed is expensive. The Westgate Mall was a tragedy in part due to the fact that Nairobi had formidable enemies yet lacked a condign security infrastructure. As noted, the Thalys train terrorist, El Khazzani, had been flagged by the French, Spanish, German and Belgian security services, but none thought they had reason to make him a priority. Resources simply do not exist to follow up on every potential threat. From the public perspective, one may reasonably ask how much of society's energies should be devoted to containing potential threats. Once the threat becomes actual, and from the perspective of the secret college for which the attack represents failure, one story is almost always the lack or misallocation of resources.

Some years ago, Mark undertook an ethnographic project that shadowed daily policing practice in and around airports, from front-line management to foot patrol, during a moment in which counterterrorism was taking priority. The project was coterminous with efforts to conduct joint exercises with counterterrorism emergency armed responders. From Mark's perspective, this project aimed for a holistic view of airport policing, using ethnography to bring down the partitions that separate agencies with overlapping areas of concern. The objective was to gain the inter-silo (and thus institutionally multi-sited, even if all in one airport) public perspective, theoretically discussed on p. 00. From the perspective of the police, ethnography promised to be a way to think through values and good practices, making explicit the tacit dimensions of their work, while also getting an academic to contribute to training, *pro bono* (Maguire and Pétercsák 2018).

Interestingly, during recorded interviews with airport security managers, "security" was not mentioned with any great frequency. Instead, managers spoke about issues familiar to any of their counterparts around the world or even in other sectors: the obligation to achieve excellence and compliance with insufficient means, the degrading need to play politics to get additional resources, and the ongoing challenges of difficult humans. Everyday experience for this cohort is filled with worries about money and the costs of things, quality assurance reports, and "building business case after business case." Even in informal conversation, managers sometimes would slip in and out of corporate speak, but then such is the official language of an increasingly standardized world of regulation and process, and often no other words are suitable. Yet at other times, these senior figures, each with decades of experience, reflected on the scale of their jobs and the need to square their individual ethos with "reality" – reality being dominated, evidently, by the constraints of the business.

Things only get worse – for local security managers – when there is an actual attack, when security fulfills its *raison d'être*. In the aftermath of the Glasgow airport attack of 2007, in which two terrorists attempted to detonate an SUV filled with explosives and shrapnel into a huge crowd of holidaying schoolchildren, police investigators had to identify potential suspects, potential witnesses, and evidence of potential networks. On top of all of this, as the security manager put it: "3,500 people. The biggest crisis evacuation of people since the Second World War!" Glasgow airport reopened in less that 24 hours, but it is worth recording the words of the senior security manager in order to realize the enormous and often hidden skills and expertise that are required to keep the contemporary moving:

> … so we had to work out a shift pattern, work out safe ways to get people in because you could no longer come to the airport the normal way, so we had to create additional car parking outside of the airport and we had to ferry staff. … So, again, you've got to think about new processes and systems, resources in place, before the area is handed back from the police. … We had to start thinking about did we have to buy tents, did we have to … how we were going to procure things, what was it going to look like, we had to get water and food for the folk because they'd very quickly eaten everything that was down there already for passengers. We had to get people off planes because there were people on planes. Airlines were serving them food and drink on board the aircraft because obviously they didn't know how long this was going to happen. So our Business Recovery Team was set up.

Media – we had to determine our media strategy, what was our media strategy going to be? What were our key messages? The website went into overload because people were looking for information on loved ones, all that sort of stuff. Unprecedented media interest, up to 800 media calls within the first 24 hours. ...

Seventeen hours into the incident we allowed our first arriving flight to come in ...

The stress of managing an incident, the tiredness, the amount of energy that people were putting in, not wanting to go home, would go home for a couple of hours and then try and get back in and you're saying "No, just stay away, we might need you in a few hours' time" because we didn't want to get everyone tired and no use when we opened up and no one was able to process passengers. ... My role, [once] leaving crisis management and business continuity became: how do I protect the airport now from another attack? So, I had to work to start looking at landside attack measures ...

Leviathan is not what it seems. Once the Emergency Ordnance Disposal – the "bomb squad" – had handed control over security back to the local police, and the police to airport security, the business of counterterrorism returned to being a matter of individuals and institutions looking out over the wall and trying to find cost effective ways to protect the public. The bureaucracy reset:

the total cost of the attack had to come off your bottom line. Nobody comes along and says to you "Oh you've had an attack here, have the money." We had to fund that attack. We had to fund everything that happened on the days after. We had to fund the new bollards. So, all of that came from Glasgow Airport.

★★★

Limited Agency. A great deal of scholarly writing and indeed political discourse is rhetorically structured as offering wisdom to the powerful, who can do something because they are powerful. In this structure, agency tends to be presumed rather than demonstrated, i.e., power is a trope. Leviathan could do the right thing, he just needs to be educated. The trope facilitates expressions of various sorts to various ends that do not concern us here. Instead, ethnographic work within the secret college transforms what is usually a trope into a question: to what extent does a government official (or any powerful person) in fact have agency?

At first glance it may seem odd to question the agency of officials who can deliver, or worse, summon others to deliver, "kinetic force," i.e., people who control operators who are professionally trained to kill.

That would seem to be agency, and it is, of a sort and in certain situations, as explored in the next chapter. At the same time, security is haunted by the possibility of dramatic failure, a possibility that cannot be laid to rest. Less dramatically, and as already indicated, officials have very limited room to maneuver. Their domains are conflicted; their resources are limited; and therefore, so are their capabilities. It is a very big world, and sometimes, nothing can be done, even if Leviathan's consul is sympathetic. A story from a counterterrorism conference Mark attended.

When we returned to the conference venue from our brief excursion to the US/Mexico border at El Paso del Norte, most of the delegates seemed poised to seize any opportunity to state their position on the topic of border control (which was not the topic on the afternoon's agenda). A young scholar, who had earlier presented her research on irregular migration routes from Central America to the USA, spoke of the physical and emotional scars created by the US border. To emphasize the point, she recalled interviewing female border crossers who described taking preventative birth control pills before setting out for Texas, because rape was expected, almost inevitable. "You, I assume," she said, directing her intervention to a senior intelligence officer from Australia, "never get to hear stories like that at work." The Australian did not seem in the least bit surprised that he had been singled out, seeing as he "came out" as a "former spook" the night before. "Well, actually, yes," he said. "We heard horror stories all the time: people dying in boats over there; a massacre over there. But my job was national security. If it wasn't a matter of national security, then it wasn't my job." He pre-empted the next challenge with, "I mean, do you want us to just go around interfering in everything?"

Later that evening Mark found himself sitting with the former "spook" over dinner. Inevitably the earlier confrontation came up. "Doesn't bother me," he said, without having been asked if it bothered him. You see, he explained [paraphrasing here], I have enough to keep me awake at night already. He began to discuss his life story, describing his family life in considerable detail. His wife took up a senior academic post away from the national capital and he agreed – it was his "turn" – to follow her in her career, so he scanned the appointments section of newspapers. A senior policing position was advertised, to which he applied successfully. At interview, the police force, delighted that they were recruiting someone from the intelligence world, offered him a bespoke research-based role – he was to head a new human trafficking unit. Two days into his new job, he realized that the "database" he was responsible for was in fact a poorly coded Excel spreadsheet, and he had never been trained to use Excel. He took a class in Microsoft packages during the evening, hoping that he wouldn't be found out, but grew to realize that many of the codes were nonsense, and some of the information was entered into incorrect cells. As quickly as possible he reorganized the data and the unit, but, he admitted, "I had a lot of sleepless nights, I still do. Those numbers were children, young women, and maybe they're still lost out there somewhere. That was my responsibility."

★★★

Agency is often presumed to exist, elsewhere of course, usually in some version of "the state." Social problems, then, are moral rather than practical. Leviathan does not know what to do, does not want to do the right thing, or perhaps he is downright evil. In any such case, the job of the engaged intellectual's task is to bear witness, to preach truth to power, in the hope that the king will do the right thing, or at least that the intellectual may be numbered among the righteous, the loyal opposition. And it is the case that great things can be done with enough political will, from Churchill's rousing the British to fight them on the beaches to Kennedy's call to put a man on the moon. But all too often, the King is absent, and the minister operates under severe constraints. The problem is not only what to do, but how to do anything at all.

References

Maguire, Mark. and Reka. Pétercsák 2018. "Airports, from Vital Systems to Nervous Systems." In Setha M. Low (ed.). *Routledge Handbook of Anthropology and the City*. London and New York: Routledge.

Ortner, Sherry B. 2016. "Dark Anthropology and its Others: Theory since the Eighties." *HAU: Journal of Ethnographic Theory*, 6(1), 47–73.

Westbrook, David. 2008. *Navigators of the Contemporary: Why Ethnography Matters*. Chicago: University of Chicago Press.

Chapter 9

Leviathan Sometimes

Late in the afternoon of June 3, 2017, Khuram Butt rented a white Renault van over the telephone. He had earlier attempted to rent a seven-ton truck but couldn't provide sufficient details for payment. Butt was a Pakistan-born British citizen, reformed drug user, and known member of the constantly morphing al-Muhajiroun jihadist group. Indeed, he was so well known that he appeared, briefly, on a Channel 4 TV documentary about the domestic jihadi threat in the UK. The 27-year-old Butt collected the van, accompanied by two friends, 30-year-old Rachid Redouane and 22-year-old Youseff Zaghba. Redouane was a failed asylum seeker who moved to Ireland briefly before separating from his wife and child (he was a domestic abuser), while Zaghba, a dual Moroccan and Italian national, was under surveillance by the Italian security services as a known ISIS sympathizer. The three men, their bodies fueled with massive doses of drugs, loaded the rented van with bags of gravel to make it a heavier "battering ram," and then loaded 13 Molotov cocktails made from old wine bottles and lighter fluid. Each man wore a fake suicide vest and was armed with a carving knife, with a ceramic blade and a handle bound with leather, strapped to their wrists. It is not clear what the intended target was, or if any indeed had been chosen. The three men cruised around London for around two hours.

At 21:58 they drove the van across London Bridge, turned and crossed the bridge once more. Then they performed a dramatic U-turn. At 22:05 the white van, travelling at speed, mounted the pavement and ploughed into pedestrians. A BBC reporter who happened to be on the bridge that night told a journalist of seeing bodies being flipped into the air and into the River Thames. Several died instantly, while others, including a late term pregnant woman, received grave injuries. The terrorists zig-zagged the van along the pavement and the road in order to hit as many people as possible, before eventually crashing on Borough High Street. The three terrorists then exited the van, ran to the Boro Bistro, a small restaurant, and began stabbing customers.

In terrorist attacks of this kind, there usually are many acts of great courage, some of the obvious kind celebrated as heroism, but others of a less-recognized kind. In this case, Transport Police Officer Wayne Marques initially thought he was running towards a pub brawl, but it was soon apparent to him that he was running towards mortal danger. Yet he kept going. Marques fought with the terrorists armed with only a baton, and suffered horrific wounds. Further into the market area, one man threw a crate at the terrorists to distract them, and then hid 20 people in his bakery. Most famously, when the terrorists came to the Black and Blue restaurant and began their attack shouting, "This is for Allah!," Roy Larner did not flee. Instead, he stood up and shouted, "Fuck you, I'm Millwall!" (Millwall is a football team notorious for its violent fans.) Larner received multiple stab wounds while fighting the attackers with his bare hands. But not everyone grew up hard on the terraces. One is tempted to think in terms of "micro-heroics" to describe the customers who threw bottles and chairs at the marauders in order to buy time for others to assist and evacuate the injured. The attackers seemed to be everywhere at once. At one restaurant, an attacker walked in and calmly began to murder a woman. Customers fled out the back, where witnesses claim to have seen unarmed police run away. For several minutes in the medieval market streets, the scene was of blood and screaming and dying.

Eight minutes into the attack, however, armed police were moving through the streets, and journalists saw a strange helicopter land right in the middle of London Bridge. In London, unarmed police must be able to call upon armed officers and receive assistance within a few short minutes. If armed support is required to deal with a major terrorist incident, ideally there is time to bring in elite Counterterrorism Specialized Firearms Officers (CT SFOs). A retired London-based counterterror police officer described CT SFOs to Mark as "anticipatory" in that they responded to "pre-planned events." London also has roving Authorized Firearms Officers (AFOs), who respond to the "spontaneous" dangers that might arise. The events on London Bridge and in Borough Market on June 3, 2017 were spontaneous, and so it was units of AFOs that arrived on scene.

The final moments of the attackers are caught on film. A man strolling along the pavement is confronted by a figure wielding a large knife. The attacker attempts to stab the pedestrian in a manner that lacks determination. Then two other terrorists arrive to assist with the gruesome work. A large armed police car arrives at speed. Within one second, all three police occupants, including the driver, exit the car and open fire. The police move so quickly that they forget to apply the car's brake, and so it keeps rolling. The terrorists turn on the police officers. There is nothing cinematic in the poor-quality CCTV footage, blurred by the flashing police lights. Terrorists slash with their knives, the police fire, moving forward and back to control the distance. Men fall down. Another police car arrives. A body is kicked to check for signs of life. All three terrorists lie dead on the streets. Others are injured too: the man who was stabbed bleeds heavily; a passer-by was grazed by a police bullet ricocheting; and the driverless AFO car rolled over a policeman's foot.

The London Bridge and Borough Market attack lasted less than 20 minutes. Armed police "resolved" the situation some eight minutes after the first emergency call was made. The political questions raised by and consequences of the violence, however, extended beyond the incident itself, like ripples that spread outwards from a stone dropped in water. Were the attackers acting alone, or was a larger plot afoot? Multiple buildings were evacuated, and numerous underground tube stations were closed. Fragments of news emerged to suggest that the dark emergency helicopter that landed right in the middle of London Bridge was carrying a 12-man Special Air Service (SAS) patrol. In the days that followed, the tabloid newspapers carried images of the Dauphin helicopter – nicknamed "Blue Thunder" – and a photograph of a heavily armed man in camouflage gear, bulging arms covered with tattoos, an athlete of a special kind, running alongside armed officers. Because the situation was uncertain and "fluid," it was deemed necessary to open the "tool shed" and deploy men whose job is to deliver certainty, of a kind.

★★★

In London on June 3, 2017, Leviathan acted according to the script. Terrorists disrupted the civil order and were killed on the command of the sovereign. For Hobbes, the core problem of politics was the creation of order. Hobbes wrote out of the English Civil War, from which one could imagine a war of all against all, which he likened to the state of nature. Not incidentally, Hobbes was a brilliant translator of Thucydides, another tough mind in a tough time, the Peloponnesian Wars. Such wars taught that social order could not be presumed, it had to be created. Recognizing this, men came together to pool their powers and create a sovereign state. But men were subject to violent enthusiasms that they could not resolve peaceably. Order, once established, had to be defended from such conflicts, which could spiral out of control, as they had in England, within living memory. Therefore, argued Hobbes, for people to have any hope of a commodious existence, Leviathan had to be boundlessly strong, unopposable on any field of contest. The sovereign, in short, must be absolute. The alternative was civil war, the return to the state of nature and the failure of politics itself.[1]

Absolute power has its own, rather obvious, dangers. The political tradition that informs the US Constitution, among other things, has struggled to create a state that is both powerful enough to establish and defend order, and yet so constructed that it does not descend into a tyranny. To paint with a broad brush, the effort from Locke and since has been to ameliorate the Hobbesian argument for absolute sovereign power, without much denying the Hobbesian imagination of politics. Checks and balances, limits on various sorts of discretion, the enumeration of human rights, and so forth are thought within the Hobbesian frame. Central to that frame is its dualism: Leviathan on one side; the people, including academics, on the other. This same dualism structures much political imagination and social thought today, as discussed in the preceding chapter.

As has been pointed out innumerable times, while Hobbes is a mighty political thinker, *Leviathan* leaves much to be desired as sociological description, of his day or ours. Much of life takes place between citizen and state, in the institutions of civil society (see Westbrook 2008). And "the State" itself turns out to be many things, only with force of imagination conceived to be unified, a sovereign king, Leviathan. The multiplicity of political authority has only increased with the growth of administration and bureaucracy, and the intermingling of powers under headings such as federalism, integration, and international law, as suggested in the last chapter. Whatever the failings of the Hobbesian imaginary as description, however, in some contexts and for some purposes it makes sense to think, speak and write in terms of Leviathan (or, for that matter, a monolithic neoliberalism).

But sometimes it does not make sense to express oneself as if to Leviathan. Sometimes one needs a sociologically, and in that sense, politically accurate description. Sometimes one needs understanding (*Verstehen*), and a little sympathy, in order to have authority to be heard. Sometimes speaking truth to power is the surest way to be ignored. The difficulty is that new political imaginaries do not come along very often, and existing ones evolve slowly if at all. How else might we imagine political authority, if not as Leviathan?

This book has argued that a great deal of politics, including security politics, should be imagined in terms of the culture, institutions, and individuals that do the work at hand, collectively and not completely satisfactorily, "bureaucracy." To that end, we have attempted to portray some of the challenges facing institutions and individuals as they attempt to provide security. The conceptual difficulty here is that the political imagination of bureaucracy is far less familiar and less developed than is the political imagination of power understood in terms of the sovereign. To the extent that our conceptions of bureaucracy are developed, and by extension many of our ideas of the modern state and much of the contemporary itself are developed, they have been articulated most famously by Weber. As should be clear by now, however, the portrait of the bureaucrat here is both in detail and in principle considerably at odds with Weber's ideal-typical understanding of bureaucracy. The scholarly task, then, seems to be to move away from Hobbesian dualism into a more sophisticated social, institutional, and indeed psychological landscape. For politics, this will require a turn to bureaucracy, but considered less reductively, and more sympathetically, than Weber did.

★★★

Power, Differently. By way of illustration and a grounded place to start, consider unarmed "community policing" in an airport, sometimes conducted under the banner of "policing by consent." The same airport may also house extremely lethal close combat counterterrorism units, Leviathan in familiar guise. But not the only guise, as illustrated by a manager of airport police:

> We want to be the community police, like you would have in a village. We want to be the consistent community police presence. But we do have requirements under legislation, we do have compliance issues under EU legislation. But we have a population here of 25 million passengers, we've just surpassed that this year, plus another ten million meeting and greeting, so that's bigger than any … it's bigger than lots of countries. That's a lot of people passing through here, 15,000 office people work around here, so it's a community, and what I want to do is have my police officers out there as the problem solvers for people. But I don't have enough police officers. That's not, it's enough to do the job, but it's not certainly not gold lined when you think about the size of this campus. In any given day, I have up to a thousand staff here …

This manager, like many others, tended to elide the term "security" by pointing instead to an extraordinary range of incidents and experiences. Before the ethnographic project even formally began, he warned:

> You know you will see lots of the incidents, you can get the stats you know, six, seven thousand incidents we go through in the year. Two thousand of them could be medical incidents, we go to every medical call, because we've all done First Aid … training … cardio pulmonary resuscitation. … I would always try and celebrate, I shouldn't say celebrate, but recognize … how many times can you say, someone was dead and you saved them? But we now have incidents where we've got a huge increase in mental health issues arriving on our doorstep. And it's getting more and more acute. People in very, very distressed states, we've had five suicides in the airport, which is something I never saw. … There's been an occasion where one of my officers had to talk a 14-year-old boy off the roof of the car park, standing outside ready to go, talk him down. You know we've looked at trying to give them counselling, and that's why we are trying to get more and more of yourselves in, the expertise to give us. … You know?

Tens of millions of mobile individuals in an airport raise a range of problems of astonishing breadth and depth. Heavy weapons and tactical gear fade into the background as other skills are put to more regular use. Here is another senior police officer's memory of dealing with an incident, which was recounted as advice to a trainee:

> Now you can imagine yourself getting the call, [she's] totally distraught, totally incoherent … Well the first thing is I'd ask them, "Can we sit down to one side?" Sit them down, and then talk gently. And then look for a name, and then once you find it out or get a scrap of information, try and concentrate on that.
>
> [He recalls:]
>
> And as it transpired, I dealt with this woman who had been up for 26 hours. Her husband, who she was estranged from, had put up stuff on Facebook, which related to her children, and she was trying to get back to the United States, to try and get to her children to tell them that, you know, they weren't being abandoned by her. And everything, and she just … everything just piled up and was on top of her … tantamount to a nervous breakdown. But by having, you know, she talked through the whole thing, talked it down and knew that at that stage the airline wasn't going to carry her that day, because it was too much of a risk. … The children, we made a phone call to them, let her talk to them; reassured her that they were okay. And then said to her now we need to look after you, so convinced her that it was a good idea to stay overnight, organized a hotel down the road here beside airside, which is next door to the medical center, because the airline would require a medical certification of fitness to travel, I said you can pop in there and get that, and then tomorrow when you come up, I'll look after your luggage.
>
> [He turns to Mark] Now that, if you want, is an example, that to me is community policing.

Airport policing is a mix of customer service, community relations and paramedical service. Over a six-month period, Mark accompanied airport police as they dealt with drunk passengers, abusive partners, lost travel documents or lost children (the latter occurs more frequently than one might expect). One day, reflecting on over 20 years of experience, one police officer had this to say:

> Around ten years after I was first here – early 2000s I suppose – it started to shift. … I suppose then the methods then of policing have changed dramatically. I suppose in terms of a lot of what we do now is technology-led and is also I suppose intelligence-led. CCTV … Body Cameras… The days of an idiot like me dressing up like a fool has proved to be ineffective and is not really good. I mean there's always been that battle as well, that on the one hand you're working with a commercial organization … and a state … then you have these huge

and vast powers to stop, detain, arrest and search, which is what is required of an airport, and then you are trying to marry these two together, and it's not a comfortable fit.

[...]

If you are armed, there's a huge amount of responsibility and expectation involved in that, you know? At this stage, I'll be 50 this year ... married with three kids, two dogs, mortgage, etc., so I have a lot to consider ... I came from an armed institution. I was in the Corps for six years before I was here so it's not that I'm adverse to it or that I've any objection to it but ... I think, for me now, I don't know, carrying a firearm around kids, around families, it's just I'm at odds with it now.

This sense of sands shifting beneath one's feet is pervasive, and is felt across professional generations. Younger police officers discussed threats and responses using martial terminology more freely than their older peers, as illustrated on p. 00, but they also expressed some doubt about being able to fulfill a counterterrorist role. These men and women are professionals with considerable experience, but the idea that one day they would have to face off against suicide attackers with explosives and machine guns understandably gave them pause. They saw the probability of a catastrophic event as low, but they knew they had to train for such an event, and did so with a stoicism born of a certain powerlessness. Word had come from on high apparently, elsewhere for sure, that aviation and airports were under threat, and that airport police were now part of a global nervous system. Here are the words of the most senior security officer in the airport:

"To safeguard civil aviation from actual and awful interference." So, that's the overall terminology for all the staff that I deal with from a security perspective. That's the overarching goal, that's why they are here. That's why worldwide there is so much money pumped into security, because, obviously, we have a number of different threats that occur from terrorists and then we have other threats from people who would have a sort of revenge motive or you have a disgruntled employee or you have people with mental health issues. So, there's just so many different avenues of threat against civil aviation and again as I said the 1,200 people that we're talking about there, their role is to safeguard civil aviation from actual and awful interference and that's laid down in legislation from both ICAO and ... the European Civil Aviation Conference, and then you also have the EU regulatory framework and then you also have national legislation. ... At the end of the day the role of the officer downstairs from a screening point of view is to make sure a gun, bomb or any item won't get through and the role of the airport police is a proactive policing role and then if something does happen they react to that and then solve the problem.

[Describes a recent incident during which a man hijacked a car at knife point, drove to the airport, and somehow managed to force his way through the fence and airside to the runways. The situation was resolved peacefully, but protocol demanded that the security officer place the black-clad counterterrorism close quarters combat group on standby. All he was willing to say was, "It could have ended differently."]

So, again, you've the two elements. We have landside and airside, so landside is a movement area where anybody can move in and airside is a restricted area so only staff and passengers can go through. You have two layers of security within the airport. You have the security screening staff and then you have the police. So, the police role, wherever he or she is, is proactive policing which would then be reactive to a scenario.

As threats airside and now landside accumulate, those charged with security are required to imagine, anticipate and act with an eye on the horizon of the near-future. Police concretize their roles by thinking about what could go wrong. They are searching not just for solutions to immediate problems, but also for deeper responses to inescapable anxieties. Leviathan, indeed.

Note

1 Note that Hobbes also used "Leviathan" to mean the body politic as an enormous whole, organs engaged with one another, hence "Leviathan." In this sense, Hobbes participates in the classical organic imagination of politics which he is usually credited with supplanting, by creating a more mechanistic understanding. Nor is covenant the same as the more atomistic sense of contract that would come later. Be such things as they may, in contemporary public discourse, "Leviathan" is usually simply equated with "the State."

References

Westbrook, David A. 2008. *Between Citizen and State: An Introduction to the Corporation.* London and New York: Routledge.

Part III

A View From the Public

Chapter 10

The Glamor of Security

Throughout the ages, humans have needed to make long journeys in the company of others. Quite apart from its physical hardships, travel has often been socially awkward. Distinctions and especially hierarchies need to be maintained even while travelers huddle close to one another for companionship and security. It is this tension, and the temporary suspension of the normal order, that animates much of the classical literature on travel. Take for instance Chaucer's *Canterbury Tales*, wherein the stories told during the pilgrims' progress show the rigidity of class, while mocking and subverting the three estates. Distinctions, obviously, may be on lines other than class. In eighteenth-century Ireland, sectarian differences ran so deep that separate coaches ferried Protestants and Catholics along the same routes according to separate but identical timetables. *Plessy v. Ferguson*, the Supreme Court case that announced the doctrine of "separate but equal" in the United States, similarly involved train cars, segregated by race. It is hardly surprising, then, that the great transportation revolutions of the nineteenth- and twentieth-centuries – the ocean-going passenger liner, the long-distance rail line, the airships and flying boats – instantiated existing social distinctions even as they made travel more widely available, not least to facilitate the movement of the laboring poor.

Today, air travel is clearly stratified, from beginning to end. From the point at which one purchases a ticket and picks various options and preferences to pre-clearance, security fast-tracks and executive lounges, airports separate travelers based on two core elements: their ability to pay and the security of their identity, two forms of "clearance." Most people see stratification when a "priority" customer boards an aircraft before them, or when someone turns left rather than right after boarding. But differences run much deeper than this. Aviation systems, aircraft design, and even the architecture of terminals express and extend social stratification. If liberalism is, as some folks argue, the name one gives to the effort to reconcile individual freedom with the demands of a hierarchical social order (the rule of law, and hence security), then the global air world is a truly liberal one. The world is open to all who can pay for access; the more one pays the greater the access; and, the greater the access one has, the more security is required. Who are you exactly? What are your intentions? Are you where you should be? These are the questions of classical liberalism – the questions are formulated explicitly by Jeremy Bentham, for example – and the same questions are asked by airport security.

The greater the number of secure or "trusted" travelers, the fewer individuals have to be actively watched and assessed by expensive security personnel or systems. By pinning down an identity, knowing who a person is, biometric systems can begin to approximate intentions. Much work beyond this can be done by algorithmic systems. The more one conforms to type, the more obvious it is when fakery or abnormal behavior is occurring. The IBM expert who designed the UK's security fast-track system for "privileged" travelers explained his approach thus: "In order to find a needle in a haystack, you must first get rid of the haystack" (see Murphy and Maguire 2015: 161). In order to find a terrorist, one must first remove the vast majority of non-terrorists from view, using clear, orderly, and stratified systems. Stratification thus conceived is itself a form of security, because it tells security watchers what a person's place is in the order of things.

One group in particular poses difficulties for the liberal vision of individual freedom under mass regulation – the very wealthy. This has long been the case. The precursors to the modern passport were massive letters of introduction from one sovereign representative to another, usually festooned with saucer-sized stamps and seals, insisting that the bearer should be trusted. (Until relatively recently, the British and Commonwealth passport included a standard note of introduction from Her Majesty on the inside of the front cover asking that the bearer be afforded assistance and protection.) From the late nineteenth-century onwards, security measures capable of handling the masses, including standardized passports and technological identification, became the norm. Perhaps unsurprisingly not wanting to consider themselves among the masses, wealthy citizens resisted the process of applying for passports at all by sending domestic staff in their stead. Standardized photography and anthropometric descriptions were also resisted, and more flattering images and descriptions of facial characteristics were insisted upon.

It is banal to decry such behavior as snobbery, and it is, but consider the bother and indignity of air travel. The endless waiting in lines, either in person or on the phone. Deferral to unhelpful websites. Constant fees, constant compliance. The unpacking and packing, undressing and dressing, the X-rays (frequent travelers wonder about the long-term effects of the radiation) at checkpoints. Questions. The incessant barking from bored security staff who do not have a more respected job. Getting through security is insulting, and seasoned travelers learn how to go limp, passively drift through it, their minds as elsewhere as possible. The contemporary airport often treats people as objects rather than autonomous beings, means

rather than ends in themselves, to sound Kantian. Mass security dehuma-
nizes, transforms people into something less, perhaps like cattle in chutes, to
provide an image one might not want to take far.

Accommodations, unsurprisingly, have been reached. No society can deny
its elites altogether; that is what it means to be elite. (Elites may be replaced
by new ones, however, that is, a new society may be constituted.) Simply
buying an expensive ticket tends to expedite security and boarding. Most
such travelers, however, are repeat players, enrolled in programs that facilitate
the passage through security both domestically and internationally (familiar
US systems are TSA Pre and Global Entry, respectively). Customs is also
expedited. For the day to day purposes of security personnel, such travelers
are the haystack referred to above. They have been examined, inventoried,
and are lightly monitored as they check in, collect luggage and the like, but
such travelers generally are out of mind. Not the problem. For the elite traveler, lines are short or non-existent, security and customs agents ask little,
and are generally welcoming, even friendly. "Welcome home." It is, for want
of a better word, nice. Security not only relies on stratification, it expresses it,
in friendly terms, no less. In some regards, there may have never been a finer
time to be *haute bourgeois*. Perhaps this is as good as it gets.

Today, we are used to the image of what Virgin rather too frankly brands
"Upper Class" travel as a proximate but largely inaccessible realm where
champagne flows and veal dishes are pronounced "excellent." Here, the
language of class is used explicitly, and a strange moral order prevails.
The traveler is someone who "appreciates" the finer things. She "deserves"
the "experience." The wine, the food, the personal attention, are generally
not purchased, they are provided because she is in "the club" or "first class"
or whatever the privileged space is called. She is thanked by staff for
"being" "platinum" or even "diamond," transformed by the gods of commerce into a new sort of person. (A mere baronet may dream.) More subtly
but ultimately more importantly, the elite traveler gets more responsive
staff, perhaps more skilled, certainly less worked, probably better paid. On
dedicated phone lines actually answered in a short time, articulate airline
representatives help the traveler work through the inevitable fluctuations in
schedule, mistakes and cancellations. Lounges abound, where one can walk
away from one's belongings for a few seconds, and of course eat and drink
and be entertained. More interestingly, the better lounges are almost like
home or a spa, with showers sporting excellent body wash, and quiet nooks
for napping. Perhaps the future will see more terminals devoted entirely to
such travel, such as the "premium" one that opened in Doha a few years ago.

Obviously, such luxuries are luxuries in large part because they are not
shared by all. Luxuries are frequently called, without irony, "exclusive," to
be enjoyed, sure, but more to be displayed in the hope of being envied.
A European airline recently made the centrality of exclusion all too clear to
David, on an older plane with only one class of seating, tiny seats three

across, aisle down the middle, the length of the plane. Sometime after acquiring the plane, the airline evidently decided to offer an elevated class of travel. Perhaps this decision was driven by the airline's competitively required code share arrangements. It is hard to tell a traveler on an international privileged class itinerary to squeeze in over there, and perhaps you would like to purchase some chips? Rather than spend money and do the obvious, i.e., gut the front of the plane and put in a few commodious seats, electronic gadgetry and ample room, however, the airline simply put a bar across the middle seats in the front of the plane. "Business" means nobody sits next to you. Simple, cheap, done. Exclusion is the essential luxury, evidently. Everything else is icing. Chaucer would have smiled.

Perhaps less obviously, however, privileged treatment situates the traveler differently in social space, not just on the plane or in the lounge. Personal attention is just that, personal, that is, not bovine. Calling a businesswoman by her name, en route from Los Angeles to Shanghai, does not mean she is family (though airlines are not above using that language, too), but it does mean that she is *somebody*. In a big airport, to say nothing of the global contemporary, being somebody is not to be taken for granted. From this perspective, the luxuries enjoyed by elite travelers are not just conveniences, although they certainly are, nor are they merely modes of separation from the hoi polloi in an increasingly materially unequal society, although they are that, too. Even in societies with some egalitarian manners, humans need identities, and identities are established largely vis-à-vis other humans, that is, humans need status, need to be recognized, to sound like Hegel.

In the hierarchy of social status, travelling commercially, even luxuriously, generally ranks below traveling privately. A great number of airports around the world operate separate internal airports for those who arrive by private aircraft, be it a helicopter or a jet. Of course, small aircraft are in everyday use across the world for numerous commercial or private reasons, such as farming. And in some parts of the world, e.g., the American West, more or less private air travel, in various configurations, is not solely the province of the very wealthy. At issue here, however, are the freedoms of VIP travel, and the problem of VIP security. When one lands in a precleared private jet, bodies and baggage are handled efficiently and discretely, often by dedicated security operators who are somewhat separate from the policing structure in the main airport. Sometimes aircraft carrying important individuals land, refuel and take off, remaining on the tarmac over national soil for long enough to fulfil residency tax requirements. Sometimes the media is alerted to the presence of the wealthy and famous, yet another category of person, and a category that is especially troublesome for security personnel, however they travel. An ethnographic vignette that Mark sent to David:

> In 2011, I was sitting in on a counterterrorism training program in a UK airport. The training group was a typical mix of elite police

officers, "borders" agents and intelligence officers. The module was a live exploration of spatial dynamics. The location was baggage Carousel 5, which was the carousel at the end, and near emergency exits onto the airport apron. Undercover officers dotted the area. Flight after flight landed, and the details appeared on the baggage screen, with passengers arriving soon thereafter. The same scene replayed itself over and over. People positioned themselves near to where they anticipated the baggage emerging, looked down at their phones or chatted. Children swung from trollies or sat on the carousel and were forced by their parents to behave themselves. The baggage was always five minutes later in arriving than one would expect. We, the team, were the cleaners, the two impatient businessmen, the individuals who stood next to one another discussing the contents of a tourist flyer. Each cohort of passengers found us at Carousel 5, and none seemed to question how we got there first. One of our tests of spatial dynamics was the security equivalent of Mary Douglas's "matter out of place" – we looked like we belonged, therefore people assumed that we belonged. We also tested a few other ideas about physical reactions to armed police or dog units. It was not a dramatic day.

Late in the afternoon, our group leader touched his ear piece, and then relayed a message. The arriving passengers from a transatlantic flight would be delayed in coming to us, to allow a female member of the British royal family to collect her baggage and exit the airport discretely. She had no access to private aircraft that day, for reasons undisclosed, so she was forced to travel first class instead. The royal was travelling on her own, with a close protection officer.

Close protection is a very particular and highly skilled form of policing. Much like the domain of specialist counterterrorism policing, elite units train with each other and may exchange staff. Several European states volunteer staff in rotation to assist in the protection of the Pope, in part as a training routine but also for diplomatic reasons. Close protection is a discipline with its own body of knowledge, social-scientific literature, and, of course, tactics. During a recent transatlantic exercise held in Los Angeles, various secret services ran a joint international exercise, the close protection equivalent of the Ryder Cup, which left the US side embarrassed and vowing revenge the following year against the victorious European teams.

But for all of this, rank matters. The Royal's protection officer was outranked by the leader of the counterterrorism training team, and therefore had to seek permission to walk his charge into the middle of a live exercise involving armed officers. Apparently, the protection officer was informed that a small number of undercover operators would be at Carousel 5, and that the unit would pivot to a close protection role for the few minutes when the Royal would be in that area. The Royal arrived at the carousel with a suited man close by, collected a bag, and was greeted by a very puzzled-looking airport official with a trolley. They quickly exited into a back office area of the terminal, through a purposely deactivated emergency door, rather than by going through the main exit to the arrival hall.

The unit leader then asked for our attention. We were going to call it a day. He told us that we would be going back through the staff security area, and he called for a weapons check, which is common when holsters have been moved about and clothing changed. At that exact moment, the emergency door, which had not fully closed, reopened. The Royal reentered, followed by her bodyguard, and walked towards a small bag circulating unnoticed on Carousel 5. Her pace slowed when she saw cleaners, businessmen, and dodgy-looking individuals in tracksuits comparing handguns. After a moment, everyone continued doing what they were doing as if nothing abnormal was happening. Eventually, the emergency exit swung closed again, and one of the undercover officers, dressed as a cleaner and still holding a mop, tipped his baseball hat and said, "Ma'am."

Putting questions of marriage to one side, royalty is hereditary. From birth, royalty has been protected. They may not notice it much, never having known anything else. (The question of how conscious of their security royals are has so far eluded our ethnographic inquiries.) For a commoner like me (David), however, having an entourage is enormously flattering.

Over the years I have done some speaking tours, in a number of countries, sponsored by the US Department of State. I always had a handler, usually a woman, sometimes American, sometimes local. I also sometimes had translators, usually women. In informal group settings, translators would whisper in my ear so as not to disturb the flow of conversation. Even at the moment I knew this was not good for my ego – some sort of psychic aneurism was threatening. But I came to understand why hip-hop stars acquire a posse as soon as possible.

There was always security, often intense. US embassies have in relatively recent years become fortresses, and the United States is, to put it mildly, not always loved. But that was general security. Sometimes there was close protection of me, notably in Pakistan. At the time, Bin Laden was still being hunted; there had recently been outbreaks of mass violence in every city I was scheduled to speak; there was substantial violence in each city within a week or so of my departure. There was anger at Facebook, said to be anti-Islamist. The State Department had lost at least one person in the preceding year. We had a substantial not very covert operation in Peshawar, which I wanted to visit (huge mountains and memories of Kipling and what was a frontier then, too).

Evidently, nobody in Peshawar wanted to hear my thoughts on political economy, probably being busy with other things. It was a dangerous time, and people were somewhat surprised I had agreed to come at all. I was protected in various ways, some very visible, some not so. I remember being walked from an ornate lecture hall across a university campus, accompanied by my elegant and senior host, perhaps a dean, behind a team of black clad commandos. And he asked whether I felt threatened. I loved it, at least for a few weeks. Maybe it would have grown somewhat irksome over time, but moving from translators to body guards was like shifting from beer to whisky. The aneurism ballooned dangerously.

As in a mirror, things look a bit different from the perspective of those who provide security. Security is not only flattering to the person being protected, the provision of security is glamorous. A former special forces operator recounts:

> So yeah basically I used to be the head of security for X [internationally known football (soccer) star] in Central America, at the time he was sponsored by [major multinational corporations]. He had at the time a group of friends that were all doing bogus jobs such as travel adviser, etc.,
>
> So X is the [extraordinarily famous and highly paid] footballer ... by the way I don't know who he is as I have no interest in football, all I know is that he's super famous. So we meet and are introduced and after the meeting one of his friends hangs back and says to me you don't look like you're very impressed with X. I look at him and say why should I be, he's just another rich guy that needs protection. He's slightly taken aback and goes on to tell me how amazing this X joker is. I respond ok cool, and tell him I dislike football, and haven't a clue who X is, and can't really see what all the fuss is about. This guy flips out and tells me he's going to have me replaced, so I say yep whatever floats your boat. Off he goes to return 30 mins later saying X wants to see me.
>
> So up I go to his room and we sit down he then asks me do I know who he is and I reply I do now, so he says does that impress me, I say no. All his mates are fuming and he breaks out laughing, he then throws all his hangers on out of the room and orders some beers for me and him. I obviously decline and he starts going on about how horrible it is to be so recognized and fussed over everywhere he goes, I agree with him and then say, well look, you have two of the biggest companies in this part of the world sponsoring you, so why not do everything top notch? He agrees and says you have free rein to make my life easier, to that end I chartered three helicopters, a fleet of vehicles, and a large team to look after him.

Anyway, as the days turn to weeks he starts confiding in me for all sorts of other things. I'll let you use your imagination as to what he would like me to sort out for him. So as I was running around with him I was getting photographed as much as he was, and for a while I was as recognizable as he was, you can imagine going to certain clubs on certain errands the ladies knew as soon as they seen me they were going to party with X ....

So yeah I have a few more stories working with other rich idiots, and that is one of the main reasons I distanced myself from the celebrity protection side of things and much preferred the bullets and bombs side.

★★★

For some years now, Mark has attended counterterrorism workshops in Europe and the United States. Active and former British, Irish, French, Swedish and North American police and military special forces gave presentations on specific incidents. Their goal was often to review a historical incident in which they were involved and to draw out "lessons learned." During one recent terrorist incident, for example, counterterror police used motorbikes to defeat city traffic. Also, there is much more to know about doors than one might think. And so forth. These experts often showed film footage of terrorist attacks in their presentations, and narrated events with colored digital circles appearing over camera footage to indicate an important person or feature.

Sometimes such recordings are studied and assessed by counterterrorism operators in search of broader patterns of behavior, but in some ways footage of terrorists behaving as terrorists is of limited value. Security experts tend to be more interested in how their fellow security practitioners behaved. Perhaps this is unsurprising in a world preoccupied with tactics and prowess, and hence prestige. On the *third* occasion during which Mark was shown footage of the North Hollywood bank shootout, which lasted a very long time and was well recorded by helicopter and terrestrial news crews, he asked himself, why this obsession with a bank robbery?

On February 28, 1997, Larry Phillips Jr. and Emil Matasareanu robbed the North Hollywood branch of Bank of America. At approximately 09.24 am, the two men left the bank, leaving terrified staff and customers in their wake. They were no ordinary thieves. Phillips and Matasareanu were wearing elaborate (homemade) body armor; they carried a deadly assortment of pistols, semi- and fully-automatic rifles, together with an M16 Dissipater, and were festooned with ammunition pouches. High on barbiturates, they were ready for battle. On leaving the bank, Phillips and Matasareanu were confronted by a waiting police cordon composed of officers armed, primarily, with an assortment of 9mm handguns and older .38 revolvers. In the special forces, such weapons are called "boom sticks" – good for making noise but little else. In short, the police were outgunned by the bank robbers, and badly so.

The shooting began. The cars used as cover by the police began to disintegrate, and so they hugged the tarmac. In a life-threatening situation, a few brief moments can feel like a lifetime. In North Hollywood, on February 28, 1997, over 15 minutes passed and still the shooting continued. The standard rules of engagement and operating procedures faded into irrelevance. A few brave souls crouched and ran to a nearby gun store to ask for heavy weapons.

Three minutes later a SWAT team arrived on scene, a full 18 minutes after the initial alert went out. Circling helicopters captured footage of the SWAT officers rescuing the wounded with a commandeered armored cash-delivery truck. Reporters also noticed that some of the tactical officers wore shorts and sneakers under their body armor. This was later put down to the alert having reached them during a training session. But nothing is ever exactly as it seems, especially when the deployment of violent force sends shockwaves through what we see, what we hear, and what we can comprehend as real. In such situations, reality fractures into partial truths.

The famous North Hollywood shooting ended when Phillips, severely wounded and with a jammed rifle, drew his pistol and shot himself, simultaneously being shot in the spine by a police officer. Matasareanu, who was by now a considerable distance away, attempted to carjack a Jeep. But SWAT officers cut him off, initiating an exchange of fire for several more minutes. At one point, a tactical officer hit him with a "double tap" in the chest ("central mass"), only to have the gunman, protected by his body armor, rise up once more. Eventually, he surrendered after a SWAT officer, wearing shorts and what looked like flip-flops, "skipped" bullets under a car and into Matasareanu's legs. The news cameras watched as the prone gunman bled to death during the 70 minutes it took for police to permit an emergency medical team to attend to him.

In Europe, in counterterrorism circles, the North Hollywood shootout looks like a "worst case" terrorist attack, whereas in the United States, or many cities in the Global South, it looks like a horrific policing incident. At a workshop with international counterterrorism and policing participants the footage of the shootout has something for everyone in the audience. It makes its own points: we failed to prepare; we were out gunned; they are watching and learning. But, more subtly, and perhaps more importantly, film of the North Hollywood shootout does not have to be explained contextually. We do not see people with a political history of oppression or with a "just cause," or even with a cause. Instead the action begins at 09:24 am when Larry Phillips Jr. and Emil Matasareanu exit the bank. From there on, the contemporary is visually available as tactics. The film is long enough to watch, not like a suicide bomber caught on CCTV. In a milieu of intense peer competition, the tactics of the SWAT team performing, rather than merely training, are endlessly fascinating. Even the colors are bright. Security achieves an odd form of purity. Action. No questions asked. This is, after all, Hollywood.

★★★

Security is glamorous. It is trite to say that we live in a violent culture. Children are trained to keep shooting victims from bleeding out. "Tactical" clothing is available in department stores. Recall, from Chapter 3, the adoption of SWAT and counterterrorism teams internationally and out of all proportion to reasonably anticipated dangers, even in a world with low tolerance for security failures. There are reasons, political and otherwise, but one of the reasons seems to be fashion. Movies are dominated by highly stylized, literally cartoonish, violence. Even while Americans, British or French citizens cannot name the countries where operations are being conducted, much less discuss the wisdom of such interventions, "we thank you for your service" has become a *formule de politesse*. Actions that used to be reviled, notably assassination, are now celebrated.

It is almost as trite to note the difficulty of making an antiwar movie or even writing an effective antiwar novel. The drama exerts a strong pull, like the glassy water just before the crest of Niagara Falls, mostly just contemplated with a shiver. Mostly. It must be and often is said that, most of the time, the violence at issue in security practices is only anticipated. Security forces train far more often than they fight. For the rest of the culture, in movies, video games, and the like, violence is generally represented, not enacted. Violence is presumably easier to stomach when it is not real, when there is no risk to oneself, and no possibility of loss or material wrongdoing. True enough, but merely negative.

It is also commonly said that no strong correlation exists between representations of violence and actual violence, certainly not enough for predictive policing. Japan has a great deal of very violent culture, but in recent generations at least, is a notably peaceable country. (Statistically at least, the suicide cults and the sarin gas attacks can be bracketed.) To say that a video game about jungle warfare is more fun than jungle warfare, however, says nothing about why the video game is attractive at all.

What does this mean? Perhaps some presentation-style bullet points would be helpful:

- Security is about violence, perhaps justifiable as some sort of self-defense once it starts but violence nonetheless; and
- Security is glamorous; and

- The glamorous is desired, not just by an individual, but by many people; then

- Do we not desire violence, at least to some extent, not just as individuals but as a people?

References

Murphy, Eileen and Mark Maguire. 2015. "Speed, Time and Security: Anthropological Perspectives on Automated Border Control." *Etnofoor*, 27(2), 157–177.

Chapter 11

The Resilience of the Individual

On June 29, 2007 at around 01:30, an ambulance crew was called to a minor incident at the Tiger Tiger nightclub, in London's Haymarket. The crew noticed fumes coming from a car that was parked nearby. They reported their suspicions to the police, who in turn alerted armed officers and the bomb disposal unit. Later, forensic examiners secured the car and found a mobile phone set to trigger a large quantity of petrol, gas and nails – the Mercedes-Benz had been turned into an effective V-IED, a vehicular improvised explosive device. At roughly the same time, a similar scene played out in London's Cockspur Street, where another suspicious car was identified. Domestic intelligence officers, so it is believed, immediately began to reconstruct the phone's location data. It was clear that a terrorist network was responsible and at large. Today's counterterrorist philosophy is "attack the network." Phone calls and messages suggested the presence of "cells" in London and Birmingham, and at the periphery of the network two names appeared, those of Bilal Abdullah and Kafeel Ahmed, two medical professionals working in Glasgow. Perhaps they were involved somehow?

Bilal Talal Samad Abdullah was born to a middle-class family in Buckinghamshire, UK. While still a boy, his family moved him to Iraq, where he enrolled at al-Mansour high school and later Baghdad College. He qualified in medicine in 2004 and returned to the UK to practice in 2006. Those who study terrorism are always keen to search individual stories for features that indicate a generic "path to radicalization," although the existence of a single path is disputed by many, including by MI5. Bilal Abdullah explained his path as a response to watching innocent people die as the result of sanctions during the Saddam Hussein regime, followed by the violence and destruction that followed the US led invasion. But Abdullah's violent radicalization cannot be attributed solely to a "blow-back effect" from the UK's overseas military adventures. Abdullah held deeply hostile attitudes towards those outside of the narrow Wahhabi-Sunni version of Islam, including great numbers of his fellow Muslims. In a private note, reconstructed from his laptop, he speaks as a moral crusader about to set himself to the bloody work of purification. His network's primary target was London, specifically those "safe" spaces where people lived, loved, and danced in praise of different gods. When that failed, Glasgow airport would have to suffice.

His accomplice in the failed London attack was Kafeel Ahmed, originally from India. A trained engineer, Ahmed was awarded a PhD in technology design from a UK university before returning to Bangalore in 2005. It appears that Ahmed received his training in jihadism in India. Both men were determined to die while causing the maximum loss of life. Although they had been "tagged" by MI5 – Abdullah for downloading material from a jihadi website while at work in Royal Alexandra Hospital – and were under active surveillance during the lead-up to the Glasgow attack, it is not known how thoroughly they cased the airport if at all. This is important, because they attacked the airport on the first day of school holidays.

At 15.10 on June 30th, Bilal Abdullah and Kafeel Ahmed swerved their black Jeep Cherokee, packed with gas canisters, fuel and nails across a lane and towards one of the main doors of Glasgow airport, and towards many hundreds of school children waiting to go on school trips. Had they succeeded in their mission to crash through the door and trigger their V-IED, the result would have been horrific. Fortunately, however, only a few weeks prior to the attack, the airport installed steel bars outside the doors. These "security bars," as officials liked to describe them, were installed primarily to keep the expensive doors from banging in the wind. The black Jeep Cherokee hit door number 2 at 15:11, and became impaled on a security bar.

Stuck on a door bar and staring at their intended victims, Abdullah and Ahmed lashed out. Abdullah threw Molotov cocktails from the passenger side of the car, setting the pavement ablaze; Ahmed drenched himself with petrol and set himself ablaze. A fracas ensued outside the passenger door, while a burning Ahmed walked to the rear door of the Cherokee, opened it and attempted to ignite the explosive material. By this point, some individuals were attacking the terrorists while, simultaneously, others were attempting to rescue them from what looked to be a car accident. The situation became confused until police officers gained control several minutes later.

In a well-known stand-up routine, the Scottish comedian Billy Connolly reenacts the failed 2007 terrorist attack on Glasgow airport, occasionally breaking down in uncontrollable laughter at the shear lunacy of staging an attack in the former murder capital of Europe. "Religious fanatics?" he wonders, "and they don't even have a football team!" His routine centers on the heroic actions of John Smeaton, an airport baggage handler who happened to be "out smoking a fag" when the terrorists struck, and his efforts to stop the attack by punching one attacker in the face. Smeaton was subsequently interviewed by the BBC. In (subtitled) answer to the bizarre question of what would he say to any other would be terrorist, Smeaton looked to the camera and said, "This is Glasgow. We'll set about ye."

★★★

There is a lapse of time between an armed attack and armed response, counterattack. If the attack is on security forces, as at Orly in 2017, or any number of embassies, the response may be immediate, i.e., the lapse may be very short. More often, however, Leviathan takes time to arrive, as discussed earlier with regard to the London Bridge and Borough Market attack. Sometimes security forces take a very long time to control the situation, as at Westgate mall in Nairobi. During the period between attack and counterattack, be it short or long, members of the public confront the terrorists in various ways.

As is well known, acute stress produces clear physical reactions that give the body capacity to act. For example, when stressed, the primitive amygdala instantly triggers the nervous system to give a dramatic energy boost for violent muscular exertion. In the psychological literature, there are efforts to recognize reactive behaviors beyond the body's "instinctive" and therefore immediate "fight-or-flight" response. Some social scientists speak of "tend-and-befriend" reactions, which occur later, are more sociological in origin, and are, apparently, more common among females. "Freeze-and-fawn" responses have also been studied. Such characterizations tacitly tend to assume a single and relatively non-dynamic threat. A marauding terrorist attack, however, involves multiple stresses, and usually multiple waves of recognition flowing over those involved, over a period of time. In that time, human behavior can be highly variable.

As noted in Chapter 9, in the London Bridge and Borough Market attack, terrorists were met with countervailing savagery: "Fuck You, I'm Millwall!" Roy Larner was willing to fight, bare fisted as needs be, against multiple armed murderers. To say that this response is brave, apart from being an understatement, does not tell us very much. Some people indeed are physically brave, but here as elsewhere, nurture and nature seem intertwined. Millwall Football Club, whose stadium in Southeast London is called "The Den" is famous for the "rowdiness" of its fans. This was not Larner's first fight. We have discussed the importance of training, and then more training, to conditioning the responses of elite special forces operatives. Under certain stresses, they go. These are perhaps extreme examples, but in many attacks, some people perform surprisingly "well," exhibit what psychologists call "resilience." Both the Glasgow attack of 2007, discussed above, and the Thalys train attack of 2015, below, provide striking examples of resilience, to which we now turn.

★★★

The following section is drawn fairly directly from Mark's fieldwork into the Thalys attacks, done in the course of the project "An Anthropology of Ten Minutes." In order to demonstrate both the confusion of terrorist attacks and the need for resilience, it seems better to let individuals who have experienced terrorist attacks use their own words, demonstrate the confusion of the attacks, the need for resilience, and oftentimes, their own resilience – bravery.

★★★

On August 21, 2015, on the Thalys train from Amsterdam to Paris, Ayoub El Khazzani attacked passengers in Car No. 12, the car in which Anthony Sadler, Airman First Class Spencer Stone and Specialist Alek Skarlatos happened to be passengers. The following is Spencer Stone's account, the first of the three young men to react:

So, you know, I was initially woken up by the train employee running past me towards the front of the train and that commotion kind of woke me up initially. I didn't know exactly what was happening when he ran by, I just knew that it was, like, you know, really odd behavior, like just how fast he was sprinting down the aisle kind of alarmed me. And then I looked at Alek and he was kind of looking towards the back of the train and then he kind of had, like, a shocked, you know, look on his face and then I looked at Anthony and he was just kind of like still looking up and kind of had the same look, like what the heck is going on? I took my headphones off and I heard glass breaking, people screaming, and then I turned around and looked behind me and the first thing I see is a guy coming in to our train car bending down picking up the AK and he's trying to load a round in and, you know, I noticed he was kind of like … something was going on with this guy. I didn't know what, but I was just, like, he's having some type of trouble. Then I kind of looked down the aisle, and there's people sitting right next to him, looking at him, and I'm kind of like doing this short little scan, and I say, you know, like in my head, you know, like going, you know, do something, you know, like give them a second to like get up and react and then I quickly realized that they are just in too much shock to do anything, so I pretty much took it upon myself, because I just thought our time was running out, that I'd make a move, pretty much, and so I just took off in a full sprint down the aisle towards him and then, you know, I could hear him trying to work the gun again and even more like he actually ended up pulling the trigger on me but there was a bad timer on the bullet so it gave me more time to be able to make it to him, which is like probably the biggest miracle in the whole story …
As I came up to him, he kind of like butt-strikes me with the gun, like as I'm tackling him, so I can't really see out of one of my eyes now, and we kind of both fall to the floor as I tackle him, and then, you know, like the main fight starts, and I'm trying to grab the gun from

him and, you know, I feel I'm kind of like, kind of losing grip, I guess, I mean, I was trying to grab it but I never had full control of the gun and so then my instincts just went to what I know and I just remember my Ju Jitsu and I just was trying to choke him out, you know, put him in a rear-naked choke, and then I flung myself to the right side of the train and kind of bashed my head against the window a little bit – I'm surprised I didn't knock myself out when I did that – and then Alek ran up as I was trying to choke him and you know he started to help me out by taking the pistol from him before he could shoot me with that. And then I started to get slashed on the back of my neck and I had my left finger, my left thumb, cut to the bone and it severed my tendon and nerve and you know once I saw my finger I looked over ... because I'm on his back now ...

Reviewing the sequence of discrete actions, one cannot help but be struck by the fact that everything happened within a very narrow temporal window. More simply, things happened fast. Spencer sensed a disturbance, made a snap decision, and was then racing down the aisle of a train carriage towards a half-naked man with an assault rifle. Alek Skarlatos recalls the odd effect the attack had on time, and gives his perspective on the first minute of the confrontation:

It was fairly obviously that it was a terrorist attack ... We saw the train employee run past us and we just looked back to see what he was running from and there was like a shirtless Middle Eastern guy with an AK-47 standing there. I mean it doesn't take a genius to figure out what was going on. And it was just, kind of, like, there's no way this is happening! And so, then I tapped Spencer and I said, "Spencer, go!", or something to that effect, and then he immediately gets up and runs up to the guy. I kind of had tunnel vision, so I didn't even realize Spencer had left until he was already almost halfway to the guy.
... To be honest I don't even remember it. But, basically, Spencer tackled the guy. I caught up to him. We fought with him for a little bit. Then basically Spencer finally got him in a chokehold, and once he got him in a chokehold, the terrorist then pulled out a handgun to try to shoot him with it. I was standing right in front of him, so I pulled the hand gun from out of his hand before he could shoot anything and then put it to his head and told him to stop resisting. He didn't, so I pulled the trigger and the chamber was empty. So, then, I basically just threw it and then I picked up the AK that was on the ground, because I think Spencer was getting stabbed around this time, so I tried to shoot him with the AK but it was on safe so instead of messing with it anymore I just started to hit him in the head with the muzzle ...

Skarlatos's efforts to subdue El Khazzani are magnified in his memories, but during those exact moments, his friend was fighting for his life, uncertain of the outcome. Spencer Stone expands on those critical moments from his perspective:

> It did happen very quickly, from where I was in a fight for my life and, you know, I very much wanted to kill the guy, you know, just I mean naturally in that type of situation: if someone has tried to shoot you twice with multiple different guns and has slit your throat, you're kind of like seeing red at that point and like you feel like the only option is to the kill the person because it doesn't seem as if he is going to stop, so you've got to win …

Bruised and bleeding, with his friend's help and the drive to win, Stone hooked his legs around the attacker and applied the chokehold until El Khazzani lost consciousness. At this point, the friends' memories fade into one another. Spencer continues,

> At this point now kind of, like, we're all standing up, we're all, like, semi-surrounding Khazzani and we just started to punch him, kick him, do whatever we could. And now he's got no weapons in his hands, and he kind of, like, winded himself on me, … and then we, like, threw him over a table and then Alek and I kind of like were holding him by the back of the neck against the table and you know we were screaming at him "Stop, stop, stop resisting" …
> And, then, that's when I saw Mark Moogalian bleeding, and I was also confused because I still had been looking for the gun shots; I didn't know if he had actually shot anyone yet or if I was actually kind of confused. I didn't know how he had even been injured, so I thought maybe he got a belt with the knife in the scuffle or something and then I just screamed, "Hey, I'm a medic. I'm a medic. Get this guy off me and then hold him down and make sure he doesn't wake up." I crawl over and I see blood kind of gushing through the neck, and I took my shirt off, originally I was going to use it as a bandage to hold pressure with but once I realized it was pressure coming from his neck, you know, like pulsating with regard to his artery, and then I put my fingers in his neck and I could feel the artery pulsating in there and I found it and then clamped it down and the bleeding just completely stopped and then we kind of just went from there.

The friends acted quickly, and within a matter of minutes the two servicemen had taken control. From the perspective of others onboard, the events seemed even more dramatic. This is the account of then 62-year-old Christopher Norman:

I was travelling from Amsterdam Airport. ... I was going to change trains in Paris and carry on down to the South. So, I was in the train and I was working on my PC. ... I heard this bang, if you like, and I wondered what is that, and I heard glass falling. ... The Thalys seats are very large so you don't actually, you don't see what's going on in the rest of the compartment. Then what happened is immediately after I'd heard that I think it was the train manager was rushing back up towards the engine in the front, running very, very fast indeed. He, sort of, almost broke through the glass door at the end of the carriage and he was shouting something. Now I don't remember exactly what, I think it was, "He's crazy," or something like that in French so. ...
I stand up and I see this guy coming up the aisle with his beard, bare chested, carrying an AK-47. Well it wasn't an AK-47, carrying a sub-machine gun, and so I sit down again. I'm actually dead scared. ... There was no question in my mind, you know my first thought was, "Oh my God, it's happening to me". ... You know I remember the Tunisia thing, immediately before it, where people didn't get up and do anything and basically they were all shot down anyway. So, my thinking was you know what do I do, how do I react in relation to this? Is there anything I can do that will basically save our lives? At the same time being very, very scared. So, I was kind of trying to get myself ready to do something but I didn't know whether I was going to do anything or not and then ... I stood up I saw Spencer wrestling with the guy, and I saw Alek in front of him hitting him and I saw the guy looking like he was trying to reach down to what I think was a gun on the ground and I said if there's one thing I have to do is to stop him from getting that gun or we've had it. It was a silver hand gun. It looked like a silver hand gun. So I jumped in there. I guess about ... well it seemed quite a long time actually ... I guess it was about 30 seconds, maybe even 60 seconds ... no, no sorry two minutes, so one minute or two minutes, something like that, the guy stopped struggling completely and from then on it is history.

With the terrorist subdued, and with his friend applying the crudest of clamps to Moogalian's artery, Alek Skarlatos set about clearing the train of any other threats:

So, then I put a new round in the AK, and then I took the AK to the back of the train, just, like, making sure there weren't any other terrorists or anybody else that was shot. When I got to the back of the train and there was a bunch of people crowded kind of packed in the back, like sardines, so I just asked them if anybody spoke English, and two guys raised their hands, and I asked them if anybody else was hurt, and they said no, and so I told them just to tell everybody else to kind of stay where they were and not to come up front, and then I left. I went back up front, starting clearing the AK and looking for the handgun ... I gathered all the weapons of ammunition, put them on a seat and then I went over and helped Spencer take care of Mark, to get his shirt off altogether, and look for any other injuries, and mostly just hung out and kind of talked with Spencer and Mark and tried to make sure the terrorist stayed unconscious.

The third of the American tourist friends, Anthony Sadler, arrived with the train's medical kit and, following Spencer's directions, cut off Mark Moogalian's clothes and checked for secondary wounds. The train was rerouted to Arras station, where, approximately 15 minutes later it was met by armed officers and emergency medical teams. The scene was secured, and the tourists stood down.

These individuals, who drove themselves at a heavily armed terrorist, were members of a fairly rare breed on a contemporary European train, people who know what it is to experience violence. Alek Skarlatos is clear on how his upbringing in California shaped his actions:

> We were kind of like paranoid growing up I guess. We've thought about and talked about situations like this happening before, that if somebody ever decided to like shoot up our school what would we do you know, things like that, would we try to tackle them? You know just things like that, we just ...we've thought ahead about it I guess.

During a separate interview Spencer Stone opened up this topic in more detail:

> I think like obviously pretty much what I described was like a little bit of, like, mental preparation, and it's, like, you know, for some people that could be kind of, like, a scary thought, and they don't want to think about those types of things and, like, hey, I get that. You don't want to be walking around, doom and gloom, thinking the worst is always going to happen, but at the same time it's very realistic, you have to prepare for situations like that, like at least have thought about it once or twice in your lifetime. ... So, for instance, one thing that happens in Europe, which I think might be slightly different to the US, is that when bullets are fired, right, Europeans don't necessarily recognize that for what it is, initially, because we don't hear it very often, because, you know, there's very little shooting as you can imagine, because we don't just get that many gunshots.

Apart from his youth in a milieu when violence was thought, we can account for the serviceman's actions by attending to his training, both medical and firearms, and perhaps his knowledge of jujitsu, but what of the others? Christopher Norman, at 62, entered the fray quickly, but he too had a sense of what was happening, a muscle memory from childhood in Kenya and time spent in South Africa. "I lived a long time in South Africa," he explained, and "I was fairly preconditioned to the idea that violence could happen, which I think is a rather different conditioning than the majority of people in Europe have." If these preconditioned individuals were not onboard, it is difficult to see the terrorist meeting any friction.

Yet, as discussed in Chapter 7, their actions would not have been enough if it were not for the luck of the day. Spencer Stone reflected on the sequence of events and how things could have been otherwise:

> The fact that we ended up in that exact spot with so many different variables; ... you know the AK, the bullet not in the AK, the primer not working and giving me that opportunity to make it to him. You know, there's stuff, I don't think I mentioned during my explanation that he tried to shoot me in the head with the pistol and he had just got done shooting Mark Moogalian with the pistol, and there should have been ammunition in it but he must have dropped it when he shot him or in the scuffle or something. I'm also sure there wasn't a bullet in the chamber so, you know, that essentially didn't work for him, and then he was able to attack my neck when I was trying to choke him. As he was cutting me he wasn't able to cut my artery and then there's just so many different things.

★★★

In short, individuals who have resilience tend to behave very differently from those who do not, as illustrated by the Glasgow and Thalys attacks. A final example comes from Anders Breivik's attack on Utøya Island. Breivik chose his target because the island was hosting a youth retreat for the Norwegian Labor Party. In his mind, he was slaughtering a future generation of Norwegian "socialists." Among the large number of children, however, were two 16-year-old Chechnyan refugees, Rustam Daudov and Jamal Movsar. The two friends attacked Breivik with rocks and brought 23 children to safety. When the incident was resolved, one of their friends, also from Chechnya, calmly smoked a cigarette. He was arrested because the police became suspicious of his relaxed attitude. It is simplistic to compare children from war-torn regions to their counterparts in extremely safe countries during what is arguably the most peaceful period in human history. But it is not a matter that one can simply pass over.

If resilience is assessable, or might be surmised from past experiences, one can imagine making resilience an explicit criterion for recruitment in critical infrastructure sites, especially mass transit systems. Insofar as resilience is learned, as these attacks strongly suggested, one can imagine teaching it. One can imagine training schoolchildren and others how to be more resilient. One can even imagine the "public" finding this more or less acceptable. To some extent, this is happening in the United States, with schools doing "lockdown" drills. One can imagine arming, and training, more "civilian" public servants. One can also imagine paranoia within reason.

Discussion of resilient individuals raises another issue. In terrorist attacks, violence and associated virtues come from many angles. Violence, even legitimate violence, is not the exclusive purview of something called "the State." To that question we now turn.

Chapter 12

Violence, Legitimacy, and the State

Economies of Force. Max Weber, in *Politics as Vocation*, influentially defined the modern state in terms of a monopoly on legitimate violence within a territory. This rather complicated idea became deeply ingrained in the critical social sciences, and it is with that familiar idea – the Weber that we think we know, professionally (*als Beruf*, as it were) – that we are concerned. As so often is the case in professional discourse, the little matter of the truth, whatever the "real" Weber may have thought, or more politely, our best reading of Weber, must be placed safely in its alcove. Nonetheless, by way of entry, the famous passage is worth quoting at some length:

> Violence is, of course, not the normal or the only means available to the state. That is undeniable. But it is the means specific to the state. And the relationship of the state to violence is particularly close at the present time. In the past the use of physical violence by widely differing organizations – starting with the clan – was completely normal. Nowadays, in contrast, we must say that the state is the form of human community that [successfully] lays claim to the *monopoly of legitimate physical violence* within a particular territory – and this idea of "territory" is an essential defining feature. For what is specific to the present is that all other organizations or individuals can assert the right to use physical violence only insofar as the state permits them to do so. The state is regarded as the sole source of the "right" to use violence.
>
> (Weber 2004: 33)

The state here is an "ideal-typical" notion; Weber is trying to define what the *concept* of the state means. As an ideal concept, the state cannot be defined by describing the particulars of its various instantiations.[1] If Weber's concept of the state is ideal, however, it is not the sort of timeless ideal sometimes called Platonic. Instead, Weber's ideal types are rooted in social affairs, history. Weber's ideals are abstractions from the messiness of the world. Perhaps it is useful to remember that Weber was a legal historian and professor of law before the sociology he helped found as a discipline was institutionally established. From the perspective of law, the statement of a rule organizes, suppresses, distills what happened and what should happen, but such statements are nonetheless engaged with a situation, sometimes decisively so. Ideal types, like law, thus strive to be simultaneously practical and responsive to the world, pragmatic, and yet just, true, and logical, or more bluntly, both in and out of time.

Turning to the world, however, is little immediate help with constructing a generalization that we can confidently call "the state." There is too much data, as it were. There seems to be no rule that organizes the activities of those things we agree on calling states. Weber is explicit. The state:

> cannot be defined sociologically by enumerating its activities. There is almost no task that a political organization has not undertaken at one time or another; but by the same token there are no tasks of which we could say that they were always, let alone *exclusively*, proper to the organization that we call political, and nowadays refer to as states, or that historically were the forerunners of the modern state.
>
> (Weber 2004: 33)

Instead, Weber turns from the activities commonly undertaken by governments to the means available to the state as an organization trying to work in the world. "It is rather the case that in the final analysis the modern state can be defined only sociologically by the specific means that are peculiar to it, as to every political organization, namely, physical violence" (Weber 2004: 33). (A certain kind of reader will immediately recall that Carl Schmitt defined politics as the distinction between friend and enemy.[2]) The state can use such force itself, or it can grant "the right" to use force to other actors. But actors other than the state have no right of their own, i.e., other than as licensed by the state, to use violence.

For purposes of defining the state, however, a difficulty with violence is that "widely differing organizations" have legitimately used violence, as Weber recognizes. But the era of various forms of collective violence, Weber is careful to say, is over. The entire passage is riven with historical qualifiers. He defines the state "nowadays" – just after the World War I. The state's monopoly on legitimate force is "specific to the present."

Thus, Weber's famous monopoly of legitimate force turns both on a normative claim, legitimacy, and on an understanding of history, and specifically modernity, at least as understood by Weber after World War I. The state is defined in terms of the monopoly of legitimate force because it is the modern organization with the right, i.e., the legitimate authority, to use, or to delegate the use of, violence as a means. Conversely, modernity is the era in which force is monopolized by the state. The tautological quality of the complex of ideas does not make the complex untrue. Indeed, something like this is the dominant and largely tacit worldview in any number of self-consciously "modern" contexts, like North Atlantic universities. Still, each word, modern, monopoly, legitimacy, and territory, are problematic, in intertwined ways, in the contemporary fields in which we find ourselves.

To elaborate this understanding of history, whence this notion of modern comes, let us tell a story. Depending on when and where, the King certainly expected people to be armed in his realm – just not in his presence. And violence was to be expected, but not every day. The Church especially forbade fighting on various holidays. Over time, the disarmed areas were expanded. Similarly, the number of days on which fighting was prohibited increased. And who might bear arms also became curtailed. Peasants were disarmed, at least to the extent possible, given the violent uses to which workaday tools may be put. During the course of this evolution, bearing arms was often a privilege granted by the sovereign to nobles, who were thereby associated with and extensions of the crown. The privilege of carrying swords, and other noble privileges, were abolished as society modernized. Eventually, the citizen was expected not to bear arms, anywhere, or fight, ever. Violence was the rarely used prerogative of the sovereign, carried out by minions. (Today such minions are called "soldiers," "agents," even "assets," i.e., understood to "serve" or even be the property of the state.) Many Europeans and others today think like this. In "modern" settings, perhaps by definition, ordinary people are not prepared for violence. They are not armed, and often want the law to ensure that other people are not armed, either. This rather Hegelian view of the evolution of the state reaches its logical and world-historical conclusion in Bismarck/Weber's Germany, or shortly thereafter.

Upon examination, this progressive conception of the arc of history runs into problems. Most states in most times and places are, by this logic, only partially achieved. Non-state actors use force all the time, and states use force in the territory governed by other states. Weber insists that the state must be "successful" in establishing its monopoly, so one might save the definition by insisting that in such places, such states are only embryonic. But then there are few real states, and we are left without a name for the form of organization that governs much of life in much of the world. In short, the prevalence of collective violence undercuts the sociological ambition to describe "state" organizations in societies as they are encountered, not as they might be imagined.

It is possible to salvage much of Weber's definition by dismissing non-state violence as "criminal" or otherwise illegitimate, and it may well be as a matter of law, i.e., from the perspective of the state. But the law may be contested, too. Al Shabaab, ISIL, the Nicaraguan Contras, Timothy McVeigh, the IRA and any terrorists who claim to be "freedom fighters" of one sort or another are precisely contesting the legitimacy of the state. And any number of what might broadly speaking be called mafias must have some degree of local legitimacy, whatever their crimes, in order to function. Such organizations may be more or less legitimate, and more simply, they may win or lose, but that seems to be a question of strength on the ground, not whether a territory had a state.

Nor does the link between legitimacy and violence seem all that tight. Paradigmatic states, such as France and the United Kingdom, key sources of our very notion of what a "state" is, exercise violence that is not, or not entirely, felt to be legitimate. US history provides any number of sobering examples, yet it is difficult to argue that the United States is not a state, whatever the legitimacy of its violence. Perhaps the modern state has a monopoly on all the legitimate force, and may also use some other, not so legitimate, force beside? But when it uses such force extraterritorially, as all of these countries do, does that mean that the territories involved do not have states? Does a drone attack "de-state" a place? And so forth. Lawyerly games aside, Weber seems to have had in mind a very well-ordered society, headed by a strong state, in which organized violence is exceptional and everyone knows what side to be on. Germany, perhaps, gave such an impression for a while, but that hardly seems enough for a general rule, or a definition of the state as such.

Even in the heart of Europe, however, it is not at all clear that violence is legitimate only when and as authorized by the state. In Glasgow, on the Thalys train, on Utøya island, people stood up and used forced against their attackers. Did they not do so legitimately? No government granted them the right to do so via some legal process. Neither the United Kingdom nor France nor Norway objected, of course, but surely the legitimacy of a young man's defending himself against a marauding attack does not spring from the Kingdom of Norway? But conversely, the existence of such violence does not mean that Norway (or France, or the United Kingdom) is not a state.

Since *Politics as Vocation*, significantly delivered between the World Wars, history seems to have gone down a path different from the one presumed by Weber. In the United States, the largest economy in the world, many people are armed, in public, every day. Nor does this right flow from the state, at least as a matter of law. As gun aficionados never tire of saying, the Constitution says the "right of the people to keep and bear arms shall not be infringed." Whatever the 2nd Amendment means, the people had guns before they had a constitution. Worldwide, security is a huge and growing private enterprise. When it protects a home or a business, ADT Armed Response presumably operates with a license from, but is hardly an agency of, the government, except in the general sense that the government is "for" property, order, and the like. Civil society, in short, employs force as a means in any number of situations. It just does not seem to be the direction of history that physical violence is "the specific means that are peculiar to" the state.

When it does employ violence, the state has a huge range of ways to do so, from the classic national military to unarmed police with arresting powers, and various forms of contractors in different situations. It is only with difficulty that these are all thought of collectively, as a unitary state. In particular, the recent revival of the use of mercenary forces, often organized as corporations and called contractors, is due in part to the desire of the United States at least to be able to deny direct knowledge of or participation in certain actions. In a conversation, where David naturally stands in for the US government: "You hired us because you didn't want your soldiers to do those things." At the same time, professional soldiers can be meticulous about the terms of their contracts, leading to some strange stories, like the tale of the leader of a terrorist organization who was somewhat accidentally captured by a group of contractors in a "theater of operation," a story told to David by one of the contractors. The contractors radioed in to ask for direction; their client said release him for diplomatic reasons that need not concern you. Somewhat bewildered, the contractors released the leader, and he lived on to direct the fight for quite some time. What, exactly, is "the State" here?

Perhaps most importantly, the end of World War II saw the erection of the modern political order, that David (2003) has elsewhere called the City of Gold, i.e., the enormous project of European integration/globalization in lieu of politics centered on the nation-state. Part of this integration was explicitly military. The UN Charter outlaws war in general, and then provides numerous useful exceptions to the rule. The claim of public international law after World War II, however, is that the choice to go to war does not belong to the state. Operationally, the North Atlantic Treaty Organization takes over a great deal of what had once been thought of as "national" defense, especially in Europe – the United States has a wider purview. And the Germans themselves were largely disarmed, and remain somewhat limited in their choice of weapons today. It is hard to say that all of this means that Germany is not a state.

It is true that Weber, in the German tradition, is talking about the idea of the state. On the ground, variations are to be expected. But Weber is the sociologist. The concepts of sociology are supposed to be empirically grounded, not mere philosophical hypotheses. One could find places that fit the Weberian ideal of a unified state with a monopoly of force, perhaps China. But such places hardly represent the ideal, or the course of history, in the globalized world. By and large, even after the rise of so-called populism, most continental Europeans do not want a unitary state. Instead of a monopoly on physical violence held by well-organized states, the contemporary seems to be marked by a rather mixed political economy of force, in which states (whatever those are) are often enthusiastic if somewhat fractured participants.

Insults. And yet Weber points us to something very important: people often do think of the state in terms of physical security, and hold public authorities responsible for providing it. The state is expected to use force as necessary to protect airports, for obvious example. Actual attacks are perceived and largely discussed as failures *of the state,* which did not detonate the bombs or start the shooting. Nor is the state allowed to claim the status of victim, even though the state incurred losses, and in a democracy at least, the state might be thought to be "we the people." At least in Western societies, however, attackers are often treated as, if not exactly blameless, somehow beyond moral judgment, and not worthy of much discussion. In fact, discussion of attackers is often actively discouraged, lest they get too much attention. Attackers are perfunctorily called cowards and the business of blaming the state begins. Knowing this, as discussed in Chapter 5, security professionals operate under the specter of their own failure.

The expectation that the state is responsible for security effectively brackets "the terrorist" and sets it in opposition to the state. Bizarrely, or perhaps not, the particularities of those killers now known as "terrorists" recede. They must have had particularities, not just because everyone does, but because very few people cast themselves as the doomed protagonists of their own violent dramas, and then act their dramas out upon an involuntary populace. It is special behavior. But all such particularities are submerged by the vast category of terrorist. For this reason, it seems unlikely that political sensitivity often plays much of a role in shifting the focus of public discourse to the state's many failings. People may be unwilling to inflame ethnic, racial, religious, or other animosities, but how often do they think the terrorists or their ilk have much to give them, or that they be engaged? How would they be engaged? And, frankly, many terrorists are idiots. Special forces soldiers speak simply of the "bad guys" that they are prepared to eliminate, sometimes point blank in one of the less domesticated cities of the world. Some of this language, this simplification of people to cartoons, expresses ordinary lack of concern for the foreign, or the dehumanization required for combat. Much such abstraction, however, is tactical and operational, and often bureaucratically managed. From a security perspective, a [terrorist] is a subset of [bad things, violence, etc.] that could happen in or to [area, infrastructure, persons] to be secured. Perhaps a marauding shooter is just crazy, in theatrical style of many American attacks, or perhaps he is some sort of white nationalist racist, or who knows what is going on (as in Las Vegas) – none of this matters operationally, at least not in the event. Shoot first. At this juncture, "terrorist" is little more specific than "adversary" or "threat" – it names an opposition to the state, a kind of failure.

As faults of the state, terrorist attacks, or even the threat of terrorism, require governments to act, and to be seen to have acted. Security theater is required in fulfilment of the people's expectations that government provide security, or at least try. Otherwise, those that speak in the name of the people (also known as candidates) will insist on change. After an attack, nobody says "what else could you have done? Those guys were really evil motherfuckers, and talented, too." Not even after 9/11. Instead, Congress established a massive commission to investigate the failings of the security apparatus, albeit with some attention to the identity and motivations of the attackers. The terrorist as such is not completely irrelevant, but is primarily defined in opposition to the state.

Shifting the focus from terrorism to security, from the attackers to the watchers on the walls, also transforms the stale academic question of what "is" terrorism. The question has never been answered satisfactorily, and cannot be answered precisely insofar as the question is understood to require an answer in the form of a neutral or objective description of the attackers and their violence. The variations of attacks that might be called "terrorist" are endless. Moreover, even if we were to define terrorism precisely, surely our completely right answer would not affect how airports are built, or more generally, our understanding/experience of the contemporary. "Terrorist," much like "security" itself, is not a noun that names a thing, but a placeholder that allows a certain kind of discourse. Terrorism names an ill-defined set of actors and actions opposed to the state. That is, terrorism is an antagonistic concept, which cannot be defined or even adequately described in isolation.

In the effort to be scientific, objective, much social science scholarship makes just this error. Once we define terrorism, we can really get to work. But definition never comes. The lines between terrorism and crime, or war, or revolution, are too murky. Madness and ideology cannot be untangled. Principled consensus does not arise. Meanwhile, always, the work of security has already begun, with or without adequate definition. The bollards are ordered, the new guards are being interviewed, and so forth. The "terrorist" is already being defined, not in principle and ex ante, but antagonistically, as the presumption of the defenses under construction. The terrorist, today, can be discerned in the shape of the castle going up, even if we know that tomorrow may require a new castle. The scholar, in her own good time, publishes another effort at definition, at drawing sharp and defensible lines.

The failure to understand terrorism as antagonism, framed by Weber's understanding of the state, creates another problem. Much security scholarship is of the form: X number of people die from A, Y number of people die from B, X<Y, so we should worry more about B. We should worry more about, say, ordinary crime than terrorism. We do not, and the social scientist shakes her head ruefully, and repeats herself. The error in such thinking is the politically plausible (secularized) Christian but wrongheaded notion that all deaths are created equal. Lives may be equal in the mind of God, but they certainly are not in politics. While "all men are mortal," as the syllogism has it, deaths from natural causes do not really figure in security discourse. An epidemic or a hurricane may receive political

attention. AIDS did, albeit far more slowly than it should have. Hurricanes get air time, perhaps some federal aid, perhaps not so much, if the place hit is, for example, Puerto Rico.

Even violent deaths are not all equal. Ordinary murders, domestic spats gone horribly wrong, hot headed kids outside bars – so sad. Gang violence in the barrio is not a good thing, either, but – and you can certainly imagine this reaction, privately or at least in small groups – what is one to expect? The same gang in the airport, however, is not at all acceptable. SWAT teams will be called. That's what "critical infrastructure" means – critical to our operations, worthy of being violently defended, without much by way of legal nicety. Islamist militants targeting office towers, or the Pentagon, is really, really not acceptable. Wars will be started. To be blunt, from the perspective of the state, some violence is not only a failure to provide security, but is also an affront, an insult. While many killings get filed under "shit happens," insults to the state are labeled "terrorism."

Terrorists know this, at least implicitly. Insult is entailed in the conception of a terrorist act, not least bodily insult, but often also more overtly "public" than the killing of innocent ordinary folks who happen to be in the wrong place. The September 11th attacks were specifically designed to destroy symbols, i.e., not just to kill people, but to be as insulting as possible, and indeed to drag the United States into a war it could not win. And the insult was felt. The United States reorganized a chunk of government, started some wars, which it has not won but which as of this writing appear indefinitely manageable for some long period of time, hence "Forever War" and shadowy operators moving through much of the "developing" world. In this, at least, the terrorist insult was successful.

The degree to and ways in which the state can be insulted says something about the state. It turns out that some people, at least in civilized places, get emotional about the "monopoly of legitimate force," indeed may refuse to concede other possibilities. The United States, as noted, gets insulted, as does New Zealand. Attacks may be discussed with rather embarrassed language. More interestingly, the insult may be explicitly denied altogether. "Don't say his name," the Prime Minister of New Zealand intoned. After the Manchester Arena attack, in which 22 people, many young girls, were killed, crowds sang "Don't Look Back in Anger." What?

In other places, almost nobody, certainly not the government, has much confidence in the state's capacity to provide security. In Kenya, in Jamaica or Mexico, in Ireland for most of its history, nobody is very surprised by breaches of the peace. The government of Kenya catastrophically mismanaged the Westgate Mall attack, and then moved on. A great many children died needlessly. Many places do not have much of a government. Life is dangerous. In such places, physical safety may be understood to be personal or at least local, and provided by the people themselves, rather than by a more or less distant state. At some point along this continuum, it becomes senseless to talk about security, and one speaks of "war zones." That is, physical security is not least a moral claim upon the state, and different states have different capacities to deliver on their obligations.

States are not equally obliged to provide the same level of security throughout their territory. Different places within a given territory may be more or less safe. Airports are considered to be safe, but clubs and bars less so. Traditionally, schools and houses of worship are safe, places of sanctuary. This brings us closer to where Weber was trying to go, or went in theory: modernization (from the perspective of the modern state) is importantly the claim of the state to provide security, which starts in "safe" places, and then extends to the entire territory. Conversely, "terrorism" is not a question of political agency (get out of Israel or Somalia or found the Caliphate) but the extent to which the state's claim to provide security is publicly frustrated, and the state is embarrassed. To sound postmodern, terrorism strictly understood is not possible until the state claims to offer security, and such claims can be violently disproven. "Surprise," say the terrorists." "Surprise, Motherfucker!" – goes the counterterrorists' favorite reply. Intolerable.

Terrorism as Cloudy Mirror. Imagine that we are inclined, still following Weber, to equate legitimate violence with the state, as discussed above, even if this seems to be an inadequate understanding of contemporary violence. Imagine further that we understand the state in rationalist, Enlightened terms, or at least hope to do so. The widespread fury over recent populist political developments suggests that many people believe in the rationality of politics, which makes many contemporary developments outrageous. Imagine, in short, the worldview of many a European or American academic.

From this perspective, it can be hard to comprehend not only recent politics, but state actions that are less rationally or at least transparently organized. We are somewhat at a loss dealing with snipers, irregular fighters, contractors, Vietnam in general, and latterly, JSOC (Joint Special Operations Command) everywhere in Africa. What happens when a passing operator, a foreign national with a car trunk full of specialist weapons, makes a "reasonable" decision, given the horrifying scene before him, then over roughly 18 hours, violently resolves a large-scale al Shabaab attack by fighting, building by building and floor by floor, through an upmarket office/restaurant/hotel campus that could have been in any well-heeled global city, and not a few urban combat video games? Or when police officers in Dayton happen to be outside a bar, so that when a man begins firing, so do they? Within 32 seconds of the first shot, the attack is over. Ten people, including the attacker, die in consequence. Or perhaps SWAT team members attend a barbecue, weapons in their vehicles of course, enabling them to respond quickly to heavily armed bank robbers. We may defend such actions *in toto* and after the fact, but the point here is epistemological and not normative. If we are honest, there is not a lot of bureaucratic rationality at work, skipping bullets in flip flops. And just why do off-duty or even visiting special forces operatives drive *toward* terrorist attacks? Because that is just what such people do, not because that is the rational plan of the Enlightened State.

In calmer and more public moments, and working in the other direction, we tend to attribute organization to violent actors, i.e., to make them state-like, and to give them political (in the ordinary sense) interests. In short, the enlightened and rational political imagination is likely to imagine terrorists in the familiar terms with which the state is imagined. In particular, terrorist violence is interpreted in political terms. Terrorism, as Clausewitz said of war generally, is thus a form of political expression, a kind of language that must be decoded. To make matters worse, terrorists often accompany their deeds with words, often styled as a manifesto. But as is so often the case, rationality may be less than claimed, and it would be silly to assume that a terrorist's language means much. Maybe the terrorist has a point, putting the question of slaughtering innocents aside for a moment. Surely Irish independence can be defended; there are lots of bad things about technology which may yet be the end of us all, as the Unabomber pointed out, and so forth. But suicidal killers of innocents reposition themselves on the normal distribution with their final act, and a tight relationship between what may or not have been said by way of political theory or justification of violence simply cannot be assumed. (The Dayton killer cited leftist politician Elizabeth Warren, an erstwhile Harvard Law School professor, as justification for mayhem. Elizabeth Warren?) Why should terrorism be engaged as politics? Obviously, this is an error of political thought, yet it occurs with each attack.

Terrorism, if it is effective at all, demands interpretation. Survivors struggle to "make sense" of an attack. As already suggested, the interpretive frame is likely to be political. Almost unavoidably, killings are interpreted in terms of available political commitments and understandings. Survivors have little else with which to work. So, why would not one see antisemitism, or racism, or rage about Palestine, or what have you, especially if the attacker says such things on his way out? The *New York Times* read the El Paso attacks as a white nationalist "call to arms." Less sympathetically, violence also provides an opportunity to rally the troops, and generally further one's own interests. David's University President used the killings, distant though they were, to extoll our (and his) virtues of diversity and inclusion. Bad taste, but understandable – diversity and inclusion are good things, racist shooters at Walmart are bad things, and presumably we should all bear witness.

If one instead wants to think, however, there remains the question of how to "read" terrorism. As Olivier Roy has been arguing for decades now, political languages are few and far between. So, the discontent of young white Europeans tends to be articulated in terms of the Jews, even in places where there are virtually no Jews – a great deal of anti-Semitism has been achieved in fact. Many Europeans convert to radical Islam, which provides a different vocabulary. In the United States, especially in the age of Trump, one should not be surprised to see familiar racist tropes. Political speech here is in the nature of fashion, a sort of "in the air" availability of a language. While this language is expressive, and of course dangerous, it is generally silly to take its argumentative form seriously, expect that a terrorist's argument can be refuted or satisfied on its terms. By the same token, terrorist speech (and action) may be "politics" in the broadest sense of engaging and affecting human relations, but such speech is not and does not even aspire to the state of political discourse as that phrase is understood in the polite corners of a modern republic. Terrorist violence is political, but it is so in the sense that Jung, say, is political, or fashion is political. The python of culture/consciousness recoils itself; it is a mystical enterprise.[3]

And this is a problem for us, for we have our limitations, too. The French Revolution literally declared politics to be the source of transcendence, explicitly supplanting religion. At the same time, politics was supposed to be rational, although the Jacobin and later Napoleonic taste for spectacle should have raised suspicions. (Melville cuttingly ends *Billy Budd, Sailor* with an encounter with the French warship the *Athee*.) Such Enlightened aspirations for politics, nowadays often called "liberalism," did not completely take, of course, although both the rejection of religion and the broader claims to science wandered into Marxism, a dominant political tradition and the dominant tradition of social critique. From this perspective, the ground of human experience must be understood to be politics, and politics must in turn be understood in a fairly rationalistic sense, not, for example, as hatred of another race, however politically salient such hatred may be.

Thinking that violence, never mind terrorism, can be delimited by the terms of rationalistic politics is, as was once said of metaphysics, nonsense on stilts. The problem is that as a polity, we have little else, or at the very least, little else that we can say publicly while talking politics. (Novelists can at least convey that whatever else it may be, collective violence is not rational. Again, consider *Slaughterhouse V* or *Catch-22*.) But at the level of public discourse before and after an attack – what should the government do? – the presumptions of the Enlightened state and polite discourse must be maintained. So, we see the transposition of events into a familiar political idiom, and unsurprisingly, often a self-serving (partisan) one. We criticize the state, and badge the killers terrorists, to be understood in terms of states. Jurisdiction is expanded, and officials are hired. Sometimes whole agencies are founded. Let no mass killing go to waste, as it were.

Again, terrorism is not a cultural phenomenon on its own account, but is instead defined antagonistically, named by its victims. Terrorism is an insult, a shadow, perhaps a nightmare, but an image without an independent existence. Therefore, terrorism, as a genus of collective violence, cannot be defined, in part because reaching such a definition requires us to define ourselves. Rephrased, we have any number of definitions of terrorism, as of the self – but none are ultimately satisfactory. The ceaseless failure to define terrorism makes sense in the same way that being unable to catch one's own shadow makes sense. The state is opaque to itself, even (especially?) the putatively Enlightened modern state, as novelists never cease reminding us. Weber sensed this irrationality at the heart of politics – the struggle with Nietzsche, the sense of disenchantment that might be relieved by the emergence of the charismatic leader. Weber did not live long enough to see how dangerous such leaders could be.

To be clear, none of this is meant to imply that attackers do not have politics. Collective action requires organization, something of a politics. As Weber says, violence can be organized by many different kinds of organization, and was, in the premodern era (and is now, too, as we have seen). Attacks deemed "terrorist" are carried out by a bewildering variety of groups, with wildly varying levels of rationality, and countless ways in which their intentions are articulated, even justified. We may imagine violence in terms of a continuum of rational organization, with maybe Richard Reid, the would-be shoe bomber, at one end of the spectrum and the Prussian General Staff at the other. Those things we denominate "terrorists" occupy any number of points along the spectrum. The IRA was a bureaucracy – their Army Council was always squashing innovation in South Armagh, or excessive fundraising in Boston. Richard Reid was, as special forces members would say, "a Muppet." Somewhere in between one finds the Red Army Faction, and the Shining Path, and the Lufthansa pilot who flew a planeload of schoolkids into a mountainside, to say nothing of people who drive through Christmas markets or bomb marathons. It is hard to generalize, people will disagree anyway, and at some level, who cares? That is why we call them all terrorists and stop thinking. Enlightened modernity only goes so far, not much further than Weber got, if any.

Notes

1 It must be admitted that there is a streak of Weber's thought that cannot shake off Kant, and perhaps even more deeply, Luther. But on the other hand, Weber is essaying sociology here, not pure philosophy nor, at least explicitly, theology. Here again, however, one must pause. A century on, the existential aspects of Weber's thought have come to the fore, while the "empirical" insistence of the first translations seem artifacts of bygone academic ambitions, viz., the foundation of sociology in the American university at mid-century.

2 The relationship between Weber and Schmitt – and the course of Germany and social thought writ large – was dramatized at the 15th convention of the German Sociological Society, held in Heidelberg in 1964, and centered on the centennial of Weber's birth (see Engelbrekt 2009).

3 As an aside, this is the sort of thing that anthropology, at its best, grapples with: the "felt necessities," to use a great phrase from Oliver Wendell Holmes, Jr.

References

Engelbrekt, Kjell. 2009. "What Carl Schmitt Picked Up in Weber's Seminar: A Historical Controversy Revisited." *The European Legacy: Toward New Paradigms*, 14(6), 667–684.

Weber, Max. 2004. *The Vocation Lectures*. Eds. David Owen and Tracy B. Strong, trans. Rodney Livingstone. Indianapolis, Indiana: Hackett.

Westbrook, David A. 2003. *City of Gold: An Apology for Global Capitalism in a Time of Discontent*. London and New York: Routledge.

Chapter 13

Security and the Humanization of Bureaucracy

Much of this book has tried to articulate the situation of and predicaments intrinsic to the enterprise of providing physical security.[1] The drama of terrorism and counterterrorism captivates the imagination – is literally the stuff of movies and games – but as we have seen, the security enterprise is also, and just as essentially, bureaucratic, and can be quite boring. Indeed, as both *Catch-22* and *Eichmann in Jerusalem* make clear, the juxtaposition of killing with paperwork is itself dramatic, expressed also by military maps, in which small squares represent large units of fighting men, and how many casualties? How many orphans? Mostly, however, the work of security is intensely ordinary, the daily activity of professionals who work tirelessly so that nothing happens. Boredom is the point, as discussed in Chapter 5. Unlike Sisyphus's rock, which is pushed up and rolled back down, ideally the attack never comes, and the ceaseless training is done for a reason that never materializes. Meanwhile, however, the security apparatus engages the public it is designed to serve, and it does so by rule – both regulation, and physical imposition. Restricted areas, protocols, iris scanning, mostly electronic stripping, the presumption of physical control over the traveler's body and belongings ... while drama is implied, security is generally experienced as the more or less irksome execution of policies established elsewhere, maybe just an expensive waste of time.

The common image of the bureaucrat, and by extension the business of not only the state, but also "white collar" symbol manipulation, and by further extension, the contemporary condition, is not pretty, and not altogether wrong. Consider Bartleby the Scrivener, Scrooge, the inchoate dread of Kafka's characters, or Weber's rationalism and its attendant disenchantment. In contemporary popular culture, consider Dilbert or "The Office." Over a generation ago, the North Atlantic turn to the right highlighted by the ascendency of Reagan in the United States and Thatcher in the United Kingdom was fueled, at least rhetorically, by opposition to bureaucracy, to the fussiness of the contemporary condition. Whatever it may have done for specific economic interests or society writ large, deregulation certainly, and satisfyingly, removed regulators. More recently, the various political movements grouped together under the heading "populism" have gathered adherents and international solidarity from their shared antagonism to the mandarin elites with which large polities rule (see Holmes 2000).

Despite this frustration, bureaucracy shows no sign of going away. Shifts in political economy, for examples, the recent urbanization of billions, or the rise of the internet, or pointedly if trivially, the emergence of offices with ping pong tables and beer in the afternoon, may change the aesthetics of the office a bit. We now have casual Fridays, and more "diverse" workplaces, where "excellence" is pursued as relentlessly as "innovation." None of that means that bureaucracy as a mode of social, economic, and political life is fading at all. If anything, the world is becoming more and more bureaucratic, as digitization allows near universal record-keeping. Consider, for more examples, the rise of the administrative university, or the contemporary hospital, where functions like "teaching" and "medical care" have become routinized, and placed under the jurisdiction of webs of officials speaking HR. All symbol manipulation by elites, all the time. And what alternatives do we have, other than chaos? (Which is perhaps why so many believe that anarchy will come, brought about by global warming, or some virus, or a rogue state, or the big electromagnetic pulse, or ...)

By the same token, and as noted in the Introduction, "security" is ubiquitous. Security names a bureaucratic preoccupation for the dangers the future may hold for the enterprise, of running an airport, of maintaining a health care system, or a food supply, or an election – as more and more of life is placed under bureaucratic rule, the number of ways such rule may be insulted, disrupted, multiply apace. The empire is stretched; there are many reasons for worry. "Security" is the armature for such worry, the bureaucrat's somewhat self-serving emphasis on the public protected. (It is always "for your security" that you must do this or that, i.e., a bureaucracy's recognition of a security concern simultaneously challenges and reiterates the bureaucracy's own jurisdiction.) But there are reasons for worry in fact. We do have problems, and therefore many ways in which we must work together, lest there be chaos. The question, at this juncture, is how such worries can be conducted to lead to productive participation, perhaps even cooperation? Maybe, to use old words out of their traditional contexts, we can view security and even bureaucracy writ large with sympathy if not quite solidarity or community?

A more familiar and also convenient way to tell this story, at least the physical security part, is that our current preoccupation with security results from the *form* of contemporary violence, namely terrorism. (To invert Shakespeare, the fault lies not in ourselves, but in our stars.) So a long list of famous social scientists and philosophers have proclaimed ours to be an age of security.[2] This new age, apparently, begins during the immediate post-Cold War period, a period marked by wishful thoughts – perhaps the peace dividend would be paid out, history would end, and liberal democracy would reign free? To many, however, the new world order of the late 1990s looked suspiciously like advancing Western hegemony, albeit without the political friction of socialist totalitarianism, or the critical friction of a credible Marxism. Cassandra-like books and essays were published by the likes of William Connolly and Samuel Huntington, but these voices were drowned out by the high priests of liberal globalization, on the one side, and the neo-Marxists, on the other side, who saw nothing to celebrate about *pax Americana*. Then 9–11 happened, and things became something else. Our time became the age of security, or so the story goes.

There is a growing body of anthropological work on the impact of "state security," especially the US variety (e.g. Masco 2014), and on the intrusion of security into everyday life in various field sites (see Goldstein 2010). Those who study security directly, as such, tend to emphasize the street level. This approach dovetails with the new wave of anthropological studies of state bureaucracy that focus on the everyday materiality of the state (e.g. Gupta 2012). Studies of state bureaucracy, just like security research, tend, monotonously, to devalue the ideals espoused by officials and see their actions as a form of "theatre," of the "absurd" variety. State security is clearly a nefarious form of power that should be opposed, and it is up to anthropologists and others to find ways to temper power, perhaps by demystifying its myths, pointing to its failures and absurdities. John Bourneman and Joseph Masco (2015: 792) express this as a moral injunction:

> In our postcolonial, post-Cold War moment, there is a theoretical if not practical anti-state bias in most national traditions of ethnography. ... [M]any anthropologists sense a calling – if not an ethical obligation – to side with the victims against society and the state.

The elisions in this theoretical and methodological literature are many and striking. There is a lot of loose talk about the street level experience, but far less about operational, to say nothing of the executive, levels. Do front-facing staff understand the technologies they use or the policies they enact? What about the formulation of policies and procedures, or even the drafting of regulations, the proposal of laws? Is it possible to consider taking a seat at the table in contemporary organizations where the near future it at stake? This is an especially acute question in the domain of security, where seats at the table are rare but influential, and where the near future is, literally, a matter of life and death.

This is an old problem in political philosophy, returned in new clothing. A few signposts are useful here. In *Thus Spoke Zarathustra*, Nietzsche sees nothing sacred in the worship of the new, artificial master. He has this to say:

> Somewhere there are still peoples and herds, but not with us, my brothers: here there are states. ... State is the name of the coldest of all

cold monsters. Coldly lies it also; and this lie creeps from its mouth: 'I, the state, am the people.' … Where there is still a people, there the state is not understood, but hated as the evil eye, and as sin against laws and customs. … The state, I call it, where all are poison-drinkers, the good and the bad: the state, where all lose themselves, the good and the bad: the state, where the slow suicide of all – is called 'life'.

(2005: 45)

The phrase "cold monster" is striking and thereby also distracting. Important for our purposes is this notion that outside or perhaps somewhere below is where one finds the "people" and thus freedom, whereas the closer one gets to power the more artificial things become, and the more one finds little more than "clambering apes" (Nietzsche's term) who worship power.

During his lectures to the Collège de France during the late 1970s Michel Foucault starts out by discussing technical matters of security and how they are directed towards the "population," before pivoting to an attack on those who ascribe too much power to the state. Indeed, he insists that his objective is to "put a stop to repeated invocations of the master as well as to the monotonous assertion of power. Neither power nor master, neither Power nor the Master, and neither one nor the other as God" (2007: 56). Indeed, he wonders, "if the state is not that kind of cold monster in history that has continually grown and developed as a sort of threatening organism above civil society, [but rather] is a way of governing … a type of governmentality?"

This is not to reduce everything to techniques and technologies, however, because the modern bureaucratic order, like any order, requires transcendental ideas. Foucault is well aware of Kant's insistence on *focus imaginarius* in the *Critique of Pure Reason*,

> the illusion that the lines have their source in a real object lying outside the field of empirically possible knowledge – just as objects reflected in a mirror are seen as behind it. Nevertheless, this illusion (which need not, however, be allowed to deceive us) is indispensably necessary if we are to direct the understanding beyond every given experience (as part of the sum of possible experience), and thereby to secure its greatest possible extension, just as, in the case of mirror-vision, the illusion involved is indispensably necessary.
>
> (Kant 1929: 533; see also Foucault 2007: 286)

Even clambering apes need something to hold onto, apparently. Meaning matters. In short, in these late imperial times, we must humanize officials, and conversely, understand ourselves as part of the order that we take seriously.

★★★

Surely the critical social sciences must have something to say about bureaucracy, and surely those insights require some sort of *Verstehen*, understanding entailing projection and in that sense sympathy if not agreement. And if that is the case, then absolutist dismissal of bureaucracy is off the table. But absolutist dismissal has moral clarity on its side; nuance can look like a moral failing. Splitting the difference between sympathy for the devil, on the one hand, and radical rejection of contemporary society (on which they depend), reasonable souls often look within the key structures of modernity. So, it is said, modernity would not be so unbearable but for the fact that neoliberal technocratic types infuse our institutions like aliens or even zombies among us, and we good folk need to "push back" against them. But how? The most critical among us swear that they can show us a "hidden terrain" of governance composed of "ethical and affective claims and conflicts," a sort of samizdat network or even illuminati for these dark times.

We are skeptical about such descriptions of our situation. Consider M. _____. He is the head of security for the airport in a key global city that, not incidentally, has suffered a terrorist attack. He is also his government's liaison to an international professional association with substantial *de facto* regulatory power over airports like his. M._____ is a bureaucrat. He is not what operators sometimes call a "capable" individual, meaning "capable of hurting people quickly." Nor does he enact violence. (The history of airports is not especially rooted in militarism, colonialism or sexism – though all played roles in creating the present.) M._____ is, rather, the kind of guy who will implement an efficiency model, or optimize patrols so as not to interfere with the passenger experience. He knows that passengers are customers, consumers, and he has to keep them safe. His job is one characterized by responsibility more so than "power." Indeed, he sees himself as a person with surprisingly little room to maneuver. Where is M._____'s "hidden terrain" of "ethical and affective claims and conflicts"? Does the abstract ethnographic incantation of ethical and affective claims and conflicts take the concrete form of a story about a senior bureaucrat disagreeing with a new governance measure? How often?

Much the same story emerges when we move from the tail toward the tip of the spear, to speak with capable individuals, which are thick on the ground in places like Nairobi. We have found soldiers of various sorts, and at various stages in their careers, to be very interested in talking. The circumstances must be right. Introductions are often required. A bit of background is useful. But most importantly, people must sense that they are being taken seriously. And "right, wrong or indifferent," violence is serious. (The current American adulation of its armed services is offensive in large part because it is so unserious, forgivable only because we have so few alternatives.)

Less dramatically than the shadow wars, there is seriousness too in protecting an airport, or commanding a reserve unit. And here we come closer to the everyday character of the modern, the institutional routinization of the well-lit portions of the globe. Perhaps the public good is in keeping things going in the absence of a compelling reason to do just that. It is hard to keep things going. The virtuous terrorist attacks a castle with a God-shaped hole. Inside, some people provide security because that is what they do.

★★★

Suppose, rather than preach truth to power, we speak with those who hold power, maybe even ask how their days are going? As this book has detailed, if we actually talk to bureaucrats and security operatives, a very different picture emerges. What follows is a reprisal of some key ways in which official power, power over modern life, is both quantitatively less and qualitatively different from what often is assumed.

★★★

Knowledgeable Uncertainty. As discussed in the opening of this book, in contemporary data-rich domains, information (sometimes boggling amounts of information) often coexists with significant uncertainty. While uncertainty may be part of the human condition, consciousness of uncertainty is hardly constant. Let us return to our mythological history of the latest *fin de siècle*. In hindsight, the end of the twentieth century was marked by an astonishing level of confidence. Experts knew what they knew. Catch phrases, "the end of history," "the Washington Consensus," and "the Great Moderation" express the spirit of the age that has passed. The attacks of September 11th and any number of computer hacks made us aware of insecurity in new ways. (The US Department of Defense began funding efforts to develop a "science of security," largely concerned with cybersecurity.) The emergence of unlooked for political developments like the Arab Spring and the insolvency of Greece and Brexit, to say nothing of the election of Donald Trump to the Presidency of the United States, made experts look foolish in real time. And most importantly, the Global Financial Crisis cast entire disciplines and core systems into doubt. Almost a full generation after September 11th, experts speak more hesitantly. One would have expected COVID-19 to see the return of the expert on horseback, but even the humble face mask proved too much to know, and conflicting advice flowed. Experts certainly know that their conceptual frameworks are compromised, but they are not sure how, or to what extent. New paradigms are in short supply.

And yet we have more information than ever before: more capacity to surveil, collect, and process data, capacities which themselves raise problems. In such contexts, a host of conceptual and expressive tools are deployed to make sense of the world and act upon it: narratives and models, scenarios and exercises. Much of our research concerns the range of tools available, and what such tools teach their users. Too often social scientists have assumed that the tools of governance are either faulty or are followed slavishly — social scientists have tended to ask after the validity of the outputs, with an eye to challenging the legitimacy of the exercise of power. Bureaucracy is of course based on expertise, and expertise in turn rests on claims to the truth, so this line of attack makes some sense. But while validity is obviously important, bureaucratic expertise is a practice before and after it is a substantive proposition to be falsified or not. So, in an age of uncertainty, another truth has emerged: the map may be necessary even if it is to some substantial but unknown degree wrong. The bureaucrat must continue to navigate, that is, to exercise power, even if expertise is dubious. Failures of security — being caught by surprise — do not lead to admissions of error, much less the abandonment of jurisdiction, but lead instead to more security, starting with measures designed to prevent the last failure ("closing the barn door after the horse escapes").

Regardless of the tools used, bureaucratic thinking in this hesitant age is often conducted with a view to conceptual horizons that seem difficult, if not impossible to define. "Security" emerges in field after field, not as quite the same word, but with the same problems. Insecurity is obvious in the event, whether or not something is secure — really secure? — cannot be known. Is the airport secure? What did the last attack teach, or fail to? Did the systems and structures built in response address the vulnerability? Cannot we imagine other vulnerabilities, waiting supine, to be exploited once discovered? Haunted by such questions, experts across a range of domains know that they do not know as much as they used to think they did, but must proceed nonetheless.

Domain, Limited Agency, Resource Allocation. As discussed in Chapter 8, how do the relatively senior figures in which we are primarily interested locate their authority and specify their jurisdictions within a common contemporary, albeit one that is fractured or separated into "silos"? How do they organize their activity vis-à-vis other institutions; what relations do they have to manage? Who are the clients, consumers, or competitors? To whom do they ultimately answer?

The scope of official agency is often quite narrow in practice, much narrower than implied by words like "state," "government," or even "law." Such words are abstract, unspecified, and hence unconstrained, implying freedom of action. Actual officials, however, are specified in countless ways, hemmed in, their options limited. Actual officials never see the agency, and in that sense freedom, promised by the abstract "state." As further discussed on p. 00, officials often have little capacity to do much besides what they already do, which may or may not be the right thing. (Soldiers are similarly situated.)

In order to keep doing what they are doing at all, officials generally must struggle for resources. Many of the activities in which we are interested do not, in themselves, make money or otherwise generate resources. A compliance program is a cost center. Airport security is expensive, bothersome, and by its nature raises concerns about privacy, discrimination, and an overweening state. Much like a well-drafted legal document, or a weapons system, not until things go badly wrong does a well-designed airport security system prove that the cost was worth it. Until such failures, the erosion of the institution's justification, and hence its funding, is the order of the day. This process of erosion is not unique to airport security. During a bull market, an understaffed US Securities and Exchange Commission ("SEC") could, and did, ignore whistleblowers, and Bernie Madoff would operate a complex Ponzi scheme for years and years.

The Public. "The public" is neither neutral nor trivial nor often clearly specified. How do officials imagine their public or audience in terms of representation, the justification given to license actions or resource allocations, or to legitimate actions that may result in risk or failure? For whom are the experts expert? What counts as success or failure? And how does the success of the enterprise affect the future of an office or the trajectory of a career – how is the official rewarded (or punished) and how are such actions publicly legitimated? Such questions are familiar, even traditional, in various governance contexts. The same questions take on added urgency in security contexts, when lives are often at stake and the usual mechanisms of transparency and accountability may not be available.

★★★

The Weight of History. In their scholarly, as opposed to institutional, mode, academics tend to understand present situations to pose questions. Critical social scientists in particular may think their mission is to articulate incisive questions. The luxurious presumption of such thinking is vast and rarely acknowledged. In the Ivory Tower (again, as distinct from the careerist concerns of actual academic life), the time is always now, the time in which questions are posed. History is to be questioned, which is another way of saying that history is not particularly imperative. Similarly, the future is a trope, not thought to require too much of us, today. That is what it means to live safe within the Tower, to be able to indulge such thoughts.

A core faith of so-called engaged scholarship and Enlightenment politics more generally is that such thinking ultimately will resolve itself, correctly or at least corrigibly, and give rise to action. Politics will be, in short and literally, rational. We will know what security is, and take rational steps to achieve it. Indeed, that is the point of the secret college understood to be a college, not least a group of thoughtful people. But as any honest professor knows, thinking often does not resolve itself. Thinking may be successful, but usually is not – one reaches an impasse, or more commonly still, matters become ambivalent, uncertain, and many things might be said, inconsistently but with some truth. Thinking harder may not bring one closer to decision. Expertise often fails. Here I stand, says Weber, echoing Luther. Thought, and therefore putatively Enlightened politics, is not rational, but existential.

Political actors, in comparison with academics, do not enjoy the long now of thought. They are much more burdened by both the weight of the past and the immanence of the future. They have little time, and must act anyway. Therefore, habit is substituted for imagination, office for merit, tactics for strategy, and custom for morality. The bureaucratic future tends to be like the recent past, only more so, and improved. In contemporary settings like security, not only is the future not new, it is on the contrary quite often old, and consequently constrained.

For dramatic example, the US war in Afghanistan is now the nation's longest running campaign. The "Forever War" has become not something transitory (to be won and so ended), but the norm, the context of business. How is the future of the war envisioned? What is the nation trying to accomplish? What is our preferred scenario? During the heyday of the neocons there was talk of nation building, optimistic at the time and simply no longer credible. "Getting Bin Laden" provided a purpose, if a grisly one, but he was finally killed. Political speeches continue to rely on abstractions – security, protecting freedom, etc. – but they do not suffice to explain this policy not that. "Get the job done." But what is the job? President Trump ran on getting out of Afghanistan; he later supported sending another 4,000 troops. But why not zero? Or 14,000? Or 24,000? At some point the US will "leave," albeit presumably will still be there, more or less, as operations demand. So, a substantial part of the US security community, spending nearly 5% of the gross domestic product of the world's largest economy, operates without an articulated future, in some real sense without a strategy. Strategy is subsumed by tactics. Or, to be more precise, the future looks like the status quo, a continuation of what we've been doing, only maybe more (or less!) so. Getting the job done, even if the job is not specified. This is what we do.

The continuation of the enterprise is also part of what it means to be professional. As suggested already, there are profound organizational and institutional constraints on what can be seriously thought or said, or not. Scenarios are formed by people in institutions, and the institutions import form, telos, commitments, and a host of assumptions surprisingly independent of the world ostensibly mapped. The US military provides security through the capacity to project force globally, making it difficult to ask what the purpose of US engagement in Afghanistan is, and therefore making it impossible, at least under ordinary circumstances, to judge success or failure. Success or failure at what? Security, presumably – the conceptual horizon recedes. From the Pentagon's perspective, "militarized global hegemony" is deeply synonymous with security. Nobody in the room has the authority to say, well, why don't we devote substantial resources to thinking about doing something else? People who say things like that do not get in the room.

The institutional drive towards reiteration is not just a military matter. Could Alphabet (Google) seriously entertain the idea of not digitizing things? Each university, under the banner of "innovation," does exactly what every other research university does, monetizing inventions, adding administrators. To generalize, in many powerful settings, consensus is often profoundly sociologically and professionally constrained. The social horizon is far shorter than the intellectual horizon. Institutions do what they do until they are forced to do something else, or, in Darwinian fashion, they are replaced.

Thus, our inquiries are leading us from the future to the past, from power to constraint. Bureaucratic "rationality," the "iron cage" of modernity, and even "politics as vocation" – warhorses of the sociological imagination – now seem insufficiently nuanced, at least as such terms are usually used in the academy.

★★★

Towards the Reimagination of Bureaucracy. Much contemporary governance is actually done through decidedly undemocratic bureaucracies, what we might collectively call the administrative state. In this regard, at least, the liberal democratic order is much like the old Soviet order, whatever it is Russia has now, or China, or even a large corporation or university – actual governance is bureaucratic. It is true that in liberal democracies, administration is legitimated by reference to … liberal democracy. Representatives are elected by "We the People," more or less, and those representatives delegate power to administrative agencies and bureaucracies. This, at any rate, is the story we tell in any number of regulatory law classes in the United States. What the US Environmental Protection Agency, or the Securities and Exchange Commission, or any agency does is presumptively legitimate because it is done by bureaucratic officials hired – or their bosses were hired – by people who were elected by the people, or who were nominated and approved by people who were elected by the people. For present purposes, the point is that "liberal democracy" is not the mechanism of governance, it is the mechanism of, at most, distant oversight over the bureaucracies that actually wield power, and the mechanism of legitimation for such bureaucracies. A similar dynamic plays across the European project – whatever the Commission does is said to be democratic because of the democratic process in the Member States. It need hardly be said that such legitimacy is thin, believed by few.

Harold Berman argued that the twentieth century "social" revolutions, especially the Russian Revolution, experienced in the United States in attenuated form as the New Deal, gave rise to a new understanding of the state. In this understanding, the state is directly responsible for civil society writ large – health and welfare and such. This vast expansion of the role of the state required a concomitant expansion of the apparatus of the state – the growth of the modern bureaucracy. This can be seen architecturally, in Washington DC, if one heads northwest from the White House, in the rows of fine apartments built for civil servants in the 1930s and 1940s out Connecticut Avenue. One might also tell a parallel story about the rise of the giant modern corporation.

The changes wrought by the English, American, and French Revolutions – and a great deal of civil life and law in between – carried with them their own legitimacy. These revolutions made the set of ideas for which "liberal democracy" is a shorthand a presumptively legitimate armature or model of governance. A judiciary ought to be independent, a legislature democratically elected, and so forth and so on. Such understandings have become part of the collective unconscious, at least in many societies. The twentieth-century social revolutions that ushered in the modern administrative state, however, were not as successful as a matter of culture and collective psychology. In particular, the social revolutions were not very successful in legitimating the administrative state. Although it came to be widely understood that the government should be responsible for education, health care, and social rights generally, the social revolution left us with little normative ordering of bureaucratic governance along the lines of the legitimating tales told for liberal democracy. Bureaucracy was and is generally seen as alienating, Kafkaesque. Weber speaks of disenchantment. Russians have endless jokes. Populists decry distant elites. Talk gets rougher; violence may break out.

Even within the capitals, bureaucracy is almost always legitimated not on its own terms, but instead by reference to liberal democracy, the achievements of the earlier revolutions. In particular, legislatures are said to "delegate" specific regulations and other decisions to administrative agencies. The exercise of power is legitimate because decided – in the abstract and not in detail – by the duly elected representatives of the people. The legitimacy of bureaucracy is thus derivative, even parasitic. If elections are seen to be less than genuine, as they sometimes are, and as the distance between election and bureaucracy grows, as it seemingly inevitably does, the idea that bureaucratic power is either democratic or liberal becomes harder and harder to sustain. Thus "government," "elites," "Europe," and so forth are easily cast as the enemy of democracy, indeed the enemy of the people. In other words, the "crisis of liberal democracy" is largely a crisis for the administrative contemporary state, understood operationally in bureaucratic terms. For a long time, states, that is, bureaucracies, could use stories about "liberal democracy" to legitimate themselves. In many societies and for many people, such stories no longer seem convincing. Instead, bureaucracies are seen to be self-perpetuating expressions of elite power.

What is to be done about this situation? One answer, beloved by people that in the United States are called liberals, is to "try, try again," that is, to make bureaucracy more directly subject to liberal democracy. Require more transparency. Limit the discretion of officials. Subject administrative action to legal review. There is much to recommend this approach, which is basically the approach of US administrative law, but it has its limits. Judicial review, transparency, and limitations all tend to produce more bureaucracy, more of the same complexities, delays, and inscrutable exercises of power that were the source of frustration in the first place.

The opposite approach, ostensibly beloved by many conservatives (also as popularly used in the United States) is to do away with bureaucracy whenever possible. Shrink government! Drain the swamp! There are times when this makes some sense, or is at least appealing, but the limitations are equally obvious. Bureaucratic institutions, whether deemed public or private, are often required to make life possible in complex societies, indeed constitute complex societies.

Rather than thinking about bureaucratic legitimacy in derivative terms, perhaps bureaucracy could be at least partially legitimated by directly addressing the central philosophical problem of liberalism itself, the absence of a shared notion of the good? Like other critics of liberalism, Alisdair MacIntyre argued that modern political and legal thought moves from substantive commitments to particular ideals of the good towards procedural commitments, and perhaps to purely formal goods, such as equality, defined in terms of such procedures. This abandonment of notions of the good and settling on procedure, preeminently contract, in fact, is what makes the writings of Hobbes, or the Peace of Westphalia, "modern" rather than medieval achievements. If the wars of religion cannot be solved by disputation or on the battlefield, perhaps we can agree to disagree.

But, as MacIntyre delineates in *After Virtue*, such peace comes at a great price. There are things that cannot be thought or discussed without some shared notion of the goods appropriate to such things, and ultimately important to human fruition. That is, ideas of whether this or that is better for some X presumes a knowledge of what X, ideally, should be. A telos is an end in terms of which a thing may be understood, a watch in terms of keeping time. The watch may also be jewelry or a paperweight, but it is "timekeeper" that defines the watch as watch. This is teleology, Aristotle through Aquinas. It is classical and medieval, but by definition not modern, thought.

One way to understand bureaucratic delegation is that it implicitly creates spaces in which such thinking or such conversations can happen today, that is, spaces for teleological discourse within a frame of liberal democracy that explicitly denies the possibility, much less achievement, of such discourse. For example, a legislature may decide that "it would be good if" we had clean water, or secure borders, or stable financial markets, or what have you, and then – in an organic statute such as the Securities Exchange Act of 1934 – creates an institution devoted to such ends. In this view, bureaucracy is not illiberal merely because of its distance from liberal processes and its employment of elites. Bureaucracy is illiberal in intention and in principle – it is the way liberal societies manage to have teleological political discourse. The problem – especially for diverse polities like the United States, or Europe, and perhaps less obviously, Russia or China – is that teleological discourse, agreement on the good, is hard to come by. People think differently about such things. So vague abstract standards suffice to authorize a regulatory agency, but must be ever half-articulated, somewhat disingenuous.

Telos is associated with the stake towards which Greek footraces were run – out to the stake, around it, and back to the start line. So the idea of "telos" has not only purpose – run fast – but a temporality built into it. The stake is a goal, the thing to be reached, the not yet achieved. The future. So, with only a little violence, we might understand teleology in terms not of purpose secured by consensus on the nature of the good, but in terms of preferred futures.

At this point it is no more than a vague hope, but perhaps people can come to understand their bureaucracies as places where different futures are collectively thought and worked upon, places of – at least on good days – good faith and team effort, with a good will. Rather than Hobbes' Leviathan, or Weber's rationalist disenchantment and petty power politics, we might think of bureaucracy as public service towards some, always yet to be finally articulated, notion of the collective good. Bureaucracy humanely conceived could thus compliment and buttress those forms of government that we, somewhat misleadingly, now call liberal democracy.

Notes

1 Much of this chapter first appeared in talks, including David A. Westbrook, "Security and Bureaucracy in a Time of Populism" presentation to the 157th IMA Detachment, Rayburn Office Building, Washington, D.C., June 19, 2019; Mark Maguire and David A. Westbrook (2019) "'Those People [May Yet Be] a Kind of Solution': Late Imperial Thoughts on the Humanization of Officialdom. "[Keynote Address], 11th Slovenian Social Science Conference: Observing Social Transformations: National and Transnational Perspectives, Ljubljana, Slovenia, May 29, 2019 to June 1, 2019; David A. Westbrook, " Those People [May Yet Be] a Kind of Solution': Late Imperial Thoughts on the Humanization of Officialdom" presentation at *Tempered Power, Variegated Capitalism, Law and Society,* Baldy Center for Law & Society, UB School of Law, November 9–10, 2018; David A. Westbrook, "Happy Endings? (Partially) Reconciling Ourselves to Bureaucracy through Teleology," at the Telos/HSE Moscow Conference, "After the End of Revolution: Constitutional Order Amid the Crisis of Democracy," National Research University Higher School of Economics, Moscow, September 1–2. Much of this was published as an essay (see Westbrook and Maguire 2019).

2 A variety of commentators have proposed that this is the "age of security", e.g., Lentzos and Rose (2009), Gros (2014), and most recently Didier Fassin (2020)

who sees security as one of two contemporary responses to inequality, the other one being "social justice," a hypothesis that somehow manages to be so ambitious that it is unprovable while also being instantly verifiably false. But Fassin is correct insofar as he understands security as an expression of deep problems in the contemporary order.

References

Bourneman, John and Masco, Joseph P. 2015. "Anthropology and the Security State." *American Anthropologist*, 117 (4), 781–794.

Fassin, Didier. 2020. "The Age of Security." In D. Asjer Ghertner, Hudson McFann and Daniel M. Goldstein (eds.), *Futureproof: Security Aesthetics and the Management of Life*. Durham, NC: Duke University Press.

Foucault, Michel. 2007. *Security, Territory, Population: Lectures at the Collège de France, 1977–1978*. London: Palgrave Macmillan.

Goldstein, Daniel M. 2010. "Toward a Critical Anthropology of Security." *Current Anthropology*, 51 (4), 487–517.

Gros, Frédéric. 2014. "The Fourth Age of Security." In Vanessa Lemm and Miguel Vatter (eds.), *The Government of Life: Foucault, Biopolitics, and Neoliberalism*, 17–28. New York: Fordham University Press.

Gupta, Akhil. 2012. *Red Tape: Bureaucracy, Structural Violence, and Poverty in India*. Durham, NC: Duke University Press.

Holmes, Douglas R. 2000. *Integral Europe: Fast-Capitalism, Multiculturalism, Neofascism*. Princeton, NJ: Princeton University Press.

Kant, Immanuel (and Norman Smith). 1929. *Critique of Pure Reason*. London: Macmillan.

Lentzos, Filippa and Nikolas Rose. 2009. "Governing Insecurity: Contingency Planning, Protection, Resilience." *Economy and Society*, 38 (2), 230–254.

Masco, Joseph P. 2014. *The Theatre of Operations: National Security Affect from the Cold War to the War on Terror*. Durham, NC: Duke University Press.

Nietzsche, Friedrich. 2005. *Thus Spoke Zarathustra*, trans. Graham Parkes. Oxford: Oxford World's Classics.

Westbrook, David A. and Mark Maguire. 2019. "Those People [May Yet Be] a Kind of Solution: Late Imperial Thoughts on the Humanization of Officialdom." *Buffalo Law Review*, 67 (3), 889–909.

Chapter 14

Is Security Modern?

Introduction. Yes, or so our title says. And from the beginning, this book has situated itself largely in airports, symbol of the modern. The book opens with a text about modern art. We have implicitly been arguing all along that there is something intrinsically modern about the familiar experience of security operations, and so it seems too late to deny the proposition now.

But what does it mean to say security is modern? At the simplest level, and using "security" in its most ordinary fashion, security does not seem modern at all. People have always worried about their own physical safety and that of their family, relatives, friends, tribe. In this we are no different from many other animals, and "security" is a trans-historical concept, if a primitive one. In this light, it might seem silly to talk about the modern character of airports. People in airports want to be safe, just like people everywhere.

All true, but "security," as in "airport security," means much more than the fundamental desire for physical safety. We began by thinking about security as experienced in airports, as a process, much of which is visible, even tactile, to which our bodies are subjected. Security, in this sense, is not least a relatively new sort of construction, the armed border zone between landside and airside that one must go "through" in order to travel. Moreover, the imposition of security procedures is done not just to us but for us. Security is a social good, provided by a bureaucratic state, which employs cadres of professionals with wildly varying competencies for the purpose. Security thus entails a notion of social space, and a notion of authority that not only asserts dominion over the territory, but that also tends to, cares for, its inhabitants. Furthermore, in understanding terrorism as insult, we maintain that the state has not merely been attacked, it has been embarrassed. Failed. Such thinking and political expectations presume a fairly strong state, both bureaucratic and legitimate, that is, modern in the Weberian sense. Less lawful parts of the world where airport security cannot be presumed are often called "developing," i.e., not quite there yet, and so a little premodern.

On the other hand, and as also discussed, security in the contemporary sense, the Weberian imagination of the state, and even commercial air travel have all been around a while. Do such things still seem modern, or have they become merely ordinary? If these are distinctly "modern" things, they are so only vis-à-vis exotically undeveloped locales, or a past about which most of us have only read. And what about the extraordinary? While the expectation of security may seem modern, so too do the occasionally spectacular failures of security, attacks in places like Brussels and Tokyo, and the ever more technologically sophisticated measures taken to forestall such attacks, from Chinese facial recognition to US drones.

To speak of "the modern" is quite difficult. The word is almost *verboten* in certain circles in the social sciences ("progressive" is just fine) because "modern" is associated with hierarchy, colonialism, claims to cultural superiority, incipient racism, and the like. That is, modern names a past, and to embrace or even designate this or that as "modern" is to validate past suffering. Shifting discourses, more problems arise. In philosophy, or philosophy of science, one often uses "modern" to indicate the break from medieval patterns of thought. (On consideration, the moment at which such a break occurs disconcertingly moves about over several centuries.) In art, in contrast, the late medieval discovery of linear perspective as the dominant mode of pictorial representation in Western high art is taken to bracket an era that ended in the late nineteenth century, with the beginning of "the modern" – it is this "modern" that our opening quote from Gertrude Stein addressed, the "modern" in New York's Museum of Modern Art (MOMA). But that was over 100 years ago now, well before we were born, and about the same time that Weber was speaking of the "modern" state in ways that seem quite old-fashioned, given World War II and the rise of integral Europe, not to mention globalization. For a while it was fashionable to speak of "post-modernity," first as a rebellion against the "modern" architecture represented by the Bauhaus and its influence on what came to be called the International Style, especially skyscrapers, which are indeed modern, no? But something seemed to have shifted in the culture more generally; the inevitable citation is to Lyotard's *Postmodern Condition*, with its useful but somewhat implausible characterization of the contemporary (well, the late 1970s) as a widespread suspicion of metanarratives. Evidently, an era of especially skeptical and creative thought dawned back then, and is still struggling to name itself.

Joking aside, such understandings of "security" and "modern" are rather too objective, static, and simpleminded. Neither security nor modernity are things. "Modern" – or what comes to the same thing, logically, "the ancients" – reappear throughout history, presumably for as long as there has been a sense of history at all. (Maybe that is what it means to have a sense of history.) From this perspective, modern names the subjective experience of the new: we now see (we did not until just recently, maybe until this very moment) that _____. Whatever is named, on this or that instance, is not the point. No principle unifies the things called "modern." What is shared is the perception of having appeared, and therefore marking a rupture in time.

That is, modern essentially names a temporal relation that is often also taken to be the name of a thing, much like "the South," or "the Orient," names both a spatial relation and a region. And if one knows the context, such relational names can work well enough, hence "modern art," until they run into difficulties, as all these names have, for different reasons. But the experience of the modern, the shock or sometimes just bewilderment of the new, remains available, as anyone who has lived through the last few years should have no trouble recognizing.

In what follows, we discuss the modernity of security vis-à-vis three very different meanings of "modern." First, the dialectic of security discussed throughout this book's opening passages ensures continual reconfiguration of both modes of attack and security arrangements, and so modern experiences, not least in airports. Second, attacks reenact the fall, not just from grace, but into modernity, the fall with which cultural anthropology has traditionally been concerned. Third, the Napoleonic Wars displaced the *ancien régime* in much of Europe in favor of what we still view as "modern" political and social arrangements. Of particular importance to this book, Napoleon's armies essentially compelled the reciprocal understanding of public and expert understandings of violence discussed in Chapter 4.

★★★

Dialectics. The most obvious relation defining modern is opposition to "traditional." The modern marks some sort of departure from tradition. How complete a departure, and how this is subjectively experienced, varies wildly from situation to situation. Historians tend to find continuities, whereas journalists usually find discontinuities. Similarly, the fact that examination of "tradition" often shows that what we thought was true since time immemorial was quite different back then, often offered as a defense of the new status quo, is not the point. At issue is the sense of arrival, and conversely, leaving.

A given tradition has a substantive content, for the simple reason that traditional things have been done before. "Traditionally," this is how [these people] make bread, get married, go to war, whatever. Classical cultural anthropology's enterprise was to describe, record, and analyze folkways before they disappeared or were at the least corrupted by tradition's nemesis, modernity. For there is no such substantive content to the concept of modern per se. Not traditional, but ... what? To say something is modern is to suggest departure, but not to specify a destination. Merely away, no longer traditional.

At least at first: destination must be specified. To have left is to have gone, and therefore to be somewhere else. To put the same point historically, nothing looks so traditional as old views of the modern. There is a great deal of nostalgia now for "mid-century modern" furniture and architecture, for example. For another, Harvard gives historical exhibits on the

Bauhaus, that paragon of and proselytizer of the modern way of life, at least as it unfolded at Harvard itself, back in the day when Germany had already been lost. Contemplating such "modernity" ineffably teaches not newness, but the transience, vanities, of human affairs – very old lessons. Any given instance of the modern cannot last, because a departure implies a period of specification, of establishing the new normal, of the waning of the feeling of newness. What had been strange and exciting becomes familiar, maybe boring. The adventure is reduced to mere relocation and redefinition, an arrival and things working out this way, and for the next generation, the unselfconscious assumption that this is the way things had pretty much always been.

It is in this dynamic sense that "security" is an intrinsically modern concept. The epistemological problem at the heart of security – the effort to make as yet unknown dangers in an uncertain future present, so that they can be avoided or at least defeated – imbues security thinking with its characteristic temporality. Security is preoccupied with the shift from the recent past, the defense we have now, to the near future, the defense we will need. Rephrased, the "horizon of fear" introduced in Chapter 2 entails a dystopian version of modernity.

If security were merely anticipatory, then one justly might object that anxious anticipation is not the same thing as actually experiencing something to be modern, the sense that "this" is a new thing upon the world. But security is a practice in the world of places, things, and people. New dangers require defensive innovations, which in turn spur new modes of attack. The dialectic of castles and cannons ensures new developments. Hijacking planes leads to securing planes leads to landside attacks, for easy example. At each stage, one experiences the new. Not all that long ago, as history goes, there was no airport security at all, and now we have fingerprint databases facilitating "global entry." We are "cleared" by scans that see inside our eyes.

The sensation of the modern is experienced regularly because security requires renewal, so that even as new norms are established, new threats emerge, and new countermeasures are taken. Old folks like us might experience metal detectors in schools and virtually all public buildings as offensively modern, an affront. For today's students, however, being scanned for weapons is ordinary and indeed normal, i.e., a behavior that reflects and re-inscribes a norm. In contrast, the fact that we teach kids how to stop their classmates from bleeding out is, at least for now, modern. At this juncture, somebody usually defends the contemporary dispensation by pointing out past injustices, somewhat distractingly and intensely conservatively. But the point here is not to valorize the past, it is to remark the current experience of the new and different, which can only be experienced as such vis-à-vis a past that is no more. In short, while concern for physical safety is not historical, is in fact ultra-human, the effort to provide security incessantly presents humans with the sensation of the modern, of history.

★★★

After the Fall. A murder mystery: Near midnight of February 28, 1986, after seeing a movie, Olof Palme, the Prime Minister of Sweden, and his wife Lisbet were walking home together from a movie, through the streets of Stockholm, when ... [Consider the story thus far: the controversial Prime Minister of a not insignificant country was walking through city streets, at night, alone with his wife, and without any form of protection. The story ends badly, of course, but the premise strains credulity.] Palme was shot, once, in the back. He died. A second bullet hit Lisbet without causing substantial harm. Sweden was transfixed. Tips poured in, massive investigations were organized and reorganized, chief inspectors were hired and dismissed, but all to no avail. Various suspects emerged only to be let go. Thirty odd years on, the case is said to be the largest unsolved murder file in the world. Books and movies abound. Reconstructing the killing, and searching for Palme's killer, has become something of a cultural phenomenon in Sweden.

Palme represented much of what Americans and others think of when they think of Sweden, and what many people also think of as modern. He was socialist, atheist, and a philandering sexual enthusiast (at one point his wife was a suspect). Sweden was officially neutral during the Cold War, and at least in public, Palme himself was a harsh critic of the United States, even though Sweden was in fact under the US nuclear umbrella. (Preaching is another cultural phenomenon in the land of the peace prize funded by dynamite sales.) At the same time, much of Sweden, then and now, is quite otherwise. So, Palme's killing has been understood to say something about what Sweden means. At the very least, the killing marked a certain loss of innocence. Swedish politics and the city of Stockholm are still special, but demonstrably not special enough to be completely free of the violence found in politics, and in other cities.

On March 15, 2019, on the other side of the world, Brenton Tarrant attacked the Al-Noor Mosque and then the Linwood Islamic Center in Christchurch, New Zealand. Tarrant is very much the contemporary marauding attacker of the white identarian sort. He posted the now *de rigueur* manifesto with the usual complaints and references. Some of the text was cut and pasted from the Unabomber manifesto, without attribution. Tarrant also livestreamed much of his attack. Fifty-one people died on the scene and in hospital. Tarrant himself was arrested a few miles away.

Almost immediately, our interlocutors in the secret college sent around WhatsApp messages about the shooter's video, evaluating his tactical erudition and displaying their own. (Once again, this world is all about tactics.)

The use of an ammo base was duly noted, but Tarrant didn't drop his weight when firing. He took a tight, linear path. No double taps, poor conservation of energy. On the other hand, the secret college gave Tarrant points for using a shotgun at the start of his attack. Still, his victims made it too easy. He encountered no real friction, and people herded together, as they often do, making them easy targets. Worst of all, this guy, less than ten minutes in, was getting winded, tired. He quit – nobody stopped him – because he didn't have the cardio, and drove off to the Linwood Islamic Center, where somebody would throw a credit card reader at him. Another "rank amateur."

Other people, unsurprisingly, responded differently. Americans of a certain class love to visit New Zealand, and then rave about the country's beauty, and something else. They struggle to say what is just so nice about the place, apart from the scenery, and one hears references to friendliness, small roads, civility, "it's like the fifties," and so forth. New Zealand is the last unspoiled place, evidently. New Zealanders often seem to have a similar sense of themselves. Prime Minister Jacinda Ardern quickly portrayed the story as an assault on New Zealand, which was attacked because of its virtues of kindness and inclusion, and to which New Zealand must respond, as a nation, with yet more virtue. She also got a gun control law passed and additional money for mental health care in New Zealand. And how else should she have responded? Ardern quickly became an international political celebrity.

A racist marauding shooter came as a shock to the ostentatiously civilized self-image of New Zealand. Shooting Muslims in a mosque is not civil at all, not Kiwi. It was not enough to say that Tarrant was in fact an Aussie – he was in New Zealand. Nobody wants to claim to have been innocent (naïve, childish), and nobody wants to claim, at least not publicly, their belief in their own moral superiority. In an essay that made it across the Pacific, a senior Kiwi journalist wrote that "we aren't innocent, we have crime, racism, sexism," i.e., claimed sophistication and moral compromise by reciting the usual pieties accompanied by the *mea culpas* on the part of all (and none). But then he went on to say "but we never thought it could happen here, could not be done to us, feels foreign, etc.," i.e., he protested the (now lost) innocence of New Zealand vis-à-vis this kind of violence, imported from Australia/the Irish/global white nationalism, a very contemporary sort of evil.

Obviously, not every attack, in every place, is experienced as a loss of innocence. Many terrorist attacks change nothing much at all for those not immediately affected. But sometimes, as was said incessantly after 9/11, "this changes everything." There is a sense of a "fall," a sense that recalls anthropology's traditional concern with the native's loss to the modern. Consider Levi-Strauss's *Triste Tropique* (that is why it was sad), Margaret Mead's lost horizons, or Boas attempting to record Native American cultures before they were gone. All of this echoes Rousseau's suspicion that perhaps civilization was a mistake, Adam and Eve's expulsion from the garden, and the loss of virginity on which so much imagery trades. Life is marked by before and after, and "after" is always accompanied by new, rueful, knowledge. So it is with many, not all, terrorism attacks. It never occurred to us it could happen here. Until it did, and now we "know" (they saw that they were naked). Afterwards, once we know, we tend to regard our former selves as childlike, precisely because we did not know, which is much of what both "naïve" and "innocent" mean.

Not wanting to appear childlike, people like our Kiwi journalist may deny that their surprise indicates prior innocence, that they never held a sunny view of a sinless human nature, not even of their own nature, although at least they are not racist murderers. No European with half an idea of history would explicitly claim, in the abstract at least, that humans were innocent. It sounds naïve, etc., although the widespread European hope that education, perhaps along with a very slowly rising GDP and a few more doses of Eurovision, make a good life and a deep understanding, is also more than a little naïve, to be gentle. "Innocence" here means something more specific and very common, especially among the putatively sophisticated: a usually unarticulated, often unthought, sense that in this time and place, we can rely on a certain set of behaviors, relations. *Comme il faut.* So, in many parts of the United States until quite recently, people did not lock their doors when they stepped out of the house. Some people in some places still do not. Schools had no metal detectors. In the United States, as in Europe but not in, say, South Africa, drivers unthinkingly pull all the way up to a stoplight, boxing themselves in and making themselves vulnerable to attackers on foot wielding spark plugs to shatter windows, to say nothing of assailants with their own cars and weapons. Until relatively recently, the idea that people would partially undress as a matter of course, and fully undress when asked, or be photographed, in order to board a commercial aircraft (paying for the privilege) would have been crazy. In many places, especially in Europe, women assume that they can disrobe on beaches without attracting direct attention, much less being assaulted (a sort of *tour de force* of the rule of law). All of which "works" until maybe, one day, it does not. To be innocent, here, is to live amidst such unexamined, unarticulated expectations that implicitly rule out certain things, especially violence, especially invasiveness, with its connotations of rape, so that such things need not be thought about at all.

One may be disabused of such assumptions by events – that is the point of insisting on "innocence." For example, many survivors of the Westgate Mall attack report that, now, a half dozen years later, they enter malls and look for the exits. They move along the walls. Their consciousness, their behaviors, and their sense of public space have been changed by their experience, by their knowledge that it could happen again, here.

Presumably these people did not think of themselves as innocent before Westgate. Kenya is a rough place. But they were indeed innocent, as they know now – that is what it means to be innocent, to realize that, not so long ago, they did not yet see that they were naked, vulnerable, as the Bible sort of has it.

In this framing, the loss of innocence is the experience of losing the tacit faith that what, in light of the attack, now seem "premodern" forms of civility will suffice. In the aftermath we need a metal detector, personal screening, CCTV everywhere, a SWAT team, drones for the more remote areas, whatever. Actions are taken, with an air of disenchantment. Again, security is a horizon. It is thus too much to expect "the modern" to be ushered in by a single act of violence. The fall is more of a slide, and "normal" changes, perhaps to be disrupted again. What we experience as security results from: eruptions of violence; losses of "innocence" i.e., the realization that "it could happen here"; and the government's need to respond, in that order. So first there is talk about arming the police. With automatic weapons. In a helicopter overhead. Blitz or no, the British submit to a stunning degree of surveillance, and see themselves as put upon.

★★★

An Idea on Horseback. Another story: in the fall of 1806, Napoleon conquered Jena, where Hegel was a professor. Witnessing the attack Hegel is said to have called Napoleon "an idea on horseback." It is not clear whether Hegel said precisely this, in so many German words, or whether the phrasing is a gift from subsequent writers, probably Mary McCarthy in her consideration of Tolstoy considering Napoleon, years later. But if Hegel did not say it, he should have, for the sake of clarity. A cynic might point out that Hegel saw most everything as an idea. And plenty of people have said that the "idea" expressed by Napoleon is "genius," or at least that is how Napoleon was understood by any number of Romantic souls. Genius easily shades into megalomania, tyranny, and so forth. All true, but something more specific is at issue.

The backstory is familiar. The French Revolution displaced the *ancien régime*, and more generally, a society based upon orders, governed by arrangements sanctioned by tradition and belief. In its place, the French proposed to establish a new order, based upon liberty, equality and fraternity, and somehow organized by Gallic reason, operating in the name of the French people as a whole, as opposed to operating organically, through their villages and local allegiances, churches and manors and universities and guilds and so on. Henceforth, folks would simply be citizens, or so it was said. In the nature of revolutions, things did not go quite as planned, and modifications had to be made to enable autocracy, ultimately even an emperor. But the core relation remained: France had a unified state legitimated by and in fairly direct control over an entire people, centrally and properly administered. As it happened, there were a lot of the French, and so the French state gained great power. The military expression of this process of modernization was the *Grand Armée*.

> Within one decade the resources that France mobilized for war had risen to unprecedented levels. The number of soldiers now available to her generals made possible campaigns that accepted greater risks, brought about battle more frequently, spread over more territory, and pursued political goals of greater magnitude than had been feasible for the armies of the *ancien régime*.

> (Paret 1984: 3)

Modernization, as understood in Paris at the turn of the nineteenth century, would be spread by the French military, "politics by other means," indeed. For relevant example, after Jena and under pressure from the French, the defeated Prussians emancipated the peasants and undertook other modernizing reforms in 1807 and afterward.

Clausewitz always had Napoleon on his mind. Clausewitz grew up as a soldier in the proud Prussian military tradition, then dominated by the petty nobility. The French, at Jena and elsewhere, humiliated the Prussians on the battlefield. Prussian pride, evidently, was unwarranted, and for a while, Clausewitz fought against the French under a Russian flag. But what was to be done? The Prussians could not match the *Grand Armée* man for man. Prussia was, relative to France, a small country. (German unification was still a few generations away.)

The answer was to modernize in a different way. Specifically, the military became a profession, open to commoners as well as nobles. Clausewitz took over the *Allgemeine Kriegsschule* (General School of War). He wrote *On War*, not least an effort to turn fighting into an academic discipline. Clausewitz also took part in modernizing reforms of the military, and the rest of Prussian society, that had the effect of largely if not entirely dismantling the *ancien régime*. The Prussian general staff, understood as an intensely professional body, became the model of military command for Germany and thence the world. War, and with it security, became a professional discourse, which we have called the secret college. Thus, if the creation of mass democracy was one way the modern emerged from the *ancien régime*, its complement was the creation of professional elites, bureaucracies. If Napoleon is emblematic of the one impulse, Clausewitz epitomizes the other.

To be clear, this "history" is largely symbolic. One may certainly find continuities. The *demos* is an old idea. Medieval kings, indeed any potentate that wishes to exercise power at a distance, will need a mandarin class to keep track of tax revenues if nothing else. Neither "people" nor "bureaucracy" were entirely new ideas. Nor can the identification of the French with mass society and the Germans with professional expertise be rigorously sustained. Surely the French had *bureaucratie*, and the Prussians a *Volk*, around 1800. One could go on, to the effect that the story told here is not all that significant. Even if this story happened, more or less, how much of what we understand as "modern" Europe came about in this fashion? More deeply, we might be skeptical about the extent to which a revolution, however grandiose, changes fundamental human realities. Perhaps things are mostly just renamed. In "early modern" France, for present example, the King was replaced by an Emperor, and class hardly went away. *Plus ça change, plus c'est la même chose* is also a French saying, and one of the things that concerned Tolstoy.

On the other hand, the French Revolution and on a smaller scale the Prussian Reforms of the early nineteenth century did happen, and were thought at the time to represent significant discontinuities, to be "world historical" in fact. For present purposes, however, we may be satisfied that such a tale at least provides an origin myth for concepts commonly used to conceptualize the contemporary, and conveniently locates that origin in the coercive context of war. Immediately after the battle, Hegel caught sight of Napoleon riding reconnaissance. Hegel did write, in a letter of October 6th: "It is indeed a wonderful sensation to see such an individual, who, concentrated here at a single point, astride a horse, reaches out over the world and masters it." From Hegel's vantage, modernity did not appear to be a choice, and that still seems right.

The move to professionalize, to create substantive bureaucracies, has obvious advantages. With a motivated and disciplined cadre of officials, training, expertise, a practiced rationality and a useful discourse, and some degree of authority, one can at least address any number of problems, including ultimately intractable problems like "security." The contemporary world, not just governments but airports, armies, churches, corporations, hospitals, golfing tournaments, political parties, non-governmental organizations, restaurant franchises, television networks, universities, utilities, whatever, is simply unimaginable without bureaucratic specialization, the hordes of symbol manipulators that make contemporary institutions possible.

But bureaucratic specialization has obvious disadvantages, too, which are the converse of the strengths. Bureaucracies are not general, and therefore tend to understand the world on their own, often self-serving, terms. (To a man with a hammer, everything looks like a nail.) Bureaucracies are widely viewed with suspicion, not least because while claiming expertise, they tend to assert jurisdiction. ("I know and therefore I rule" is not a very attractive stance.) The mere citizen may demur, and so may rival authorities, who also claim to know and aspire to rule.

As a practical matter, we must think of these advantages and disadvantages together, because neither is going away. Herein lies the bureaucratic paradox: bureaucracies have multiple and complicated relationships with one another and with the public which, by definition, lie somewhat outside their realm of expertise and therefore authority. To use Kafka's image, the castle of bureaucracy both empowers and limits. As we hope this book has already suggested, ethnographic conversation – a kind of candor – may help to manage this paradox, and with it, ameliorate the modern condition.

Reference

Paret, Peter. 1984. "The Genesis of *On War*." In Michael Howard and Peter Paret (eds. and trans.), *On War*. Princeton, NJ: Princeton University Press.

Chapter 15

Conclusion
Will It End?

Introduction. Anarchism, as a formal social, political and intellectual movement in Europe and the United States, may be loosely dated to the second half of the nineteenth century. On September 6, 1901, an avowed anarchist named Leon Czolgosz shot then US President McKinley at the Pan-American Exposition held in Buffalo, New York. Gangrene developed, and McKinley died on September 14th of blood poisoning. Czolgosz was electrocuted on October 29th, unrepentant. By the end of World War I, this sort of anarchism was a spent force. Things with beginnings tend to have ends. So, it is tempting to ask, whether terrorism itself has a history that will come to an end. If terrorism were to end, might we see the end of counterterrorism? Perhaps the entire security apparatus built to combat terror, now grown familiar, may be dismantled?

By many measures, we – meaning at least privileged inhabitants of advanced economies, but maybe more than that – are safer than ever before. In some genres of social science writing one expects to see statistics offered as evidence or even demonstration of that proposition. Statistics of course cannot be understood without considerable examination of how they were compiled, may easily be contested, and so forth. So we do not attempt (no doubt only to fail) to answer this question by reference to various accountings that we have read and more or less believe, as the case may be. Worse, as Weber points out in "Science as Vocation," the social scientist is bound to be superseded. Temporality, even a modernist sensibility, is thus built not only into the question of whether "it will end," but is built into the way such questions are approached. And this is at least analytically disturbing, because what we mean by "modern" lies near the heart of our inquiry.

★★★

The Great Game. In the late nineteenth century, British and Russian forces engaged in a usually covert struggle for much of Asia, immortalized by Rudyard Kipling as "The Great Game." World Wars and a Cold War came and were said to have ended. There was a moment, after the fall of the Berlin Wall and shallow readings of "The End of History," when it seemed that peace at last had broken out, at least in "civilized" places. Borders might have to be redrawn somewhat. Today, British soldiers are still in Afghanistan, sometimes officially, sometimes their presence is "deniable." The Russians hack elections and invade Ukraine. The Great Game continues.

None of which is to say that the Great Game continues as it did back in the day. Globalization and new technologies have meant something. The murderously loud, spectacular wars of the early and mid-twentieth century, in which large nation states were mobilized against others, seem to have passed from the scene. In recent years the rumble of tanks has been heard mostly in parades and second or third tier conflicts, and we have yet to witness an exchange of weapons of mass destruction. Although, as with security more generally, we will not know if we were truly at peace until we are at war. (As Christa Wolf said, in *Kassandra*, how does one know when the prewar period begins?) At the present moment, violence seems fairly muted. Even drones are too loud, so that we develop glide missiles that have no motors, like murderous exploding owls. At least at the present juncture, conflicts, with and among state and non-state actors, seem to be conducted largely in the shadows.

The juvenile tendency to draw equivalences among types of violence – al-Qaeda is somehow like the US support of Israel's occupation of Palestine and suchlike – should be resisted. Indeed, normative discussion of this or that species of violence is not the point here. The point is that violence often develops. As we have seen, the dynamic of castles and cannons, perhaps hastened in an age of technical discovery, means that violence changes, and is in that sense new. But it is still violence, and is in that more fundamental sense, old. And the forms do not always change. Continuing the evolutionary metaphor (perhaps more than a metaphor?), other forms of violence do not change, no more than cockroaches. Consider manual domestic violence, or knife fights in bars. Different forms of violence, especially different weapons, are available to different sorts of actors, as in the natural world – another point made by Kipling, in *The Jungle Book*.

In the Hobbesian tradition, violence is the occasion of politics. When life is nasty, brutish and short in the state of nature, men sensibly surrender their liberty to Leviathan, the collective that can protect them. Conversely, the political must at least include the capacity to deliver violence, to deliver oneself from one's enemies, and thereby ensure what would come to be called security. For example, for Weber, as we have seen, the essence of the State is the effective monopoly of legitimate violence upon a territory. Weber's sometime student Carl Schmitt goes further, and declares the essence of the political to be the distinction between friend and foe. And so forth.

One need not go quite so far. For every Hobbes there is a Locke. Empirically, most of us do not experience much violence at all. While violence is indubitably prevalent throughout history, must it be considered essential? That is, is collective violence a trans-historical concept? In the sunnier precincts of Enlightenment thought, a sensible social order removes the causes for violence, and hence violence should evaporate. Most notably, for some generations it was widely believed that the abolition of property – an institution founded on the right to exclude other people from things and places – would lead to inclusion, "solidarity," and so peace. Less radically, surely one can imagine a safe and sane society? As American anthropologist Nancy Scheper-Hughes (2018: 3–4) put it, in the wake of the Parkland, Florida, shootings: "In 1941 President FDR articulated the four freedoms that all people ought to enjoy: freedom of speech, freedom of worship, freedom from want and freedom from fear. Our children have every right to demand that society protect them from fear and provide them with a basic trust in their ontological security in the world." "Onto" is from the Greek "to be," so "ontological security" is "Freedom to Be You and Me," as *Marlo Thomas and Friends* had it in an early 1970s children's classic. Perhaps society "ought" to be like lost places such as Olof Palme's vision of Sweden, or Norway before Breivik, or even Christchurch, New Zealand, in which the state saw itself as both very benevolent and highly Enlightened, and where it was assumed that security writ large had been provided to all.

In response to madness and loss, people understandably search for causes. As discussed in Chapter 12, survivors and especially leaders often understand bloodshed to be some sort of political speech, a more or less rational response to colonialism, or racism, or foreign policy, or the expression of a misguided ideology, Salafism or white supremacy or eco-terrorism or what have you. Terrorists often help matters along by writing screeds providing "the reasons" that they have decided to slaughter strangers, perhaps posting them to social media, or at least shouting something partisan.

Understanding violence as speech has the practical political advantage of creating the opportunity for leaders to do something, or at least to talk about doing something. In response to terrorist attacks, politicians often quickly move away from the attacks themselves, and call for improvements to the conditions spoken about, conditions that somehow – how is always less than clear – rarely but dramatically give rise to what Stanley Kubrick's *Clockwork Orange* called ultraviolence. Sometimes an attack often seems quite without roots or intentions beyond killing, especially in the United States. Consider the Las Vegas shooting, or any number of school shootings. Even in such cases, one hears plaintive calls for better mental health care, gun control, and a kinder and gentler internet, all of which are no doubt good ideas … In pursuit of security, the state conveniently turns outward. What is a terrorist? Are the Israelis terrorists? What causes terrorism? Islam? Salafi Islam? The Internet? What is to be done? Such discussions are unavoidable, sometimes fascinating, and interminable. The game of politics continues, and one is tempted to add, the very interminable nature of violent events and endless talk gives one reason to believe it will not end. But, the true believer adds, the good society has yet to be built.

★★★

Security Ontology. Shifting focus from abstract "terrorists" or even "mass killings" to the security forces who oppose them (and with whom one can talk), as this book has done, solves some problems, and raises entirely new ones. Discussions of the nature of terrorism are almost always couched as policy discussions, and therefore supposedly practical. For many if not most practical purposes, however, the essential nature of terrorism is rather beside the point. Security forces around the world do not and cannot be expected to understand the whys and wherefores of their known adversaries, much less what motivates or even occasions new threats. Tactics are everything when confronting "the bad guys."

Similarly, the political discussion of the causes of terrorism, and what is to be done about the situation, tacitly presumes the (good) state, trying to protect its citizens, and with the agency to do so. But from a defensive posture, the state's vulnerability is the problem and the focus. The state is vulnerable to insult at many points, sometimes called "critical infrastructure," or "senior officials." Terrorists are evanescent and often unspecified altogether, but points of vulnerability can be identified. Nor is the agency of the state to be presumed. Perhaps the state can respond, and quickly enough, to a terrorist attack. But perhaps not. You have to be lucky every time, as the IRA wrote after a failed attack. So the defenders practice, and then practice some more.

As we have seen, from the perspective of the defenders, security is a horizon for thought, uncertain and hence unbounded. Events are not understood completely. Tactics evolve in ways that may not yet be imagined and therefore must, in the event, be suffered. Fear of that eventuality leads to paranoia within reason. (In practice, the pursuit of security is constrained by institutional structures, competition, and lack of resources, which is a good thing, because paranoia is not in principle constrained.) The apparatus of security is designed to address, and so entails the possibility of, destruction. The danger may not arise in fact; the attack may never come, but the danger is there, articulated by the security measures themselves. "Ontologically secure" is therefore an oxymoron. The very existence of a security apparatus means that there is danger, those threats against which the apparatus attempts to provide protection. In some circumstances, the danger may be only imagined, but a wall compels one to contemplate the possibility of invasion. That is, once security is understood as a problem, and measures are taken to ensure security, then those same measures serve as reminders of the problem itself. This is another way of understanding the sense of a fall discussed earlier – they saw that they were naked, vulnerable. After the attack, despite and because of the adoption of best practices, one is not secure.

Again, ontology, theory of being, comes from the Greek "on," to be. The practice of security – as opposed to the security wished for in the sunnier precincts of the Enlightenment – entails being aware of danger, to some degree, in fear. All the sympathy in the world, to say nothing of the data collected from CCTV and internet snooping and the like, will not solve the epistemological problem at the heart of paranoia within reason. While the official incentive to collect data is understandable, and much may be prevented, "security" writ large resists solution. Security is often treated as a problem that the powers that be are expected to solve, but this is a category mistake. Security cannot be solved, so long as we remain participants in a state, at risk of violent insult, and forced to take precautions, for instance erecting screening procedures at airports, because it could happen here.

The very sort of government official who might aspire to ontological security cannot have it. For this Kafkaesque situation, a bit of Kafka:

> It's true that in the main things the blame rests with the government, which in the oldest empire on earth right up to the present day has not been able or has, among other things, neglected to cultivate the institution of empire sufficiently clearly so that it is immediately and ceaselessly effective right up to the most remote frontiers of the empire. On the other hand, however, there is in this also a weakness in the people's power of imagining or believing, which has not succeeded in pulling the empire out of its deep contemplative state in Peking and making it something fully vital and present in the hearts of subjects, who nonetheless want nothing better than to feel its touch once and then die from the experience.
>
> (Kafka 1961: 133)

Our insecurity will not end because our state is something of a failure, and may be attacked. The good society cannot do without security, even if there are no barbarians anymore.

One may, for the sake of logic at least, consider two other possibilities. First, imagine a state that is completely successful. Here is a journalist contemplating the role of Gary Schippman, former Chief of Staff of US Customs and Border Protection, then founder of Giant Oak, a government contractor providing analytical services to the government:

> if public safety was the goal, the answer wasn't to stop scanning people's data. It was to do it the right way. "Now this is my theory," he told me, "and you tell me if it's crazy or wrong. But I think that the

better we have entity resolution" — that is, the better we can compile and measure people's data — "the less of a surveillance state we'll have." Once the machine is perfect, as long as you're following the rules, you won't even have to know it's there.

(Funk 2019)

One recalls Mary Douglas (1986: 98), "The high triumph of institutional thinking is to make the institutions completely invisible." As a practical matter, one might be skeptical of the capacity of the US government, indeed any government, to do anything to the requisite degree of perfection. Nor do we have any reason to believe that governments with great power value the physical security of their territory's inhabitants – why would they? Even if a government were to achieve such power and remain benevolent, as implied by Kafka's musing on the Emperor's failings, then security would have been purchased at the cost of any sense of our own real being, which is another way of saying that our situation would be totalitarian, which nobody knew much better than Kafka.

Conversely, one may imagine a failed state, a Hobbesian situation after our civilization collapses, or perhaps just a war zone. In such situations it makes no sense to talk about security, because there is nobody to assert control, to claim responsibility for the safety of the space. By the same token, there may be violence, but because there is no state to be insulted, it is mere violence, of little significance except to the participants. What else do you expect in this hellhole?

So long as we take ourselves at all seriously and have a state, we are stuck with some degree of insecurity, and on balance, that is a good thing.

★★★

Intermezzo. Our optimist may with good reason point out that there has been a sleight of hand here. We started talking about the decline of violence, and hence decreased need for security measures, including counterterrorism, but then shifted to the predicaments of the state, which was compelled to build walls, even if failing ones. Evidently, we are fated to be reminded of violence by our own imperfect security measures, lest we suffer some worse fate. But how bad is this doom? Consciousness of the possibility of violence – or the coercion necessary to suppress violence, if needs be – may be enough to preclude ontological security, rather strictly speaking. But, our optimist points out, getting through security in an airport and so reminded of the possibility of a terrorist attack is hardly to be compared with being shot, or blown up, or having one's throat slit with a box cutter. What may be sensibly hoped by a member of the haute bourgeoisie? Is violence trans-historical, perhaps even essential to collective life, and hence to be endured now and forever? Or may we hope that violence, like so much else, has a history, a beginning and an end? Perhaps the end might be hastened by good politics?

It is too much to ask you to resolve modern political thought, our relentless optimist graciously concedes. But Weber said "here I stand." So where, at the end of this book, do we stand? To that little question we now turn, but begin in what is perhaps an odd place.

★★★

Violence as Rhetoric. Violence can be understood as a language (vide Clausewitz), and is sometimes accompanied by language (often styled as a manifesto), but it would be silly to assume that the language means what it says. Terrorists might have things to say; killers like other sinners sometimes do. Any number of causes espoused by terrorists might be thoughtfully articulated. For example, Qutb's theology, at the heart of political Islam and the grandfather of al-Qaeda, the great grandfather of Islamic State, is at the very least interesting. But while there may be ideas here and there, the suicidal killers of innocents have engaged in madness, even if up to that point they generally behaved normally, or at least displayed no obvious pathology. One cannot assume a tight relationship between what may or not have been said by way of political theory or justification and violence. Why should we take this attack politically seriously? Surely not due to its violence. Death does not entail political thought, or require a response on the level of political thought, though it might require collective action. In this regard, terrorists may be little different from floods or other natural disasters.

In many cases, people want to take the politics of the killers seriously for reasons of their own. As already noted, *The New York Times* read the El Paso attack, in which 22 people, mostly Mexican-Americans, died at the hands of a white supremacist, as "a call to arms." On the Canadian border, the President of David's university used the same attack, distant though it was, as an occasion to extoll our (and his) virtues. Such interventions are a bit tasteless, of course, but the victims and often the killer are already dead, and the attacks might as well be put to good use, for example the suppression of white supremacy as political ideology.

Similarly, progressive anthropologists might be inclined to argue that inequality is a function of the neoliberal capitalist system, and is expressed in the fabric of the urban form. Consider the recent building of skyscrapers for the ultrarich in midtown Manhattan. Extreme inequality rips the urban fabric. Society's answer is to provide security within these splintered urban fabrics (see Fassin 2020; e.g. Graham 2010). The result is secure islands, green zones, in a sea of poverty. The operational form is the militarization of everyday life. We are all living in Baghdad and Kabul now.

Or, well, no. Baghdad and Kabul are violent in ways that New York and London are not. Put more structurally, the City is where trade happens, and in slightly more advanced economies, where capitalism works. The City's other great purposes are to serve as sites for religious and political life. None of these functions – trade, worship, rule – have generally had much to do with equality as such, but what equality did arise, tended to arise in cities. Nor does this story told by progressive anthropologists, in which radical inequality fosters terrorism, fit the facts very well. Terrorists are not, by and large, poor. The Las Vegas shooter was outright rich, with private planes and a network of nondescript houses – spooky. Something else is happening on the ground, which does not mean that Hudson Yards, a secure green zone for the extremely wealthy on the west side of Manhattan, should have been built, at least not in the way it was.

For decades, Olivier Roy has confronted this sort of essentialism in the context of terrorism expressed in Islamic terms, as it often is in Europe. Many people have argued that Islam is violent, intolerant, and causes terror. It is further said that fundamentalist Islam led to the overthrow of secular states in an atavistic urge to return to a medieval (bad) social order. Against this, Roy has argued that terrorism carried out in the name of "political Islam" (his phrase) deployed an essentially Soviet/Leninist grammar of the state as vehicle to achieve an Islamic state. In particular, political Islam mirrored the structure of revolutionary Marxism common throughout the developing world in the post-WWII era, but without the atheism. As a result, the Muslim vocabulary masked the essentially modern – and Western – grammar of the political aspiration, in contrast to the political quietism of traditional Islam. Iran, Algeria, perhaps Pakistan, many European Muslims, the Taliban, and so forth were "revolutionary," as that word has been used since the French Revolution, and therefore emphatically modern, not medieval. Political Islam, Roy argued, not only expressed a contemporary (as opposed to atavistic) politics, but was a language in which profound frustrations could be articulated and violent fantasies justified.

In *Deploying Ourselves* (2015), David argued, in part from Roy, that al-Qaeda was a sort of limiting case, a politics converging upon zero. Al-Qaeda was almost devoid of ambitions to rule people upon a territory. Its signature tactic, suicide bombing, was nihilistic. The point of such bombings, it was said, was the destruction of the status quo so that the Caliphate might arise (echoing the old anarchists' claim, in which destruction was claimed to be a morally sufficient preparation for a politics yet to come). In short, bin Laden was only barely political, and therefore not much like the overtly political violence of say Ireland, or the political Islam of Iran, or even Somalia's al-Shabaab, which aspire to rule a territory.

More recently, Roy has argued that Salafi discourse, associated with Saudi Arabia, is not the cause of recent terrorism committed by French youth, and particularly, of the emigration to wage jihad in Syria and elsewhere on behalf of the bloodthirsty, and ultimately nihilistic, Islamic State. Roy fairly easily demonstrates both that French converts were not particularly devout

Muslims and that Salafi discourse is conservative, i.e., seeks to maintain an existing political situation. While it may be repressive, Salafism does not seek to end the divinely established worldly order. Islamic State, in contrast, is a cult of death, endeavoring to bring about the end of time. Thus, argues Roy, the Salafis are not to blame for the rise of Islamic State in general, and in particular, are not to blame for the conversion of French and Belgian youth into IS soldiers. Instead, in light of the evacuation of religion from French public life, religion has become a covert discourse. Out of sight, religious leaders need not be publicly responsible, indeed there is no way for them to be responsible. And so some imams are very radical indeed, and that is attractive. Islamic nihilism of the sort preached by the Caliphate has thus been adopted as the rhetoric of existentially desperate French youth.

Roy mentions Durkheim's *Suicide*, at the intersection of nihilism and culture, and at the birth of sociology. Terrorism is always also a cultural performance. Probably due to the influence of the French Revolution, which tried to place "politics" at the center of human existence (displacing religion, or trying to), most nineteenth and even twentieth-century terrorism has been phrased in political terms. Ireland is paradigmatic. But politics, at least as "politics" is used in polite society, is never the whole story. It took the poet Seamus Heaney to teach the Irish that their nationalisms expressed more profound, essentially tribal, animosities, loyalties, and anxieties, and the Good Friday Agreement only became possible when it was widely realized that political rhetoric also gestured towards yet deeper things.

As a cultural performance, terrorist violence is often accompanied by words, sometimes offered as justification, even motivation and in that sense cause. Killers, however, may not have many grammars available to them. If terrorist attacks, including the accompanying speeches, are also performances, then they must be understandable by their audiences. The text must be legible. So, killers are limited to what their audiences have heard. In Europe, we see the prevalence of the rhetoric of anti-Semitism, even in places without Jews. Antisemitism was to horrific degree achieved, and yet the language endures, and when need be, can be used to ornament a killing. In the United States, of course, anti-Semitism has always existed, and was voiced in the recent attack on a synagogue in Pittsburgh, for example. But race has always been the prevailing violent discourse. In the age of Trump, especially, it is perhaps unsurprising that mass killings are articulated in racist terms. Radical Islam can be used to narrate violence, too, obviously. Other contenders flicker on and off the stage, like the defense of the Constitution expressed by Timothy McVeigh when he bombed the Alfred P. Murrah Federal Building and its day care center, causing 168 deaths and hundreds of injuries.

An interesting aspect of the school shootings so common in the United States is the fact that violence is sometimes articulated in terms of popular culture. The Columbine shooters, and subsequent shooters, dressed like characters from the movie *The Matrix*. The recent release of *The Joker*, an origin-story movie about the arch-fiend in the Batman entertainment franchise, created a wave of anxiety that incel males, perhaps seated next to you in the multiplex, would be inspired to kill people. Of course, few people become mass killers. Study after study has shown that bad movies, or bad people in good movies, do not cause terror in any linear sense. People do not have many languages at their disposal that are felt to gain traction. If a school shooter talked like a wet British academic, about the intractable immiseration caused by neoliberal power structures, what good would that do? Syrians and the French "get" jihad. People in Colorado "get" *The Matrix*. But this is in the nature of fashion, a sort of "in the air" availability.

This is a disturbing answer. If terrorist violence is not really about Islam, or the US Constitution, or white people's rage, or Jews (sometimes in Palestine, sometimes just qua Jews), or what have you, then submitting to the demands of Islam, preserving the Constitution, making white guys comfortable, and so forth will not make the violence go away. What is the violence about, really, and how is that to be addressed? What is to be done, politically? Presumably we will build a wall. But we do not expect the wall to work, at least not entirely. We may even sympathize with the watchers on the walls, as this book does, but that does not really address the question. With what attitude do we participate in an empire that is always already something of a failure, even as it is something of a success, at least comfortable enough for some of us, some of the time?

★★★

On October 3, 2019, a man walked into Police Headquarters, Paris, where he had been an employee for over 20 years. As *The New York Times* recounts:

> Shortly after noon he calmly left his office, walked across a bridge, bought an eight-inch kitchen knife and an oyster knife, and slipped back into the police building.
> His colleagues in the office had stayed behind to have lunch at their desks. The killer slit the throat of one, a 50-year-old police major, and fatally stabbed another, a 38-year-old officer, in the abdomen. He then went into another office, stabbing a 37-year-old administrative employee, and descended the stairway toward the building's giant courtyard. Along the way he stabbed to death a 39-year-old police-woman, the prosecutor said Saturday.
> Once in the courtyard he threatened another employee with his knife. Ordered to drop the weapon by a young policeman, the killer first walked slowly toward him and then started to run, pointing his knife. The officer fired.
> The killing spree, the prosecutor said, lasted exactly seven minutes.

The man's name was Mickaël Harpon, and as usual, his story reads in many ways. French authorities did not initially release his name. He had been a convert to Islam, but police insisted that did not mean that he had been radicalized. His case was later turned over to anti-terrorism units. He was from Martinique, and deaf, and frustrated by lack of career advancement. Various "radical" texts were exchanged with his wife. He posted violent messages, some rooted in Deaf politics, some more Islamic, on social media. He had been overheard defending the Charlie Hebdo attackers. He had been accused of, but ultimately not punished for, domestic violence. Relations between the French police and civilians have soured in the context of the "Yellow Vest" demonstrations of general discontent. On the Wednesday preceding Harpon's attack, the police staged a massive demonstration of their own. The force is suffering an unusually high number of suicides, over 50 in the year prior to Harpon's attack. No doubt some narrative, with some relations to the truth, will coalesce over time, but what are we to make of this?

Against the sunny tradition of Enlightenment thought, a darker story, conventionally beginning with Rousseau, emerges, a story in which civilization, culture, is the problem. It is not merely that we are threatened by the state of nature and so submit to Leviathan. It is that submitting to Leviathan, life in society, is itself unbearable. Romantics, and cultural anthropologists, have always drawn on this sense that nature, for all of its horrors, would not be so damaging to the soul as the modernity in which we live in fact. The state of nature is not available to us, except as a thought experiment. We live in society, and that often seems to be the trouble. Evelyn Waugh, speaking on the BBC in 1961 of P.G. Wodehouse's airy comedies: "Mr. Wodehouse's idyllic world can never stale. He will continue to release future generations from captivity that may be more irksome than our own. He has made a world for us to live in and delight in." Waugh has his Wodehouse right, but it is hard to know what to make of the shadow cast by "more irksome than our own." Perhaps it bears mentioning that Waugh had several extended homosexual affairs in the same England that forcibly castrated Alan Turing, the patron saint of both computer science and codebreaking, who ultimately committed suicide? But perhaps Facebook has more suicides to answer for, already, than the anti-homosexuality laws of the United Kingdom managed to rack up during their tenure? Perhaps we are not progressing? As the legal scholar Grant Gilmore said, "In hell, there will be nothing but law, and due process will be meticulously observed" (1977: 11).

Can we live like this? Nietzsche speaks of the last man, so perfectly modern, so perfectly safe, worthy only of contempt. Weber speaks of the disenchantment of rational bureaucracy, and the resulting turn to the charismatic leader. Freud wrote *Civilization and Its Discontents*, in response to the horrors (banal: "senseless") of World War I. Freud and Weber both died shortly thereafter, and did not live to see Germany turn to charisma with a vengeance. All of this sounds overheated, and perhaps is. And as of this writing, however, in country after country, often angry charisma seems far more appealing than the sorts of bureaucracy that this book has sought to explore and perhaps even improve a little. And the rebellion, when it comes, is unlikely to look like an engagement with late Freud, and more likely to look like a man with a knife in police headquarters, or something much bigger.

Since the collapse of Marxism as a viable form of critique, it has been difficult for North Atlantic elites to imagine that all might not be right with the direction of modernity, hence the end of ideological conflict implied by the oft-misunderstood phrase "the end of history." By way of thought experiment, however, just suppose our "progress" is towards a society not worthy of affection, perhaps even to be loathed? Suppose capitalism (for all its flaws and which David teaches) is what makes society? Our legends come from Disney; all our "friends" are on Facebook. The culture industries give us all the culture we have, if not all that we need. Social media, that is, what passes for our community, is "cursed." No doubt sins are being committed in our name, though we cannot agree on a list of sins. The gorge rises.

At this point, many "progressives" feel compelled to say that the past was horrible, all vile isms and slavery and whatnot, which ends up being a very conservative defense of the status quo, along the lines of this moment should be loved because other times and places were despicable, or, in our idiom, are morally repugnant. The common defense of North Atlantic modernity is essentially: "You wouldn't want to live among sinners, would you? You are not a sinner, are you?" Progressive indeed.

This conservatism can also be expressed in more historical terms. In the middlebrow West, we frame issues in roughly the same way we have been using since the Renaissance – prehistory, a lost classical age, a brutal "middle" ages, and modernity, now cosmopolitan and post-national. Violence and the political aspirations associated with such violence tend to be historicized and then cast as a throwback, to be defeated by the march of time. Anders Breivik must be denied, because he suggests that Norway, modern cosmopolitan Norway, has to some extent failed. Who could not wish to participate in cosmopolitan Norway? Or "Europe"? This is what Fukuyama, channeling Hegel, actually meant by the end of history. After the psychic collapse of Marxism, the inhabitants of advanced liberal democracies had little conceptual equipment with which to criticize their own societies, which clearly represented the future, indeed, the only future they can imagine to be possible.

Understandably, the establishment has tended to deny accusations of failure, even if tacit, by externalizing them, often by claiming their accusers wish to return to an evil past. It is unclear what "return" means – surely what is being contested, now, is the future. Nonetheless, various attacks are summarily labelled and dismissed as futile efforts to return to some pre-lapsarian past, maybe even a medieval Muslim one. Or white nationalism, racism tinctured with the sexism of the males who lost out on globalization. One need not physically attack anything to be called medieval. Voting for Brexit was widely held to be some sort of atavistic urge to "go back" to the past. All of this is somewhat tautological: if one saw the world in the approved cosmopolitan way, one would be satisfied with this understanding of history and one's satisfying place in it … . One might even frame history itself in ways that positioned oneself as the desired outcome of the dialectic, she thought as she slid into her business class seat and ordered a bourbon.

Suppose, however, one has an entirely different idea of the modern? Or even of the significance of history itself? If the Koran and hadith express eternal truths, then straying from them is simply error, not development nor evolution. Or suppose, relatedly, that modernity (however presented in the North Atlantic) just is not enough? One can express that thought with reference to Nietzsche or Weber, as above. Or there is this: "I just couldn't live in Bratislava and serve lattes," said a head of security, Serbian, tall, bald, simultaneously friendly yet menacing, with an adventurous past, by way of explanation. If what used to be disparaged as bourgeois or suburban life doesn't satisfy, some people will seek out what does. Mountain climbers, opioid addicts, special forces guys … and terrorists.

Houellebecq's *Submission* artfully suggests that France has created a society so barren that one can imagine an attractive contemporary Islam. Or, for many police officers, evidently, a bullet. The broader question is whether France, or the United States, or modernity more generally, has lost its way, and what fills the vacuum? What are the Watchers on the Walls defending? So, the real attacks come from within. Roy tries to understand why French youth convert to a foreign death cult. Americans just lose it and go to Walmart, or set up a shooter's nest in a nearby hotel. The scary metaphor for such terrorism is modern bodies, under great stress, chemical and otherwise, in an antiseptic environment. From time to time a cell flips out, becomes cancerous, and some individual shoots up a school or a mosque or an airport. The body (politic), usually successfully, eliminates it. Sometimes, as in say Germany or Somalia, the autoimmune system fails altogether.

Or so it appears, on bad days.

Perhaps modernity is not to blame. Maybe this is merely the human condition, in that sense, nature rather than culture, our fate rather than our history, to be endured rather than overcome. The *Iliad* begins with rage. Maybe even more than war, rage is the subject of the book. War is the setting. When he was denied Briseis, Achilles kept to his tent. When he lost Patroclus, Achilles did not talk about *tendresse*. He slaughtered.[1] From this perspective, whether or not rage is in ourselves or in our stars matters little. Either way, terror is not most importantly the expression of a violent ideological logic, but instead an unleashing, a letting slip, as is the counterterrorism massed against it. Civilization, indeed life itself, and maybe especially male life, involves frustration. Rage that is always in danger of being expressed, one way or another. From this perspective, not only is ontological security an oxymoron, actual violence may be expected from time to time, like prime numbers, which are rare but in infinite supply.

That said, this is a too one-sided, and negative, reading of *Civilization and Its Discontents*, essentially a psychological internalization of the Hobbesian logic of *Leviathan*. External fear becomes internal rage at the oppression of civilization. There is truth here, but not enough. Surely people come together out of more than fear? Eros, encompassing not just lust but the desire for company, maybe even love? Against *Leviathan* (1651) we might read *King Lear* (1606). The play is about bonds forged, tested, broken, reforged, and about lives defined, and defended or attacked, in terms of such bonds. There is little or no interest in self-preservation here, quite the contrary, there is much willful self-destruction. The play is about nature, especially including love, not the flight from nature. The violence in *Lear* springs not from fear but from courage, and from its forms of imagination, from *eros* rather than from *thanatos*. Tragedies are about virtues, often love, but are violent nonetheless. And if that is right, we should not even hope, with the sunnier and softer side of the Enlightenment, to expunge our capacity for violence, for with it would go love, friendship, familial obligation, honor of many sorts, and that existential need easy enough to disparage as vanity but without which there would be little art, little science, little culture.

Mostly, though, violence does not erupt. The cancer cell is eliminated or contained. Most people, most of the time, do not take up arms. Many societies are quite peaceful. Violence is often imagined, not just in the feverish planning of the secret college, but in games, movies, even old books. Societies will find narratives that glorify violence. Race, antisemitism, honor, even counterterrorism. Let's all have a SWAT team. In US culture, especially, militarization is often a form of style. A fantasy, certainly, but all style involves fantasy. Very tough trucks, Hummers. "Tactical" clothing. Guns galore. There are even good things about this. Military virtues are virtues; Achilles is a hero.

Even Roy Laurer ("Millwall!") is brave. Not an angel, but who expected that? Whatever our virtues, we all have failings, sins. In fact, modernity cannot be understood without some acknowledgment of sin. This is the Peace of Westphalia, the entire liberal edifice of rights – we build structure, process, because fallen man cannot agree on the nature of the good, and is willing to kill over the argument. From this perspective, "liberalism" or "modernity," however defined, does not substantively transcend violence, never will, and should not seriously try. Instead, violence is the reason for the forms of the social we most readily acknowledge as modern. We therefore must seek to contain violence, to express the passions while avoiding as much of the bloodshed as possible, to allow for the carnival so that the ordinary is peaceable. Challenges abound. Perhaps we can build a society people love, so that "ordinary unhappiness" is kept to a minimum? Maybe we can limit the damage done by the narratives of violence, articulate the passion without letting blood? And perhaps our official violence can be conducted in ways less clandestine, more restrained, publicly legitimated, and worthy of respect, than is now the case.[2] There are many such questions, and addressing them would require other books. But the general question is what kind of polity do we wish to have, and how will it cope with the violent possibilities entailed in our condition? Good bad or indifferent, the watchers on the walls, whether soldiers or bureaucrats, serve the polity that belongs to us all, and to which we all belong. The question of what it is to be defended is ours, not theirs. Here, politics begins, with a latte.

Notes

1 Saul Bellow, in *Ravelstein*, a *roman à clef* about his friendship with the conservative professor and gadfly Alan Bloom, notes the importance that Bloom places on the *Iliad* beginning as a poem not about war in general, but about the rage of Achilles. And Achilles has arguments about why he is being mistreated, and maybe he is – but there is more here.
2 Westbrook 2015.

References

Douglas, Mary. 1986. *How Institutions Think*. Syracuse, NY: Syracuse University Press.
Fassin, Didier. 2020. "The Age of Security." In D. Asjer Ghertner, Hudson McFann and Daniel M. Goldstein (eds.), *Futureproof: Security Aesthetics and the Management of Life*. Durham, NC: Duke University Press.
Funk, Mackenzie. 2019. "How ICE Picks its Targets in the Surveillance Age." *The New York Times*, October 3. Available at https://www.nytimes.com/2019/10/02/magazine/ice-surveillance-deportation.html [accessed April 9, 2020].
Gilmore, Grant. 1977. *The Ages of American Law*. New Haven, Conn.: Yale University Press.
Graham, Stephen. 2010. *Cities under Siege: The New Urban Militarism*. New York: Verso.
Houellebecq, Michel. 2015. *Submission*. Paris: Flammarion.
Kafka, Franz. 1961. *Metamorphosis and Other Stories*. London: Penguin Books.
Scheper-Hughes, Nancy. 2018. "How to Talk (and Not to Talk) about School Shootings." *Anthropology Today*, 34, 3–4.
Westbrook, David A. 2015. *Deploying Ourselves: Islamist Violence, Globalization, and the Responsible Projection of U.S. Force*. London and New York: Routledge.

Index

Made in the USA
Las Vegas, NV
10 June 2025

23475372R00109